THE COMPLETE IDIOT'S GUIDE® TO

Heirloom Vegetables

by Chris McLaughlin

ALPHA

A member of Penguin Group (USA) Inc.

ALPHA BOOKS

Published by the Penguin Group

Penguin Group (USA) Inc., 375 Hudson Street, New York, New York 10014, USA

Penguin Group (Canada), 90 Eglinton Avenue East, Suite 700, Toronto, Ontario M4P 2Y3, Canada (a division of Pearson Penguin Canada Inc.)

Penguin Books Ltd., 80 Strand, London WC2R 0RL, England

Penguin Ireland, 25 St. Stephen's Green, Dublin 2, Ireland (a division of Penguin Books Ltd.)

Penguin Group (Australia), 250 Camberwell Road, Camberwell, Victoria 3124, Australia (a division of Pearson Australia Group Pty. Ltd.)

Penguin Books India Pvt. Ltd., 11 Community Centre, Panchsheel Park, New Delhi—110 017, India

Penguin Group (NZ), 67 Apollo Drive, Rosedale, North Shore, Auckland 1311, New Zealand (a division of Pearson New Zealand Ltd.)

Penguin Books (South Africa) (Pty.) Ltd., 24 Sturdee Avenue, Rosebank, Johannesburg 2196, South Africa

Penguin Books Ltd., Registered Offices: 80 Strand, London WC2R 0RL, England

Copyright © 2010 by Chris McLaughlin

International Standard Book Number: 978-1-61564-052-2
Library of Congress Catalog Card Number: 2010906823

12 11 10   8 7 6 5 4 3 2 1

Interpretation of the printing code: The rightmost number of the first series of numbers is the year of the book's printing; the rightmost number of the second series of numbers is the number of the book's printing. For example, a printing code of 10-1 shows that the first printing occurred in 2010.

Printed in the United States of America

Note: This publication contains the opinions and ideas of its author. It is intended to provide helpful and informative material on the subject matter covered. It is sold with the understanding that the author and publisher are not engaged in rendering professional services in the book. If the reader requires personal assistance or advice, a competent professional should be consulted.

The author and publisher specifically disclaim any responsibility for any liability, loss, or risk, personal or otherwise, which is incurred as a consequence, directly or indirectly, of the use and application of any of the contents of this book.

Most Alpha books are available at special quantity discounts for bulk purchases for sales promotions, premiums, fund-raising, or educational use. Special books, or book excerpts, can also be created to fit specific needs.

For details, write: Special Markets, Alpha Books, 375 Hudson Street, New York, NY 10014.

Publisher: *Marie Butler-Knight*

Associate Publisher: *Mike Sanders*

Senior Managing Editor: *Billy Fields*

Acquisitions Editor: *Tom Stevens*

Development Editor: *Megan Douglass*

Production Editor: *Kayla Dugger*

Copy Editor: *Kelly D. Henthorne*

Cover Designer: *Kurt Owens*

Book Designers: *William Thomas, Rebecca Batchelor*

Illustrator: *Hollis McLaughlin*

Indexer: *Julie Bess*

Layout: *Ayanna Lacey*

Proofreader: *John Etchison*

For my youngest, Bella, who gives up many, many hours with her mom when books are being written.

Contents

Appendixes

Introduction

I've been growing vegetables since the eighth grade. I enjoyed it mostly because it amazed me to watch plants start off as a seed and then one day actually produce food for the table. At that time, my small garden was limited to tomatoes, strawberries, and an herb or two. Still, I was pleased that I could grow anything at all.

Over the years, my love for gardening turned into passion, and I managed to add to my plant repertoire. I was well past that ah-ha! moment that I first felt when I'd made the plant/food connection at 14. At one point, my husband and I lived in the California Sierra foothills and I became friends with Allure, who was smart in the ways of the world and especially gifted with plants.

She took me to her gardens and I saw my first purple fingerling potatoes. They looked gnarled and much darker and more colorful than a potato should have been, I thought. She cooked them, and we ate the little oddities. Buttery and full of flavor, they were wonderful, and I immediately added them to my next season's seed list. She showed me other vegetable and flower varieties that I'd never seen before.

I had no idea that I was being introduced to my first heirloom plants. This knowledgeable woman shared with me many seeds that she'd collected from her own gardens and so I witnessed that universal generosity that true gardeners possess.

At the end of the season, Allure showed me how to collect the seeds from my plants so I could grow the same varieties the next year. I was smitten, and I had another ah-ha! moment. Until then I had always just purchased new seeds every year.

I had no idea that I couldn't have kept the seeds from the varieties I grew even if I *had* known the techniques—because I'd been purchasing hybrid varieties. I fell in love with these special and unique heirloom plants, although I still hadn't learned that the group had a name.

Most people haven't seen, much less eaten, purple potatoes, white carrots, or striped tomatoes. These are the varieties of our ancestors, and they grew them for good reason. Come see what makes heirlooms special and why they have earned their way into the hearts of so many gardeners.

Let me share with you hints for growing healthy and high-yielding crops and techniques for saving seeds from your own garden. In the Heirloom Vegetable Directory, meet the veggies and choose varieties that have laugh-out-loud names, rich heritages, amazing colors, and mouthwatering flavors.

How This Book Is Organized

The Complete Idiot's Guide to Heirloom Vegetables is divided into three parts.

In **Part 1, Our Vegetable Inheritance,** I give the definitions of heirloom vegetables, and there are several. I'll discuss some excellent reasons to grow heirlooms, including their fantastic flavors and why they taste better than the bland stuff in the produce section of the supermarket. I'll get into heirloom plants' incredible adaptability to specific climates. I'll also talk about their far-out names and the interesting stories behind them.

I'll explain why growing vegetables gives you some control over what you and your family eat, as well as explore how they connect us to our past. You'll learn a little bit about genetics and the important role genetic diversity plays in our future.

You'll learn how your vegetables become pollinated and the importance of who pollinates them. I'll explain the difference between open-pollination and hybridization. I'll get into what monoculture is and why commercial companies use it. If you've ever been confused by the term "GMO" and what that really is about, I'll explain it in this part of the book. I'll also talk about what makes seed banks important and why you just may want a seed bank of your own.

This part also goes over how to choose the right heritage varieties for your garden. We look at how much space you have, who will be helping you, your growing zone, and what you plan on doing with the harvest. I also have some excellent gardening practices to share with you to help your veggies flourish.

Part 2, The Birds, the Bees, and Saving Seeds, is dedicated to one of the most wonderful aspects of heirlooms: the fact that you can save seed that breeds true! I'll talk about annuals, perennials, and biennials and why it makes a difference if you'd like to collect and save heirloom seeds.

I'll get into what pure pollination is and techniques for preventing undesirable cross-pollination. I'll explain how to use caging or bagging techniques in case distance isn't available. You'll also learn how to hand-pollinate plants to ensure pure pollination or to make sure your plants are pollinated at all.

This part also discusses collecting, cleaning, drying, and storing seed to save for next year's crops.

Part 3, The Heirloom Vegetable Directory, is a collection of hundreds of heirloom vegetables for you to peruse to see which vegetable varieties appeal to you and yours. You're going to be amazed at the variety, but it's only a sample of the heirlooms available to the home gardener.

Last, I have a glossary of common heirloom and vegetable terms, as well as a resources section listing many different heirloom seed companies that are sure to carry any variety that strikes your fancy. Feel free to contact the companies with any questions you may have. These folks are passionate about what they do, and they're more than willing to give guidance.

If you'd like to see color images of the varieties listed in the directory, I have them in an online collection at www.cigheirloomvegetables.com. If you have any images you'd like to share for the site, feel free to e-mail me at the website.

More Cool Stuff

Just to keep things fun and interesting, I've added some sidebars with hints and cautions to make your heirloom growing experience easier and more rewarding.

> **HERITAGE HINT**
>
> These boxes will give you some extra ideas and tips for growing heirloom vegetables in your own garden.

> **WEED!**
>
> Here you'll find warnings and things to consider about growing heritage veggies.

> **DEFINITION**
>
> These sidebars provide definitions and details about specific heirloom and vegetable terms and techniques.

Acknowledgments

Once again I find myself indebted to my incredibly patient family and friends who are certain by now that I've lost my mind. I want to thank my uber-cool dream editor, Tom Stevens, for picking up the phone *every* time I call.

Penguin Group and Alpha Books, whose educational *Complete Idiot's Guide* series are serious fun to write. My agent, Marilyn Allen, who (like Tom) always picks up the phone. My wonderful editors on this book, Megan Douglass and Kayla Dugger. A huge thank you to Mayo Underwood for being my professional eye and an astounding heirloom pioneer in her own right.

Books are never written by just one person, and I want to also thank the garden-world-renowned Doug Green; my go-to man for pumpkins, Joe Sobel; and John Fendley of the Sustainable Seed Company. Your help and knowledge, gentlemen, is more appreciated than you can imagine. A huge thank you to Lisa Gustavson for not only helping with some technical aspects of this book, but for telling me that I'm sane.

My friendship and gratitude to Jere and Emilee Gettle and their gracious use of the vegetable images for the website that accompanies this book. No one in the world captures the beauty and colors of heirlooms the way Baker Creek Heirloom Seeds does. A huge thank you to Southern Seed Exchange and Terrior Seeds (Underwood Gardens) for generously allowing me the use of their veggie images on the book's companion website as well. I firmly believe that there is no other group on this planet as kind and as passionate as those who love the garden.

I'm indebted to Allure Jeffcoat, who showed me my first heirloom plants and shared with me her precious seeds and knowledge. I owe Jeff Winslow big time for his amazing work on *The Complete Idiot's Guide to Heirloom Vegetables* photo website and Hollis McLaughlin for once again coming to my rescue with her fabulous artwork.

My husband, Bobby, who never, *ever* complains while he picks up the slack around the house. My wonderful kids and granddaughter, whom I rob time from while I'm having an affair with a book.

As always, I'm blessed and proud to be surrounded by the people in my life. As for the new friends that I've made while writing this book, the pleasure has been all mine.

Special Thanks to the Technical Reviewer

The Complete Idiot's Guide to Heirloom Vegetables was reviewed by an expert who double-checked the accuracy of what you'll learn here, to help us ensure that this book gives you everything you need to know about heirloom vegetables. Special thanks are extended to Mayo Underwood.

Trademarks

All terms mentioned in this book that are known to be or are suspected of being trademarks or service marks have been appropriately capitalized. Alpha Books and Penguin Group (USA) Inc. cannot attest to the accuracy of this information. Use of a term in this book should not be regarded as affecting the validity of any trademark or service mark.

Our Vegetable Inheritance

1

When you think of a carrot, what's the first image that comes to mind? You're probably picturing "long, tapered, and orange." Would it surprise you to know that they also come in colors such as purple and white? Some carrots are mature at 2″ long, and some are the shape of ping-pong balls.

Although these colors and shapes may intrigue you, the flavors will amaze and delight you. When you garden with heirlooms, you open up a whole new world of vegetables that you may not have known existed. The beauty and quirkiness of heirloom vegetables has captured gardeners' imaginations and hearts with their superb garden performances, entertaining histories, and intense flavors.

The first part of this book explains just what makes heirloom vegetables so special. The fact is that your great-grandparents had it right all along: everything old is new again.

The Cherished Heirloom

In This Chapter

- How we define heirlooms
- Excellent reasons to grow heirlooms
- What genetic diversity means
- How heirlooms connect us to our past
- Your role in your family history

In this chapter, I'll explain what defines a vegetable as an heirloom (sometimes called heritage or vintage) plant. We also talk about what gives heirlooms their superior flavor, how they adapt to their environment, and why genetic diversity just might be the most compelling reason to grow them. We look at why heirlooms, with their playful names, are a direct link to our past and how you can help give them a solid link to our future.

Heirloom Vegetables Defined

To begin with, it seems important that we understand what places some of our precious veggies into the heirloom class. But the truth is that there's no official definition. Heirlooms are rich with culture and were brought to us courtesy of immigrants from every part of the world.

Heirloom vegetables are always *open-pollinated* varieties, which means that their seeds can be saved every year, and the plants grown from that seed (as well as the fruit produced) will be a replica of the parent plant. Technically, this means that you'd never have to buy seeds again after the first year, unless you wanted to try other varieties, which I strongly encourage you to do. And if generous friends share seeds with you from *their* plants, you may never have to purchase seeds for your garden.

HERITAGE HINT

In gardening circles, the term "fruit" is often used interchangeably with "vegetable." Vegetable isn't a botanical term, but rather a culinary one. Botanically speaking, if the food in question is the seed-bearing part of the plant, then it's a fruit. (Although it's true that a tomato, while technically a fruit, is considered a vegetable in the kitchen.)

It's important to note that no one owns open-pollinated or heirloom varieties. They are part of the public domain. Unlike many commercial *hybrids*, heirlooms—which are the best of the open-pollinated varieties—have no secret parentage (as is often the case with hybrids) and they're available to any gardener. Although these are general characteristics of all open-pollinated varieties, some gardeners and breeders have more refined definitions. The heirloom definitions can get sketchy. Originally, heirlooms were considered to be those varieties that are 100 years old or older. Many gardeners now consider plants that have been handed down through families to be heirlooms even if they're just 50 years old.

DEFINITION

Open-pollinated plants are those that are pollinated naturally (by insects, wind, water, birds, or mammals). These plant varieties have seed that "breeds true." In other words, the seeds from an open-pollinated plant will produce seedlings and fruit that will look like the parents. Heirlooms are a subset within the open-pollinated class.

Hybrids are the offspring of two plants of different breeds, varieties, or species as produced through human manipulation for specific genetic characteristics.

Family heirlooms are family vegetables whose seeds have been saved and passed down from generation to generation. Many of these varieties originated from *cross-pollination* in the garden or on the farm. Their seeds were saved, grown, and resaved for many years. Many of these family heirlooms have wonderful stories attached to them.

DEFINITION

Cross-pollination is the transference of pollen from the stamen (male part) to the pistil (female part) of the flower. Some plants have both reproductive parts on the same flower, such as peppers. But some plants, such as pumpkins, bear both male and female flowers separately. Cross-pollination also refers to two different plant varieties crossing.

Open-pollinated vegetables that were introduced by seed companies before 1940 are also heirlooms but are referred to as "commercial heirlooms."

Another area that can be confusing is when open-pollinated varieties are "created." This is when a breeder uses two heirlooms (or an heirloom and a hybrid) and crosses them on purpose for certain desirable traits. At this point, the plant produced from the cross-pollination is a hybrid.

But by growing, saving, and replanting the seeds for five seasons or more, the variety becomes dehybridized. At this point, when the seed is grown out, it consistently grows true to its parent and is now considered an open-pollinated variety.

So will these new kids on the block someday become heirlooms? Well, maybe. If they're kept around for generations as a highly desirable variety for whatever reason, these could end up being the heirlooms of our future.

Excellent Reasons to Grow Heirloom Vegetables

There are many compelling reasons to try out heirloom vegetables for yourself. One of the most exciting is that there are hundreds of heirloom varieties from which to choose. Hybrid vegetables that are available in the average grocery store don't begin to scratch the surface of all the different vegetable shapes, sizes, colors, and flavors.

When you *do* find heirlooms in the produce aisle, they're extremely expensive. By growing these special vegetables in your home garden, you'll save money, have the ultimate in fresh produce, and enjoy intense vegetable flavors you've never tasted before. You'll also put food on the table that has its own genes and produces true seed. To top it off, recent studies have shown heirloom vegetables to be higher in nutrition than their half-breed cousins, the commercial hybrids.

The Flavor Factor

One of the first things that draws gardeners to heirlooms is what they hear about their fantastic flavors. To begin with, *any* vine-ripe vegetable grown in the home garden (hybrids included) beats store-bought vegetables hands-down in taste. But most heirlooms have a flavor factor that the prolific hybrids simply can't match.

Although taste can be subjective, the truth is that heirlooms have excellent flavor simply because the varieties we've grown to love were selected and grown expressly *for* taste. This is opposed to commercial hybrids that are created for not only uniformity of color, shape, and size but also for yield and transporting abilities.

It makes sense when you think about the types of plants that families wanted to replant year after year. No one would keep the seeds belonging to poor-tasting vegetables or wimpy varieties. No, these heirlooms were treasured by their families for their deliciousness, hardiness, and local adaptability.

That said, not *every* heirloom vegetable's claim to fame is great taste. Past generations loved mouthwatering melons as much as the next. But they lacked sophisticated transportation and refrigeration. It behooved people to preserve seeds from vegetables that traveled well and had a long storage life, too.

In the end, the vast majority of heirloom varieties saved through today bear the earmarks of great flavor, beauty, disease and pest resistance, and the ability to adapt to their environment.

So which vegetable variety is the one that modern gardeners tasted when they became hooked on heirlooms? My first guess would be an heirloom tomato. In fact, I would go as far as to say that if you've never had the pleasure of biting into an heirloom tomato, you've never *really* tasted a tomato. Seriously.

Although, it could also have been an heirloom lettuce with its distinct buttery, sweet, tangy, or peppery flavors. If you've only munched store-bought lettuce, these descriptions may come as a shocking (but pleasant) surprise when your taste buds realize there's a vast difference between the two.

HERITAGE HINT

When cooking with any heirloom vegetable, remember they're naturally rich in flavor. The idea is to enhance their individual characters with a light hand, not cover them up. Go easy on the spices and herbs and lean toward simple sauces. For instance, many people are used to boiling vegetables, which not only dulls their flavors, but also may reduce the nutrients. Try sautéing or steaming them instead, and let the heirlooms speak for themselves.

The Accommodating Heirloom

One of the advantages that heirlooms have over hybrids is their inherent ability to adapt to their environment. This includes acclimating to the soil they're planted in as well as the specific climate. This can be confusing if you've heard that hybrids were created to be hardier plants. In general, hybrids can grow in a wide variety of environments and are genetically bred to ward off diseases.

However, what's being overlooked is that before commercial hybrids, there were individual varieties of heirloom plants that were perfectly adapted to their areas. Renowned garden writer and gardener-extraordinaire Doug Green says, "While the hybrid varieties usually have higher yields, heirlooms are adaptable to a wider range of growing conditions than that of hybrids."

Historically, as vegetable varieties adjusted to their environments, they also developed resistances to local pests and diseases—thus, *landraces* were born. Because the plants evolved naturally without being mechanically altered, the fruit was able to retain delicious flavors.

 DEFINITION

Landrace is an old-fashioned term that refers to domesticated plants that have adapted to the natural and cultural environment in which they live. The term is specific to heirlooms in that they're a crop cultivar that's been improved by traditional agriculturalists and yet hasn't been influenced by modern breeding practices.

The plants developed unique traits according to their environments, such as cold tolerance and drought resistance, as well as resistance to local pests and diseases. Heritage plants have survived everything that nature has thrown at them.

These survival traits developed naturally, so we ended up with some incredible genetic diversity. Eventually the plants went from "surviving" to "thriving," and seeds saved from these varieties became those that people handed down through the generations, as precious as any family heirloom.

 HERITAGE HINT

Some gardeners who may also be historians, plant breeders, or seed savers are actually on the hunt for heirloom varieties that are thought to have become extinct. Every so often, an heirloom variety is rediscovered in someone's garden or farm. Sometimes these are the "new varieties" that seed companies offer. They're new in the sense that they're now being made publicly available.

What Is Genetic Diversity, and Why Do I Care?

Genetic diversity refers to the range of characteristics within a species that, over time, allows that species to respond to new features of its environment. Gardeners in Alaska can have potatoes just like gardeners in California, all because there are varieties adapted for each environment. Diverse genes are also what prevent one pest or disease from wiping out an entire crop of beans, for example.

For instance, say there's a variety of bush bean called "Big Time Producer" that's susceptible to a certain fungus. This fungus moves into a farmer's field, attacks the Big Time Producer bush beans, and destroys the crop. If the farmer also has planted bush varieties other than Big Time Producer—varieties that are not susceptible to that particular fungus—he'll still harvest beans that year. If all he planted was Big Time Producer, he's in some trouble.

Why do commercial growers practice *monoculture?* Well, on the surface, it sounds like a plausible solution for producing massive amounts of food quickly and easily. It takes less time, energy, and money to seed a single type of crop. Monoculture also maximizes crop yields without other plant species competing with them. This may allow for a higher vegetable yield.

> **DEFINITION**
>
> **Monoculture** is the practice of growing or producing a single variety or species of crop over a large agricultural area.

Once upon a time, the argument was that the monoculture concept would produce more food to feed the masses. It seemed true for a while, but even that theory isn't holding water anymore. Some growers are now producing a variety of heirlooms successfully on a commercial level.

One of the best examples of monoculture gone awry is the Irish potato famine of 1845. In the 1840s potatoes were the main food staple of Ireland. Unfortunately, every farmer was growing "Lumper," a potato variety that was vegetatively cloned; therefore, every plant was genetically identical to the others. Lumper had adapted extremely well to their northern climate. During the fall of 1845, a deadly fungus was introduced to Ireland by way of North America.

The unusually warm and wet weather enhanced the growing conditions for this fungus. Consequently, every potato crop was destroyed—not a plant was spared.

Thousands of people fled their country in order to find any means of survival. For lack of diversity, more than a million people died of starvation.

It's important that we learn from this historic tragedy so we're better prepared in the future. And the key to being prepared is genetic diversity. This is where open-pollinated and heirloom vegetables come in.

Home gardeners can help preserve biodiversity quite easily. One way is to plant different varieties of one vegetable. For example, plant several kinds of tomatoes, beans, or melons, then save and share the seeds. This practice makes it much harder for any insect or disease to wreak devastation.

A Little Control, Please

Food is a basic human necessity. He who controls the seed controls the food supply. I'd like just a little control over how my food is grown, what's put on it, and which vegetable type I'll grow.

The commercial food industry has all but ignored the maintenance and improvement of open-pollinated vegetable varieties. It's also interesting to note that five companies control all of our commercial seed worldwide.

Truth be told, I'm a control freak. I'm tired of relying on external sources for all my family's essentials. Between desiring healthy food for my family, a weak economy, and a global movement toward a healthier diet and sustainable living, there's no better place to start than with heirloom vegetables.

Our Connection to the Past

Of course, heirlooms weren't always called "heirlooms." In fact, the term "heirloom" wasn't even used until the 1980s! Before hybrids, heirlooms were those traditional vegetables grown in gardens everywhere. They were the staples of life. Some of the heirlooms that have been preserved by family seed-saving go as far back as 2,000 years or more.

Stories of how these antiques arrived in our hands in this modern day and age have been written in letters or diaries. Many are mentioned in archival documents as well. But the vast majority comes with stories that have been handed down generation to generation—in the very same way the seeds have.

A large number of the heirloom varieties we are enjoying today came with immigrants from every part of the world during the eighteenth and nineteenth centuries and have been handed down through families and acquaintances. Connected to those seeds is the history of our ancestors and who they were, giving us a basic definition of who *we* are. In a nutshell, seeds are a living heritage for people. We can hand down antique furniture, jewelry, and paintings, but none of these are alive.

On the surface, it seems that there's a large number of heirloom seed companies with a never-ending supply of seeds for those who would like them. However, relying on companies to provide historical seeds indefinitely is unreasonable considering heirloom seeds are discontinued from seed companies all the time, never to be seen again. These companies remove heirlooms from their seed lists because they're not as profitable as hybrids; once the heirloom seeds are purchased, those seeds can be saved. This doesn't do much for repeat business the way hybrid seed sales do.

Many gardeners simply enjoy growing vegetable varieties with colorful history, exquisite flavor, and adaptability. And sometimes, quite by accident, someone's history is kept alive.

Case in point: The Mong tomato. Heirloom-revival pioneer Mayo Underwood of Underwood Gardens shared this story with me about the Mong tomato.

> "Many years ago at the Flower and Garden Show in Chicago, I met a man named Marvin Reiter from Palatine, Illnois. His father, in Iowa, was a neighbor of a gentleman named Mr. Mong. Reiter spoke about these deliciously huge tomatoes that his father's neighbor grew in his garden. He had never seen anything like them.
>
> Reiter mentioned that he would get some seeds for me to try from Mr. Mong. After he walked away, I chased him down the garden show aisle to ask how to contact him—I didn't want him to forget about sending me the seeds. Time went on, and it looked as if he, indeed, had forgotten until five years later, he sent me a note saying Mr. Mong had passed away. Along with the note, he had sent what he said was the last five of the tomato plant seeds.
>
> I grew the seeds out and collected more of these fantastic tomato seeds and called it the Mong tomato. A few years later, *Organic Gardening* magazine grew them in their test gardens and named them 'Tomato of the Year.'"

Who wouldn't want to be a part of something so extraordinary?

What's in a Name?

Gardeners have no problem admitting that heirloom names are a huge part of the fun. Some names simply tickle our fancy, making us smile as we repeat their names to anyone who asks. Heirloom vegetables have names such as Drunken Woman Frizzy-Headed lettuce, Moon & Stars watermelon, Tall Telephone peas, and Mascara lettuce. There's the popular Mortgage Lifter tomato, and one called Mule Team. Also, there are Beaver Dam and Lady Godiva pumpkins, plus Rattlesnake and Dragon Tongue beans.

Add these to your garden, and the party conversations will never be the same! Some varieties are named for the person who found them or the families who perpetuated them, like Grandfather Kurtz Cowhorn okra, Grace Lahman's Pink tomato, and Dr. Walter tomato.

This charming story comes from Mayo Underwood. She shared this with me about Mostoller Wild Goose Beans:

> "In the fall of 1865 or 1866, a flock of Canadian geese landed in the sawmill belonging to Joseph Mostoller. One of Joseph's two sons shot the bird and brought it to their mother, Sarah. While the boys argued over whose bullet it was that actually killed the goose, their mother cleaned and prepared it for dinner.
>
> She found bean seeds inside the craw of the bird and was curious as she didn't recognize them. Sarah then dried and planted them. The Mostoller family beans were grown by generation after generation of Mostollers before the bean became popular to gardeners all over."

While the Mostoller Wild Goose bean is a fun story, it's hardly an unusual one. There's a multitude of historical anecdotes just like it.

The Mortgage Lifter tomato also has a great story. Through the years, the exact specifics have been tweaked a bit. But the essence of the story is the same: local boy makes good getting creative.

During the Great Depression, there was a self-employed businessman in West Virginia named Marshall C. Byles or "Radiator Charlie." Mr. Byles owned a (you guessed it) radiator repair service that had gone downhill just as everything else had during that era.

Apparently, Byles didn't know anything about breeding plants, but he did grow tomatoes in his garden. He decided to experiment with the largest of the tomatoes. He chose five tomato plants and cross-bred them. For four years he experimented and rotated the breeding pattern. He then saved the seed of his signature tomato plants, which yielded a pinkish-red fruit that weighed in at 1 to 2 pounds each.

Byles then grew seedlings and sold them for $1 per plant. He claimed that this tomato variety grew a beefsteak tomato so big that it could feed a family of six. People talked, and word got around (some things never change); some people drove as far away as 200 miles to purchase Radiator Charlie's seedlings.

Within four years, the tomato sales paid off the $6,000 mortgage on Byles' home. The Mortgage Lifter tomato gained recognition throughout the United States. This sweet tomato bred by a radiator man with a failing business in a crashed economy remains one of the most popular heirlooms today.

The Least You Need to Know

- Heirlooms don't have an official definition, but gardeners agree that they're open-pollinated vegetables that have been handed down generation to generation for their outstanding qualities.
- Excellent reasons to grow heirlooms include superior flavor, more nutrition, regional adaptability, genetic diversity, pest and disease resistance, and to maintain historical connection.
- Practicing vegetable diversity in the garden helps protect food crops from being wiped out by a single pest or disease.
- Heritage vegetable varieties often have fantastic stories behind them that are not only fun, but help us keep the connections to our pasts.
- Home gardeners can make a huge impact on preserving our food heritage by growing heirloom vegetables and saving seeds from them.

What's in a Seed?

In This Chapter

- What is an open-pollinated plant?
- How hybrid vegetable varieties are created
- What is GMO?
- Why the world needs seed banks

In this chapter, we discuss open-pollinated vegetables and whether all open-pollinated plants are considered heirlooms. You learn how and why hybrid plants are bred, as well as what is genetically done to vegetables that labels them as "GM foods." We also talk about seed banks and what makes them important.

Open-Pollination

Open-pollinated vegetables are those plants that produce seed that breeds true. In other words, baby plants that come from the seeds of an open-pollinated plant will produce seedlings and fruit that resemble the parents.

They're usually pollinated by the natural pollinators of the world such as wind, insects, birds, and mammals. Traditionally, humans don't have anything to do with it. However, the open-pollination label doesn't exclude those plants that are *hand-pollinated*. Some plants actually self-pollinate, such as tomatoes and peppers. These types of vegetables have what is called "perfect flowers." This means that they have both male and female parts (a stamen and a pistil) and don't rely on pollinating insects to bear fruit. In fact, many times the flower has been pollinated before it even opens up! That said, it's possible for an insect to pollinate vegetables that are self-pollinating.

Not every plant that has both male and female parts can do this. Some plants may have both parts on one flower, but will still need a pollinator to transfer the pollen to the pistil. Vegetables such as pumpkins and melons bear male and female flowers separately, which would make it necessary for pollinators to visit both flower sexes.

> **DEFINITION**
>
> **Hand-pollination** or mechanical pollination is when a gardener pollinates a vegetable flower by hand. This is usually because they want the seeds to breed true and not cross-pollinate with other plant varieties. This technique is also used when there are very few natural pollinators around.

The fact that open-pollinated plants grow true-to-type doesn't mean that the plants are clones. In other words, they're not genetically identical. Although these vegetable varieties will have the same description, flavor, and habits, there can be *slight* differences. Still, the basic characteristics of that variety (traits that drew you to the plant in the first place) will be there.

> **HERITAGE HINT**
>
> Interestingly, heirloom varieties start out as hybrids by cross-pollinating naturally (wind, animals, etc.) or being cross-pollinated on purpose for traits desirable for their region. The farmers or gardeners would save and plant the seed over and over until the seeds would grow true to the original plant every time.

Hybrid Vegetables

In order to get constant, reliable results that are both inexpensive and fast, commercial plant breeders work with varieties that have a closely related gene pool because they've been previously hybridized and are quite similar. These modern varieties are made up of genes that have been "recycled," created within the same gene pool, so there's not much genetic diversity left in the plant. What this means for the seed-saving gardener is that the seed saved from a hybrid vegetable will not generally produce fruit like that of either of its parents. These are called *F1 hybrids*. In fact, not only will the fruit grown from hybrid seeds not resemble their parents, sometimes they're sterile and don't germinate at all.

DEFINITION

F1 hybrid means the first generation of plants created by crossing two different plant varieties or types. To produce consistent results, the same cross has to be made each year; F1 hybrids don't reproduce themselves from their seeds. The F1 stands for "first filial."

The commercial seed industry has put all of its energy into hybrid varieties, many of which are kept as trade secrets.

Consumers also played a role in the development of hybrids. For example, when grocery stores began carrying hybrid tomatoes, it was because they were bred for high yields, uniformity, easy transportation, and tough skins so they could be harvested by machine instead of humans.

Don't forget that most vegetables have to be able to withstand hundreds of miles on a truck and a week or more on the produce shelf and still manage to look fresh as a daisy. Being bred for size and appearance with thick skins for transportation makes many tomato hybrids less expensive for the grocer to bring into his store.

Humans are naturally attracted to symmetrical images and uniform shapes, and so we're drawn to the tomatoes' perfect looks and bright red color. Consumers began choosing the hybrids over the old varieties (heirlooms). Grocers responded by demanding more produce that was uniform; vegetables easy to transport for stocking—and stacking. More hybrids were created and evolved to have traits that benefited the industry instead of our palates.

Such is the case with the watermelon. Old-variety watermelons were rounder and less cylindrical than you see in today's grocery produce section. Grocers asked that the melons be bred elongated for easier stacking. It made good business sense for seed companies to accommodate this request. Of course, creating patented hybrids also made good business sense for the seed companies.

It's interesting to note that when hybrids eventually fall under attack from either a pest or a disease, it's the heirloom plant that the breeders turn to. Breeders use the heirlooms' genetics to breed pest or disease resistance into the modern hybrids. It becomes easy to see why the genetic diversity in heirlooms needs to be protected and preserved. Without it, the world's food production is left vulnerable.

This isn't to imply that we shouldn't grow *any* hybrids, or that they *all* lack flavor. Indeed, some hybrid vegetables are quite flavorful, productive, and beautiful. But perhaps heirloom vegetables shouldn't be the rarity.

And Then There's GMO

GMO stands for "genetically modified organisms." In this case, the "organisms" we're talking about are our food supplies. These are also referred to as GM foods and GE (genetically engineered) foods. The term "GM" is sometimes confused with the term "hybrid." They are not the same thing at all and should never be used interchangeably.

GM foods are crop plants that have been genetically engineered to have what are considered specific desirable traits. In laboratories, plant geneticists can isolate a single gene from one plant and insert it into a different plant to create a plant that's drought-resistant or herbicide-resistant.

The technique is very accurate, and the new plant will now be drought-tolerant or very hard to kill with an herbicide. But "very accurate" doesn't mean perfect. Genetic engineers can't control where exactly the gene will land inside an organism. They can't always be sure of its position in the gene recipient (another plant, in this case). What this means is that the introduced gene can land smack-dab in the middle of another gene, disrupting its function.

The gene-sharing doesn't stop at plants. Genes from nonplants are often inserted into the crops as well. One example is with the frost-sensitive tomato. Flounder (yes, the fish) can survive in freezing water temperatures. So scientists took the "anti-freeze" gene from the flounder and inserted it into a tomato. Presto; we now have a much longer growing season for that tomato variety.

Perhaps the most well-known genetic addition that has caused a major stir for both sides of the GM argument is the use of the *Bacillus thuringiensis* (B.t.) gene in corn (and other crops, as well). B.t. is a natural pesticide. It's a bacterium that produces crystal proteins that kill insect larvae.

By inserting B.t. crystal protein genes into corn, the corn can in essence produce its own pesticide. Pests such as the European corn borer have now met their match with this GM corn.

One of the most well known of the GM modifications may be "Round-Up ready" foods. Corn, soy, canola, sugar beet, and cotton crops have been bred by Monsanto to withstand spraying with Round-Up, an herbicide. Wheat and alfalfa are under development. Pollen from Round-Up-ready plants has already spread to contaminate non-GMO and organic varieties, including "traditional" hybrid and open-pollinated plants.

Data from the U.S. Department of Agriculture (USDA) report authored by Dr. Charles Benbrook presents compelling evidence linking the increase in pesticide use on GE, "herbicide-tolerant" (HT) crops to the emergence and spread of herbicide-resistant weeds. According to the study, there has been an increase in herbicide use by 383 million pounds from 1996 to 2008.

The cross-pollination and the advent of "super weeds" impacts all growers/gardeners—from home and hobbyist to organic and conventional farmers.

Recent studies have health experts concerned about the potential health risks and long-term effects of GMO foods on people. If you explore GMO food further (and I encourage you to do so), you'll find companies that swear by the safety of this process and groups with the polar-opposite opinion that GMs are extremely dangerous for our food supply, as well as a human health hazard.

The reality is that there are no conclusive answers. Food science is truly in its infancy, and we have no way of knowing the effects (short-term or long-term) of crossing genes from the animal and plant kingdom.

What we *do* know is that GMO foods such as corn cross-pollinate easily with the other open-pollinated varieties, and this gives cause for great concern. If the agricultural industry isn't careful about planting distances between GMO vegetable varieties, the industry could destroy our open-pollinated vegetables.

Seed Banks

"Genetic vaults" or seed banks have been put into place all over the world. They house heirloom seeds as well as native plant seeds from every corner of the earth. These seed banks are put into place for several reasons. The first reason is to protect the biodiversity of food crops. If a plant variety were to be destroyed by disease, natural disaster, or war, seed banks would be a source for regrowth of that variety.

Also, many heirloom seeds that have been developed over the years (sometimes centuries) are no longer available commercially and are becoming rare, some being just on the edge of extinction. Seed banks also house the genetics for rare species of native plants all over the world. They not only house vegetable seed, but shrubs, flowers, grasses, trees, and grain seed as well.

Seed banks of various sizes try to hang on to the world's genetic plant diversity in 1,400 buildings worldwide. Some countries have a national bank as well as smaller ones that house seeds local to a specific area. While seed banks are an efficient way to preserve the world's seeds, they can have their problems, too.

Once again, seed banks can't hold everything (at least none have yet). They also can experience equipment failures, severe weather, and money issues (like budget cuts). Banks can be mismanaged or fall apart due to wars. Everyday farmers and gardeners can help by collecting their own seeds, too. In fact, it's exciting and simple to create your own private seed bank.

The Least You Need to Know

- Only the seeds from open-pollinated varieties breed true to the parent plants.
- GMO stands for "genetically modified organisms" and shouldn't be confused with hybrid plants.
- We have no way of knowing the short-term or long-term effects of GM foods on people, animals, or plants.
- Seed banks are the genetic vaults that preserve plant species and genetic diversity. You can create your own seed bank.

Choosing Your Heirlooms

In This Chapter

- Ten questions to ask yourself first
- Start with the vegetables you're eating now
- Your growing zone and microclimate
- Varieties for fresh eating versus storing

In this chapter, we get into some heirloom vegetable decision-making. Instead of ordering vegetable seeds willy-nilly, there are some good places to start when deciding what you should grow in your garden.

The beauty about doing just a little bit of planning before purchasing is that, with a few guidelines, you're apt to choose those vegetable varieties that'll thrive in your garden—and you'll be successful in growing heirloom veggies. That is, after all, the whole point.

Ten Excellent Questions to Ask Yourself

I don't want to get all stuffy on you by suggesting you need a strict plan, because you don't. Still, before you start digging, you'll have a tremendous advantage if you take a little time to think about what you'd like to grow, where it will go, and how you would like to use it. Here are some good questions to ask yourself before you choose your heirloom vegetables:

1. Which part of your yard gets full sun (6 to 8 hours)? The least? In between? You should know at least this much before you begin. Most vegetables will need full sun, but there are exceptions (like lettuce).

2. What is the first vegetable, fruit, or herb that immediately comes to mind when you think of garden produce? This is your "fantasy crop." This is the crop you should start with, because fantasy crops bring your ideal vegetable vision to life. It doesn't matter which vegetable it is (well, for the most part). You'll want to find a variety that will do well in your growing zone before you plant your fantasy.

3. What kinds of foods do you and your family eat most often? These are the types of vegetables to grow in abundance. That said, I'm a firm believer in always planting something new to me in the garden.

4. Are you going to have help from family members? Think about how much you can feasibly do by yourself versus if you have backup from helping hands.

5. What areas in your yard can you reasonably give to raising food crops? Keep in mind that you can always mix flowers in with your veggies.

6. If your lawn is smack-dab in the middle of the best sun at your home, would you be willing to give up some of it? Nice raised beds look lovely with green lawn strips in between for walking paths.

7. Figure out your specific growing zone. Do you have a long growing season or a short one? The season's length will affect which plant varieties you choose.

8. Do you get heavy snow or none at all? Snowfall affects whether you should purchase winter-hardy types of plants versus more tender ones. It also offers clues to how long your growing season is.

9. What plants do you see at your local nursery? In your neighbor's yard? This will clue you in to which varieties grow well in your area and give you a head start without having to guess.

10. Do you want crops you can store for some months like potatoes, onions, and carrots?

The answers to these questions become a terrific custom information base for you, which makes the garden ideas and decision-making easier.

What's Your Family Eating *Now?*

Now that you have a couple of fantasy crops in mind to get you revved up for vegetable gardening, let's get down to business. In order to get the most out of your veggie garden, you'll need to make a list of every type of vegetable that you purchase *now* from your grocery store's produce section.

Then sit your family down for just 15 minutes and ask everyone what they'd like to grow that you don't purchase regularly. Throw some options out there that are new to everyone. This simple list-making task will go far in saving you money, as well as being sure that you'll actually eat the vegetables you grow.

It's interesting to take this money-saving concept a bit further and actually do the math. One way is to keep track of the produce you purchase from the store for a month or two before the growing season. Keep a record of the weight (or the number) of each vegetable that you purchase.

Then weigh (or count) how much of the same crops you get from your garden. Or you can use the same basic idea and just keep count (or weight) of what you eat from your garden one week and price it out at the grocery store.

Remember to compare apples to apples (so to speak).

You can't compare your fresh garden heirloom tomatoes to the average commercial stock on the shelf. Compare the prices of your heirloom tomatoes with the prices of *their* heirloom tomatoes. Try not to look smug as you leave the store—no one likes a sore winner.

A Question of Space

How much space do you need to grow vegetables? It depends on what type of veggies you want to grow and how many. But you'll want to know what you have to work with before you choose your vegetables. If your kids really want to grow giant pumpkins, a good size part of the yard or a large raised bed could technically be devoted to pumpkins. One thing is for sure, you absolutely do not need what usually is referred to as "land" to plant a vegetable garden. Not even close.

There are successful ways to grow sprawling veggies like pumpkins and other squash in small spaces. One way would be to "train" the vines by physically aiming them in a direction and pruning them to keep only several vines. If you prune, remember that you'll harvest less fruit than if the plant is left to its own devices.

Some veggies take to containers with ease. Carrots, peppers, and lettuce come to mind. Tomatoes usually do well in containers, although if you let them dry out to the point where the soil pulls away from the sides of the container, they may never forgive you and are likely to produce less fruit.

In fact, if you think of containers as small raised beds, it's hard to think of anything that *wouldn't* grow in them. One thing that's different about containers versus raised beds is that the container will dry out faster because its sides above ground absorb the heat quickly.

So the key here would be to make sure you keep the soil in containers moist. When choosing a container, take into consideration its composition (i.e., plastic or clay, which dries out faster), as well as the mature size of the vegetable plant. Hanging baskets along the eaves of the sunny side of your house can work, too.

If you know you're going to need more space, have you considered working it into your landscaping? What about your lawn? Many people have front and back lawns that aren't used at all. They're watered, mowed, and they add some green to the yard. But have you ever thought about actually *using* them? Step outside and take a look at your lawn. Are you willing to give some of it up?

If you're absolutely certain that you either have nowhere to garden or you just need more space, consider a community garden. Many cities have community gardens where you can lease a plot for the year (and beyond). The nice thing about gardening in a large space among other gardeners is camaraderie, guidance, and a chance to share your plants with others.

HERITAGE HINT

Before you start drawing up garden plans on your front lawn, be sure that you get a sufficient amount of light in that area. Look at the whole picture when you're planning your vegetable garden.

The Long and Short of It

Every location has a growing season you need to factor in when choosing your vegetables. The determining factor of the length of your growing season is the frost dates. Frost dates are the estimated last hard frost of spring and the first hard frost of fall or winter.

Your local Cooperative Extension office can give you some pretty precise dates as well as what's currently going on in your growing corner of the world. Some years call for changes in frost dates, and your extension office can alert you to these changes.

Nature being who she is, of course, these dates aren't exact; they're approximate dates. However, we can get pretty close to each area's frost dates by averaging them as they have occurred throughout the years. The length of your season will not only affect which vegetable varieties you plant but also how many crops you'll produce.

A long growing season is six to eight months from the last frost date in spring to the first frost date in fall. The lucky gardeners living in the warmer climates have the widest vegetable varieties to choose from. Another advantage to having a longer growing season is that it's possible to get two or three harvests in the same season. So after the first crop of carrots mature, gardeners living in areas that have that extended growing time can replant and harvest carrots again and maybe a third time before the season wraps up.

If you live in a short growing season of three to four months, be very certain that you choose those varieties that are fast growing and produce fruit quickly. It can be discouraging when you plant a long-season tomato and realize that your area has the short end of the stick, so to speak. Cheer up; you gardeners in the colder zones can grow tulips.

HERITAGE HINT

Hard frosts or "killing frosts" are when temperatures fall below 28°F for a few hours or longer. The chances of tender plants and semi-hardy plants sustaining foliage damage or worse are high at these low temperatures.

Also known as a radiational freeze, an impending hard frost is preceded by a cloudless sky, dry air, and no wind. You may notice that there's no condensation on your car windshield. If it's 10 P.M. and the temperatures are already below 45°F, Jack Frost is on his way.

Know Your Zone

Before you spend a dime on seeds, it'll serve you well to figure out not only what vegetables you'd like to plant, but which varieties will grow well in your zone.

The U.S. Department of Agriculture (USDA) provides a zone hardiness map as a general guideline for what will grow in each gardener's particular area. It's important to understand that these are very general guides. No map can guess the specific *microclimate* in your city, neighborhood, or yard.

> **DEFINITION**
>
> **Microclimates** are local atmospheric zones where the climate differs from the larger surrounding area.

In fact, the USDA hardiness zone map is most helpful when discussing perennial plants, trees, and shrubs. This is because any annual can be grown in any zone as long as there are enough warm days for that plant variety to reach harvest. Perennials need to be able to over-winter where they're planted. That said, it's important that you find out the days until harvest (or get an approximate count) on varieties before purchasing seeds. Understanding your growing zone is a helpful guide no matter what you're planting.

For instance, if you're planting a vegetable that requires 100 days of warm weather and your area has an average of 120 days of warmth or more, you're in good shape. However, if you discover that you live in a growing zone that has only 60 warm days, you need to choose varieties that harvest closer to that amount of time.

To find your zone on the hardiness map, find out what the minimum temperature is in your area (contact your local Cooperative Extension office or weather station if you're unsure). If your area can dip down to 20°F or 30°F, then you're in zone 8. Below 40°F but above 30°F? Then you're in zone 3. If your temperatures only drop as low as 50°F or 60°F, then you're in Hawaii or somewhere similar (zone 11), and we hate you.

USDA Hardiness Zones

Zone 1: Below –50°F

Zone 2: –50°F to –40°F

Zone 3: –40°F to –30°F

Zone 4: –30°F to –20°F

Zone 5: –20°F to –10°F

Zone 6: –10°F to 0°F

Zone 7: 10°F to 20°F

Zone 8: 20°F to 30°F

Zone 9: 30°F to 40°F

Zone 10: 40°F to 50°F

Zone 11: 50°F to 60°F

AHS Plant Heat Zones

Another general guide, which may be more helpful to you than the USDA map in the case of annual vegetables, is the American Horticultural Society's Plant Heat Zone Map. This guide is based on the *average* highs instead of the lows of plant survival. Here, the average number of days that temperatures are 86°F and above is indicated.

Zone 1: 1 day

Zone 2: 1 to 7 days

Zone 3: 7 to 14 days

Zone 4: 14 to 30 days

Zone 5: 30 to 45 days

Zone 6: 45 to 60 days

Zone 7: 60 to 90 days

Zone 8: 90 to 120 days

Zone 9: 120 to 150 days

Zone 10: 150 to 180 days

Zone 11: 180 to 210

Zone 12: 210 days and up

After you have your USDA Hardiness Zone number, you can come over to the AHS map and look up approximately how many days your area has for some nice growing weather. If you're in zone 7, you have about 60 to 90 days of very warm temperatures. Now you know to choose vegetable varieties that mature within that time frame—or at least *close* to that time frame. One can always push temperature for a little longer (or shorter) amount of time with microclimates.

Microclimates

Microclimates are those areas within a larger general region that may have different climates than the whole. They can be created by a number of things such as physical structures, extra windy areas, topography, or large bodies of water. For example, you may find that your zone is said to be prone to heavy frost, but become confused when your plants rarely succumb to an icy death.

Your zone might not act as it seems your zone should for many reasons. In urban areas, buildings (or lack thereof) can have a huge effect on the immediate area. They may act as wind barriers or create wind tunnels. If you have a large body of water nearby, such as a lake or the ocean, this tends to moderate the air temperatures of nearby inland areas.

Topography certainly plays a major role for microclimates. Do you live on a hill? Are you high up or deep down in a valley? Warm air is lighter than cold air, so if you live in a valley you may have more frost problems than someone living higher up.

On which side of the hill do you reside? A northern slope is slower to warm up, but a south-facing slope is a mixed bag. The southern side warms up faster, but if plants begin to bloom, they could be set back if a sudden frost hits.

Other factors that can affect microclimates are rainfall, soil types, mulching practices, paved surfaces, fences, walls, raised beds, cold frames, hoop houses, balconies, and rooftops. So if you think that a number on a map has the last word on your garden, think again. Clever gardeners will manipulate their microclimate by using any number of the preceding resources to their advantage.

How Do You Like 'Em: Fresh or Stored?

Here's a question that is often considered too late by gardeners: What's your primary goal for vegetables? Is your only goal fresh produce each season? Or are you looking to store some vegetables such as squash, zucchini, or potatoes?

What about other ways of putting food by? Do you want to can tomatoes? Make pickles? Are you interested in canning green beans, carrots, or peas? How about those beans you want to grow? Do you want those fresh with dinner, or are you looking to dry them for soups and stews? Maybe you were thinking about freezing things like broccoli, Brussels sprouts, and bell peppers.

Knowing exactly *what* you plan on doing with your bounty can make some differences in the varieties you choose. For instance, if you like the idea of having produce through the cold months, you'll want some winter squash and maybe use garden space for lettuces.

There are also pumpkin and winter squash varieties that keep longer than others. Some cucumbers are especially great for pickling, and some are best eaten fresh.

Some beans have mouthwatering flavor from the vine to the table, and some are grown primarily for drying and storing. The answers to these questions can also tell you whether you want or need a tomato that produces ripened fruit all at the same time so that canning can be done all at once, or whether a stupendously flavored tomato that ripens two at a time is desired for fresh eating.

Don't let these factors overwhelm you. Consider them as best you can, and when you begin to choose heirloom vegetable seeds, it'll become clear what makes sense for your garden.

The Least You Need to Know

- It's important to understand which vegetables you'd *like* to grow and what you're eating *now*.
- Figure out your growing zone and what kind of space you have to avoid disappointment.
- Know your particular microclimate and how to create one for extending the growing season.
- Know whether you want to plant vegetables to eat fresh, or if you'd like to grow some veggies for storage as well.

Tried-and-True Gardening Practices

In This Chapter

- What compost does for the vegetable garden
- What is companion planting?
- Why you should mulch vegetable beds
- Why you want to lure insects to your garden

Now that you've come to the realization that your grandparents and great-grandparents had it right when it came to vegetable varieties, it shouldn't come as any surprise that they actually knew *how* to grow them, too.

This chapter gives you an overview of the gardening practices that have worked for gardeners and traditional farmers over the centuries. These techniques work as well today as they did back in the day.

Whether you're a self-proclaimed organic gardener or you feel that anything goes, each of the techniques that follow will save time, water, energy, and money in your vegetable garden.

Compost Is King

Adding compost to your soil is hands-down the single best thing you can do for your vegetable bed. For healthier vegetable plants, higher produce yields, and fewer garden diseases, the first place to concentrate is the soil. Your garden soil's best friend is compost.

Soil is full of billions of living and breathing organisms that are invisible to the human eye. Simply put, soil is made up of organic matter, minerals, water, and air. All of these ingredients not only make up a stable medium for roots to hang on to, but also provide for plants' nutritional needs.

If you want healthy, productive heirloom veggie plants, you need soil that's rich in organic matter. Organic matter is the very heart of compost, and its end result is *humus*. Adding your own compost to your vegetable garden is sustainability at its finest.

Creating great garden soil is about having as much organic matter in the garden bed as possible. Compost or humus will make the complex nutrients in the soil easily available to your plants. A soil that's full of life-sustaining humus is often called "*friable*," meaning that it has a full, *loamy* texture and crumbles easily in your hands.

DEFINITION

Humus is the material formed after organic matter has broken down. Humus makes complex nutrients available to plant roots.

Friable soil has an open structure that crumbles easily in the hand.

Loamy soil generally contains more humus and nutrients than soil that's sandy, clayish, or silty. Loam is considered the ideal gardening soil.

Compost can add nutrients such as nitrogen, phosphorus, and potassium in various concentrations depending on what materials are added to the compost pile. Various micronutrients like copper, iron, iodine, zinc, manganese, cobalt, boron, and molybdenum add value to the compost (therefore, the garden soil). Good compost eliminates the need for synthetic fertilizers and helps ward off plant diseases. Compost has enormously beneficial effects on soil (and therefore plants) that's not truly translatable into numbers.

Although humus may seem to be the ultimate goal, you can use compost in your garden bed at any time as a soil amendment as well as a mulch to retain moisture, suppress weeds, and control erosion. Following are five great reasons to add compost to your heirloom vegetable bed.

HERITAGE HINT

Brown (carbon) and green (nitrogen) materials are blended together to make compost. Examples of brown materials include aged hay, shredded dried leaves, sawdust, dried grasses, straw, chipped wood, dryer lint, paper towels, newspaper, cardboard, oat hay, and shredded documents. For green materials, use grass clippings, leaves, perennial plant trimmings, tea bags, coffee grounds, houseplants, alfalfa meal or hay, and kelp/seaweed. Do not add manures from meat-eating animals (such as cats and dogs) to your compost pile.

1. *Compost can protect plants against disease* due to the beneficial microorganisms produced by composting organic materials. These microorganisms render plant pathogens inactive. Researchers have discovered another virtue of compost that doesn't get as much publicity as it should: it's valuable for plant-disease resistance. Potato blight, powdery mildew, and damping off are all examples of plant diseases that compost can help suppress.

2. *Composting extends the growing season* by allowing you to plant earlier in the growing season and harvest later than usual by providing warmer soils each end of the growing season. Compost improves average soil structure by bringing it to a loamy, friable state. Nutritionally rich soil with good structure holds heat better than poor soil. For the gardener, this means the soil warms up faster and stays warm longer.

3. *Compost acts as a pH buffer for vegetable plants.* For most plants, the most desirable pH is neutral—neither too acidic nor too alkaline. If a gardener is generous with applying compost to garden soil, the gardener doesn't have to worry about the pH levels as much—if at all.

   When humus is plentiful in soil, vegetable crops and flower beds are simply less dependent on pH levels in the soil. Due to its biochemical structure, humus acts as a buffer for soils that fall slightly to one side of acidic or alkaline. This not only takes the guesswork out of an average pH level, but in many cases, it can take the pH factor out of the equation entirely.

4. *Composting saves water* because it increases soil's capacity to hold water by a wide margin. For example, a dry soil low in nutrients may hold only 20 percent of its weight in water. Compare this to a dry soil that's high in organic content, which can hold up to 200 percent of its weight in water.

5. *Composting reduces water runoff* by adding organic matter to the soil. When soil is low in organic matter, it'll have poor crumb structure. This makes it easy for everyday watering and storms to wash it away. Lost topsoil results in even lower fertility, thus creating a vicious cycle. Compost preserves and enhances soil structure and helps fight erosion, keeping healthy soil under the plants where it belongs.

There's nothing inherently wrong with using synthetic fertilizers, but they tend to temporarily mask poor soil; they don't actually solve any problems, help hold water or stop erosion, or amend the soil. Compost, on the other hand, changes the entire structure of the soil—making it nutritionally rich for your vegetables.

For more information on the many virtues of composting as well as how to create some for yourself, check out *The Complete Idiot's Guide to Composting* (Alpha Books, 2010).

Basic Seed Planting Guide

There are a number of requirements to keep in mind as you start your seeds. Practices differ depending on what type of vegetable you are planting and where you live and garden. Some seeds are better off started indoors many weeks before the last frost. But some seeds prefer to be planted directly into their permanent beds just after the frost has passed. Following is a simple chart of common vegetables and their basic starting requirements.

Seed Variety	Month	Indoors or Direct	Soil Temp	Seed Depth/ Spacing	Germination
Arugula	April–May; Aug.–Sept.	Direct	50°F–60°F	½" deep; 1" apart; thin to 1"–6" apart	5–7 days
Bean (Bush)	June–Sept.	Direct	70°F–80°F	1" deep; 2" apart; thin to 2"–6" apart	4–10 days
Bean (Pole)	June–Sept.	Direct	70°F–80°F	1" deep; 2" apart; thin to 6"–12" apart	4–10 days
Beet	April–Oct.	Direct	55°F–65°F	½" deep; 2" apart; thin to 4"–6" apart	10–20 days
Broccoli	Feb.–April; Sept.–Oct.; transplant in April–May	Indoors; direct in late summer/ fall	60°F–70°F	¼" deep; 24" apart	4–7 days
Brussels Sprouts	March–April; transplant in April–May	Indoors; direct in late summer/ fall	60°F–70°F	¼" deep; 24" apart	5–10 days
Cabbage	March–April; transplant in April–May	Indoors; direct in late summer/ fall	60°F–70°F	¼" deep; 24" apart	7–12 days
Carrot	April–Oct.	Direct	60°F–70°F	¼" deep; ½" apart; thin to 3"–4" apart	6–21 days
Cauli- flower	March–April; transplant in April–May	Indoors; direct in late summer/ fall	60°F–70°F	¼" deep; 24" apart	4–10 days
Corn (Sweet)	May–Oct.	Direct	70°F–80°F	1" deep; 4" apart; thin to 8" apart	4–10 days

continues

continued

Seed Variety	Month	Indoors or Direct	Soil Temp	Seed Depth/ Spacing	Germination
Cucumber	May–Oct.	Direct	70°F and above	½"–1" deep; 6"–12" apart; thin to 3 plants	6–10 days
Eggplant	March–May; transplant in June	Indoors	80°F–90°F	¼" deep; 18"–24" apart	10–15 days
Kale	March–April; transplant in April–May	Indoors; direct in late summer/ fall	45°F–65°F	¼" deep; 24" apart	5–10 days
Leek	March–May; transplant in May	Indoors	50°F–60°F	¼" deep; 6" apart	5–7 days
Lettuce	April–July; Aug.–Oct.	Direct	45°F–60°F	¼" deep; 1" apart; thin to 6"–12" apart	7–14 days
Melon and Watermelon	June–Oct.	Direct	80°F–90°F	½"–1" deep; thin to 3 plants	4–10 days
Onion	March–April; transplant in June	Indoors	50°F–65°F	½" deep; 6" apart	4–10 days
Pea	April–June; Aug.–Oct.	Direct	45°F–60°F	½"–1" deep; 1" apart	7–14 days
Pepper	March; transplant in June	Indoors	80°F–90°F	¼" deep; 12"–18" apart	6–12 days
Radish	April–June; Aug.–Oct.	Direct	45°F–90°F	½" deep; ½" apart; thin to 1"–3" apart	4–12 days

Seed Variety	Month	Indoors or Direct	Soil Temp	Seed Depth/ Spacing	Germination
Spinach	April–June; July–Oct.	Direct	45°F–55°F	½" deep; 3" apart; thin to 6"–12" apart	7–14 days
Squash (Summer)	May–Oct.	Direct	80°F–90°F	1" deep; thin to 3 plants	7–10 days
Squash (Winter)	May–Oct.	Direct	80°F–90°F	1" deep; thin to 3 plants	7–10 days
Tomato	March; transplant in June	Indoors	70°F–75°F	¼" deep; 15"–24" apart	7–14 days
Turnip	April–June; July–Oct.	Direct	45°F–85°F	¼"–½" deep; 2" apart; thin to 4"–6" apart	5–15 days

Most seeds, whether sown indoors or out, want a warm soil of about 80°F to 90°F to germinate. Those like lettuce, spinach, kale, and so on that want cold soils are best started outdoors, where the freezing and thawing of the soil will break down the seed coat. The wrong temperature can destroy the ability of the seed to germinate.

Good Bedfellows: Companion Planting

Companion planting is simply any plant that is purposefully planted next to another to enhance growth, beauty, or flavor. Typically, companion plants may do any number of supportive things for vegetable gardens. If you've ever planted flowers that attract beneficial insects such as bees, or break up the plant varieties in your garden, you've companion planted completely by accident.

One example of companion planting is the traditional Native American three-sister growing technique. The "three sisters" are corn, beans, and squash. They're planted together and aid each other's growth. The beans fix nitrogen from the air and make the nitrogen available to the plant roots; the corn stalks provide support for the pole beans to climb; and large, prickly squash leaves shade out weeds. The result is productive and gorgeous plants—and the added benefit of less weeding makes this a serious win-win situation in my book.

One of the best ways to take advantage of companion planting is *not* to plant massive amounts of any one vegetable species in one section. Grow a species-diverse garden. The idea of planting with diverse plant species is to not have a concentrated area of one crop, so the destructive bugs and diseases aren't alerted to the feast. Plus, by planting varying plants, a beneficial insect habitat is created.

Another type of companion planting is to grow plants that emit a strong odor to repel unwanted bugs from the immediate area. Strong fragrances also mask the delicious scent of your tender rose buds or cabbages. Mints and Rue are great for masking the great smell of your heirloom vegetables as well as repelling insects.

Many flowers and herbs can be planted with vegetables to help repel pests, attract helpful insects, or enhance veggies in some other way. Some flowers, such as French marigolds (*Tagetes spp.*), pull triple duty in the garden.

French marigolds are one of the easiest annual flowers you can plant in your garden, and one of the most beneficial. Marigolds call in the beneficial insects, repel unwanted bugs with their strong scent (also masking delicious aromas), and have a compound they emit from their roots that battles nematodes in the soil. Other tried-and-true companions for vegetables include the following:

- Cucumbers—plant nasturtiums and radishes for cucumber beetle control

- Asparagus—tomatoes, parsley, or basil will help control asparagus beetles

- Potatoes—horseradish to repel Colorado potato beetles

- Eggplant—catnip will deter flea beetles

- Tomatoes—basil will repel tomato hornworms

- Carrots—onions control some nematodes and rust flies

- Corn or squash—peanuts interplanted will produce a higher yield for all of these crops

Bring on the Beneficials!

Perhaps the most popular companion planting style is to grow plants that attract pollinating insects as well as those that eat the bad guys. Luring beneficial insects to your yard or garden is one of the best ways to incorporate organic pest control.

The three components that bring the beneficial insects to the garden are pollen, nectar, and water. If you provide plants that have flowers high in pollen or nectar and leave some water around, they will come.

Not all insects are created equal. Some bugs, such as aphids and snails, think of your garden vegetables as *their* dinner instead of yours. These bugs are the enemy. The other guys are the beneficial insects, and they're your cavalry. The beneficials do a bang-up job balancing out the potential damage that the bad guys can wreak on your vegetable plants.

Beneficial insects fall into two groups, and some cross into both categories. The first group is the predators who carry the heavy artillery. These guys devour the pests that are devouring your vegetables. The second group is the pollinators; these insects make the garden bloom and produce fruit. Ideally, you'd like to attract as many insects from both groups as you can.

Learn to Recognize Team Players

It's imperative that you be able to recognize beneficials, so you don't inadvertently squash your own troops. Learn to recognize your creatures by identifying your local insects. Nothing book-worthy; there's no quiz. Just memorize the locals.

If you really have no idea what the heck some little insect is, catch it in a jar. Bring it down to your local nursery for proper identification. You were probably going down there anyway to see whether they brought in heirloom tomato plants.

It's amazing how many good guys we don't recognize. For instance, most people are very familiar with ladybugs and recognize them as part of the cavalry. These cheery-looking beetles will eat about 50 aphids a day, munching on plant mites and scales as well. But have you met the ladybugs' children? If you didn't shudder when I asked that question, then you haven't.

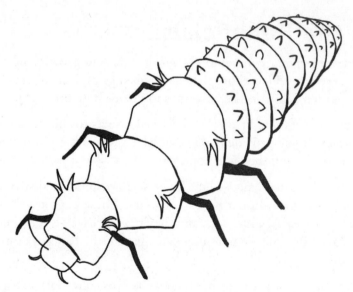

Something from a science fiction movie? Nope, this is a baby ladybug (larva) that loves dining on aphids.

I like having a bug identification page called *Mac's Field Guide* hanging around just for these situations. It's available through Amazon.com and is laminated, so it'll hold up as you take it with you around the garden.

On one side of the page you'll find the good garden bugs and on the flip side the bad ones. It also tells you where to look for both types of bugs and which plant whets their appetites.

To learn more about your local good guys (and bad guys), contact the Extension agency (Master Gardeners) of the state university nearest you.

The Art of Seduction

The garden is nothing if it isn't about sex (bet you didn't see that one coming). It's *all* about sex, if you think about it. Everything needs to procreate to stay in existence—plants included. Plants need to be pollinated in order to set fruit, and the fruit is carrying their seed.

Seeds that are scattered everywhere possible ensure that the species continues to see another day. The problem is that plants aren't equipped to go out, club a mate over the head, and drag it back into the proverbial cave. But that doesn't mean they're no good at seduction. On the contrary; they're masters at it.

Like everything, plants can be provocative for different reasons. Some have a show of bright flowers that transfixes bees. Some ooze strong nectars that make butterflies and birds drunk with happiness. Still others produce so much pollen that when the wind blows the neighbor next to them becomes instantly pollinated.

In any case, your job as matchmaker to your vegetable and its would-be suitors is to lend a romantic hand where you can. You get to light the candles, play the music, and pour the wine by planting flowering plants that are rich in pollen and nectar.

Some Very Sexy Plants

Here are a couple of flowering plant ideas in case you're not sure about what's sexy to beneficial insects. Of course, you should gather species information on the most attractive plants in your community. Some of the following flowering plants lure syrphid flies, lacewings, ladybugs, parasitic wasps, and predaceous beetles. Others attract bees, butterflies, and blue mason bees to your heirlooms for pollination.

Planting some of these flower or herb varieties alongside your vegetables will keep the pollinators plentiful and the pests at a minimum.

- Alyssum (*Lobularia spp.*)
- Anise (*Pimpinella anisum*)
- Asters (*Aster spp.*)
- Bee Balm (*Monarda spp.*)

- Coriander (*Coriandrum*)
- Cosmos (*Cosmos spp.*)
- Dill (*Anethum graveolens*)
- Fennel (*Foeniculum vulgare*)
- Feverfew (*Chrysanthemum parthenium*)
- Goldenrod (*Solidago californica*)
- Lavender (*Lavendula augustifolia*)
- Lovage (*Levisticum officinale*)
- Marigold (*Tagates spp.*)
- Queen Anne's Lace (*Ammi majus*)
- Rudbeckia (*Rudbeckia spp.*)
- Sedum (*Sedum spp.*)
- Sunflowers (*Helianthus spp.*)
- Tansy (*Tanacetum vulgare*)
- Thyme (*Thymus spp.*)
- Yarrow (*Achillea filipendulina*)
- Zinnia (*Zinnia spp.*)

This isn't an exhaustive plant list by any means. Many other flowers and herbs excel at luring beneficial insects to the garden.

Mulch Like Mad

Mulch will help you avoid a multitude of potential problems. Many gardeners think of mulching in terms of perennial beds or landscaping. But it's probably the second best thing you can do for your veggies besides composting. There are numerous materials that can be used as mulch, but remember that in a vegetable garden you'll want to think carefully about which mulch material you'll choose.

Bark chips or shredded bark works well for landscaping and under trees. But because your vegetable garden is filled with annual plants (more than likely), the garden is often disturbed by harvesting, turning, and replanting each season and sometimes more often.

WEED!

If you choose to use grass clippings as mulch, be sure that there weren't any herbicides sprayed onto the lawn that the clippings came from before you spread them onto your garden beds.

The best type of mulch for veggie beds is going to be an organic one that breaks down rather quickly. Grass clippings, straw, leaves, and even compost are great choices for vegetable beds.

Inorganic mulches such as landscape cloth and plastic can also be taken advantage of in a veggie garden, especially for the heat lovers such as watermelon, cucumbers, and pumpkins. If you choose a non-biodegradable cloth, be sure that water can get underneath it. Mulch has properties that may surprise you. Just 1" to 3" of mulch offers …

- *Weed control* by blocking out light, making it hard for weed seeds to germinate. If a weed does try to rear its head, the mulch will often smother it before you ever notice it.

- *Water retention* by shielding the soil from the drying sun, which cuts down on evaporation. Between the moisture-retaining compost you put down first and the mulch, your vegetables will be able to go longer without a soaking.

- *Root protection* by reducing the temperature fluctuation on plant roots. Mulch will also keep your vegetable roots cool during the hot months.

- *Disease barriers* by keeping any contaminated leaves or soil from a previous year from touching the plants. Sometimes even watering can hit the soil and splash bacteria back onto the plant leaves. Mulch makes a terrific barrier.

- *Soil erosion prevention* by holding your precious compost and amendments close to the ground where watering and rain can't wash them away from the plants.

- *Soil conditioning* by adding organic matter and eventually turning into compost. This is beneficial to all life forms in the soil, such as earthworms.

Remember not to pile mulch up around plant stems; this could actually encourage fungal diseases or invite bug pests to come and set up camp. Place it at the plant's *drip line* and outward.

DEFINITION

The **drip line** refers to where water would naturally drip off the leaves (tips) of the plant.

After months of heavy rain, gardeners sometimes report problems in those areas that were mulched heavily. They felt that the thick mulch encouraged slugs, wet rot, and fungus to take up residence.

While I agree that this can be an issue, for me, the benefits of mulching far outweigh the possible detriments. I remain a big fan. So if you live in an area that sees downpours much of the time, you may want to keep this in mind and mulch lightly.

The Least You Need to Know

- Compost can protect plants from disease, extend the growing season, act as a pH buffer, save water, condition soil, reduce water runoff, and add nutritional value to the soil.
- Giving a little attention to the temperatures that individual seeds require to break dormancy will help you be successful with growing heirloom vegetables.
- Companion planting can attract beneficial insects to the garden to control pests and pollinate plants.
- Mulching your vegetable bed can help control weeds, retain water, protect roots, prevent soil erosion, and provide a barrier to disease.

The Birds, the Bees, and Saving Seeds

There are some particulars to pollinating heirloom vegetables that you'll need to know. I'll explain exactly *how* vegetables become pollinated and why the origin of that pollen is important. I'll also talk about how you can have a hand in pollination in this part.

I'll get into collecting, cleaning, drying, and storing your heritage seeds through some very simple processes. Even if you've never collected and saved seeds before, there are easy vegetable seeds to get you going down the road to creating your own seed bank.

Pure Pollination

In This Chapter

- How plants are pollinated
- Thinking about the distance between varieties
- Physical barriers to prevent cross-pollination
- What is hand-pollination?

Pollination is a vegetable plant's main concern, considering that pollen will not only make it produce fruit for the gardener's table, but the fruit guarantees that the variety will be around to see another generation. *How* vegetables are pollinated is crucial when it comes to planning your heirloom garden. In this chapter, we talk about how mature plants make baby plants and why the details are important.

The Sex Life of Vegetable Plants

The primary goal in the sex life of veggies is to get the sperm cells from the stamen of a flower onto the pistil of another (or the same) flower, which has the ovary. Once this happens, the plant is said to be pollinated, which means seed will now form.

Some plants have a distinct male flower (which holds the pollen) and a separate female flower (which has the ovary). This is the case with pumpkins, melons, and zucchini. *Cross-pollination* is the term used when the pollen is either transferred between the flowers of two plants or when pollination occurs between two flowers on the same plant.

Some plants such as beans, tomatoes, and peppers have what's called "perfect" flowers. These plants have flowers that have both the stamen and the pistil (male and female parts) on the same blossom. When a flower pollinates itself, it's called "self-pollination."

While some plants do self-pollinate, that doesn't mean they *can't* cross-pollinate. They can and they will. Some plants *need* to be cross-pollinated in order to produce fruit. Vegetable plants pollinate either by themselves or with assistance from wind, water (dew), insects, birds, and mammals—including humans.

HERITAGE HINT

When two plants cross-pollinate, the result of the cross won't be seen until the next generation of plants. For instance, the variety Moon & Stars watermelon is planted next to a Chelsea watermelon, and they cross-pollinate.

The fruit harvested from that Chelsea plant, for example, will actually be the Chelsea variety. It will look like a Chelsea watermelon should look and taste like a Chelsea watermelon should taste. The *cross* between Moon & Stars and Chelsea will be in the seeds inside the melon. If you collected those seeds and planted them, the fruit born from that plant would be the Moon & Stars/ Chelsea cross—an F1 hybrid, which may not be anything like either parent.

Keeping Varieties at a Distance

There are several ways to prevent your varieties from cross-pollinating (and therefore, creating a hybrid). One way is to simply have them keep their distance. On the outset, this sounds pretty simple, but you need to keep some things in mind. To use distance as an isolation technique, two things have to happen.

If you're using distance as your barrier, unless you have a lot of acreage, you'll probably only be able to grow one variety of a particular vegetable at a time. Distance works very well for vegetable varieties that are uncommonly grown.

You may also be able to get away with shorter distances between varieties if you stagger *when* the varieties are planted. In this way one plant is finished blooming and being pollinated before another begins. The seeds from each have been kept from cross-pollinating.

Crops used as barriers in between your seed-saving veggies can work, too, not just as a barrier but as a decoy by becoming another pollen source for pollinating insects.

Unfortunately, even if you work all of this out, your worries may not end with your own garden. Take a peek over your neighbor's fence and see whether they are growing the same species but a different variety. Bees, other pollinators, and wind can carry pollen for miles. This problem is actually fairly simple to solve. In the spirit of keeping things friendly with your neighbor, choose a different technique for maintaining pure pollination.

For example, if your neighbor is growing peppers, your pepper plants can easily be cross-pollinated by any pepper, hot or sweet, growing near it. How near? For commercial purposes, hot peppers are kept over 1 mile from sweet peppers, and sweet peppers are grown $\frac{1}{2}$ mile from other sweet peppers.

In home gardens, the isolation distance is as far as possible, or a minimum of 50 feet. This is because home garden seed is for personal use, not for commercial purposes.

For vegetables that have perfect flowers and are therefore self-pollinating, you may still want to keep distance between varieties. It's still entirely possible for the pepper varieties to cross-pollinate.

Physical Barrier Techniques

In a home garden environment, it may be impossible to be sure that varieties are kept far enough away from each other to be certain that pollination has been pure. Not a problem: physical barriers or mechanical isolation can be a seed-saver's best friend.

Caging

A technique called caging is an effective physical barrier. For self-pollinating plants, it's quite perfect as far as pure pollination goes. The rectangular or square cage is made from a frame of wood or lightweight plastic. Then window screen or cloth is stretched over the frame.

The screen or cloth must be long enough for about a foot of it to be buried into the ground to prevent penetration by determined insects and ground-dwelling bees.

You can set the cage over veggies such as peppers or tomatoes when you see flowers. The plants have the opportunity to pollinate themselves without interference from insects that cross-pollinate the varieties.

The cage can be placed over insect-pollinating vegetables as well. You can use the cages in a couple of ways when working with these types of vegetable plants. The first way is to alternate which plant is caged on which day.

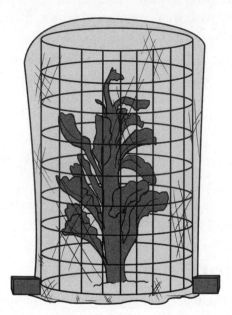

Bagging is good insurance against undesirable cross-pollination between vegetable varieties.

Say you have kale and cauliflower from which you'd like to save seed. These vegetables readily cross-pollinate. So when the blossoms are visible on the kale, cover it with the cage from morning until night.

Remember that ideally, you'd like to cover several of these plants. The cauliflower can then have all the bees' attention and become pollinated. The next day (early) remove the cage from the kales and place it over the cauliflower plants.

Now the kales have a chance to become pollinated, and the cauliflower remains isolated. This routine continues up to the point where the plants have stopped flowering. To ensure seed purity, it's a good idea to now cage both types of plants until the seeds have begun to dry.

If a bare cage is used with netting or cloth over the top, be sure that the material is long enough to have rocks or boards hold the ends down. Once again, this will make it hard for insects to get inside. It's important to note that caging may reduce the amount of fruit that's produced.

Yet another method is to cage and introduce the necessary pollinators to live in the cage. This is done quite often to prevent carrots from crossing with Queen Anne's Lace anywhere within ¼ mile.

Bagging

Plants that are insect-pollinated such as broccoli, cucumbers, watermelon, and pumpkins can be protected from cross-pollination by using the bagging technique. It also works well for self-pollinating plants such as tomatoes and peppers. Bagging is exactly what it sounds like—covering the female flower with a bag so that pollinators can't pollinate it.

In this case, you would hand-pollinate the female flower using either the paintbrush or flower-to-flower technique, then cover the blossom with a paper or light material bag like muslin or a commercial product called Reemay. Don't use plastic bags for bagging flower heads, as they can cause the flower to fry as well as get slimy and are therefore unsuitable for seed production.

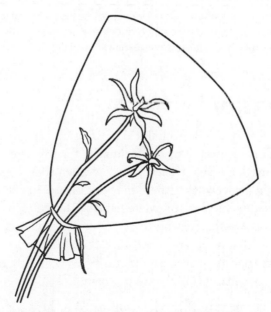

The caging technique is an effective physical barrier when you're after pure pollination.

For veggies that self-pollinate, cover the blossoms with a bag as soon as they appear. You'll need to secure the bag to the stem without hurting the plant. You can use a cotton ball under the edge of the bag and then tie it with thick thread or a twist-tie. You want the tie to be secure, but do this gently.

The cotton ball will also thwart determined bugs from reaching the flower. When you see fruits forming, you can take the bag off with no further worries. Remember to tie an identifying string or ribbon onto the stem after the flower has set fruit *before* you remove the bag! This way there'll be no question about which flower you pollinated.

Those veggies that are wind-pollinated such as beets, chard, spinach, and corn have pollen that's so small it can usually penetrate even the most finely woven fabrics.

> **HERITAGE HINT**
>
> Once in a while you'll hear someone make the comment that when they hand-pollinated their cucumbers the fruit turned out tasting bitter. To clarify, a bitter cucumber has nothing to do with pollination.
>
> Bitter cucumbers are about *cultural* influences. Cultural circumstances such as drought while the fruit is being produced puts stress on the plant and can result in the cucumbers having a bitter flavor.

Hand-Pollination

Hand-pollination is also called mechanical pollination, as it's done very specifically by the gardener. This technique is used primarily for three reasons. The first is when natural, open-pollination is insufficient, such as when there aren't many pollinators around or there's the concern that there may not be any in the immediate area. The second reason gardeners or plant breeders hand-pollinate is to ensure that varieties don't cross-pollinate. Another reason to give vegetables a hand with pollination is to increase the chances that pollination will be successful. For example, cucumbers often have problems with their fruit reaching maturity, as well as fruit deformity. So it makes sense to be sure many flowers are pollinated.

If a gardener wants to be sure that open-pollinated or heirloom seeds are being saved, hand-pollination is the easiest answer. This technique ensures that the plant was pollinated by the same variety and not cross-pollinated by another variety (which would make the seeds F1 hybrids instead of open-pollinated plants).

Flower-to-Flower Technique

This is one pollinating technique in which no tools are necessary; all you need are the flowers themselves. Vegetables like squash, pumpkins, and cucumbers have both male and female flowers. It's easy to tell the difference between the two.

You can spot the female flower by the small fruit (or "potential fruit") that sits just behind the blossom. When gardeners first see this undeveloped fruit, they sometimes mistake it for a baby fruit that's already been pollinated.

It's easy to believe that somehow you've done something wrong when the fruit then shrivels up and dies. The truth is that the flower wasn't pollinated to begin with. So if that's ever happened to you, you're off the hook. This makes the male flower simple to spot—it lacks any bulge resembling a fruit.

To hand-pollinate using the flower to flower technique, start with several male flowers. Now gently pull off their petals and rub the remaining middle part (stamen) all over the female flower's middle part (pistil).

Pick and prepare several male flowers, then use a rubber band or masking tape to hold them closed, to protect them from insects. Then, open or remove the petals of the chosen female flower and "paint" the pistil with the stamens of all the waiting male flowers, one at a time. Work quickly, and watch for pollinators. Then close the female flower tightly with masking tape or a rubber band so no pollinators can gain entry. Mark the stem of the flower you pollinated. Loosely tie a string or ribbon around its stem so that you will know from which fruit you want to save seeds. Leave the fruit on the vine until it's mature.

Brush or Swab Technique

Another way to hand-pollinate your vegetable plants is to use an artist's paint brush and gently rub the bristles all around the male flower's anthers, which is the part of the stamen that's covered with pollen. Then take the brush and swirl it all over the female flower's pistil. Again, be certain to protect the flower from further pollination by exuberant insects and mark the flower that you've pollinated immediately.

If you like playing the scientist and feeling all official, the paint brush technique is the way to go. Either way, whether you rub the two flower parts together or use a brush, the story ends the same way. Someone always ends up with fruit.

Shaking Technique

Self-pollinating plants such as the tomato can also be hand-pollinated. This is the simplest form of hand-pollination. It's done by taking the flowering branches and shaking them gently. The pollen will drop from the stamen of the flower onto the pistil.

There's no precise number of times you should shake your tomato plants. But gardeners usually do it two or three times a day to ensure pollination. Other plants that are self-pollinating and would benefit from a gentle shaking are peppers and eggplant.

The Least You Need to Know

- Some vegetable plants have separate male and female flowers, and some have a "perfect" flower that has both male and female parts in a single blossom.
- When plants cross-pollinate, the result of that cross isn't seen until the next generation of plants that sprout from the collected seed.
- One way of achieving seed purity is to keep varieties a distance apart. The necessary distance depends on the vegetable species.
- If you're concerned that you don't have the varieties far enough apart, you can use physical barrier techniques such as bagging and caging.
- Following correct hand-pollinating techniques will ensure that the plant wasn't cross-pollinated and eliminates the worry that there aren't enough pollinating insects in your area.

Collecting to Storing Your Heritage

In This Chapter

- Reasons to save seeds
- Collecting and cleaning seeds
- Drying and storing seeds
- Simple ways to save heirloom vegetables
- Sharing your seed bounty

In this chapter, we'll get into the basics of collecting and saving seeds from your heirloom vegetables. These are the seeds you'll use for next year's harvest and the seeds that I hope you'll share with friends and family.

This chapter will also describe how to clean, dry, and store your heirloom seeds. While the techniques I share will get you on your way to creating your own seed bank, there's more that can be discussed that goes beyond the scope of this book. For those interested in the fascinating details, I recommend checking out Suzanne Ashworth's seed-saving book, *Seed to Seed*, and Nancy Bubel's *The New Seed Starter's Handbook*, both of which I have listed in the resources section.

Why Save Seed?

Agricultural experts tell us that 90 percent of our vegetable varieties have already been lost. Some of this has to do with small seed companies going belly-up because of crop failure or being bought out by the larger companies. Varieties also disappear when they don't sell well for a while and are then discontinued. It's all about business. In the end, it can mean bad news for everybody.

Here's the deal: the answer is so obvious that even governments worldwide are involved with saving seeds from heirloom vegetables. These seeds are stored in seed banks around the globe in an effort to preserve the genetic diversity of food crops worldwide. That's all well and good, but there are a couple of glitches.

The first problem is that seeds don't keep indefinitely. Every few years (depending on the species), the seeds need to be planted, the crop grown out, and the seeds collected once again. If everyday gardeners don't preserve what rightfully belongs to everybody, the only places that will have heirloom seed is "the powers that be"—and that should concern us.

Also, the large seed banks can't hold *everything*. This is where you, dear vegetable gardener, come in. It may sound unlikely to you at first, but small farms and backyard gardeners can be a tremendous help in the effort to preserve heirlooms for future generations.

We can prevent any other varieties from being lost—and bring back vegetable varieties that are nearly extinct—if home gardeners, small farms, and seed banks work together.

Vegetable Character: Annual, Biennial, or Perennial

The first thing you'll want to know about a plant before you breed it is its character. Is the vegetable an annual, biennial, or perennial? This is important because not all of these plant categories produce seed every year.

Annual veggies produce seed the first year they are planted—provided you let them produce seed. Broccoli comes to mind. While this cool-loving vegetable would produce seed the first year, we harvest their heads for dinner while the blossoms are closed tight. If you want to keep seed from a certain broccoli variety, you'll have to let a couple of them bloom so they can produce seed.

Artichokes and rhubarb are examples of perennial veggies. While artichokes will flower in a single year, they don't usually produce seed until their second year. Rhubarb may produce seed the first year; however, its seeds almost never grow true to type. It's best to take cuttings of favorite rhubarb if you'd like to propagate this vegetable.

Biennial plants are those that only flower and produce seed in their second year. Carrots, cabbage, turnips, beets, and onion are examples of veggies that fall into this category.

Some of these plants can be tricky. Cabbage and turnips, for instance, need to go through a cold period before they'll even think of producing a flower.

Carrots are a good example of a biennial plant that we grow as an annual. Carrots don't produce seed until their second year in the ground. They're almost always grown as annuals as we harvest carrots for their roots. Because we pull them up before their tops can ever flower, most gardeners never see their carrots produce seed.

My point here is that it's best to know what you're dealing with before you set out on your seed-saving expedition. That said, don't let any of this put you off. Some vegetables are wonderfully simple as far as pollinating and seed-saving goes. We'll get to those in this chapter.

HERITAGE HINT

Although some vegetable species like pumpkins have both male and female flowers on the same vine, it's genetically healthier for the plant to have a male flower from a different plant (of the same variety) pollinate a female flower.

Collecting Seed

Heirloom vegetable seeds that are born inside a fleshy fruit (such as pumpkins and winter squash) can often be harvested when you would normally harvest them for eating or storage. Summer squash, zucchini, and cucumber seeds are collected well after they would have been harvested for eating.

Those seeds that rest inside husks, pods, and other casings such as beans, peas, radishes, and corn are typically left on the vine until they are completely dry.

There are also those vegetables such as fennel that, if left to dry in the garden, need to have bags placed over their tops (the greens) so the seeds don't blow away when the first strong wind comes by. The fennel tops or umbels can also be collected when the seeds form and kept until the seeds are dry and ready to store.

Although we may go about collecting seeds from individual vegetable plants differently, you should keep some things in mind while you're gathering your future crops.

The first thing to remember is that only mature seeds will end up viable, so practice a little patience and don't try to collect seeds from young fruits.

It's important not to keep the seeds from a plant that has a disease. Not only could the disease remain on the seed, but the mother plant may be particularly susceptible to it, and you could be planting the same genetics for next year. You'd like to avoid this. Saving and planting diseased seed can also weaken the future line of the heirloom variety. In fact, the whole idea behind saving heirloom seeds is to save the healthiest seeds and best representatives of the variety grown.

Another sound seed-collecting practice is to save seeds from several plants of the same variety to keep the gene pool strong.

There are two methods used to collect seeds from vegetables: the wet process and the dry process.

Wet Processing

Collecting seeds from fleshy, pulpy fruits like tomatoes and cucumbers requires a technique called wet processing. With wet processing, the idea is to squeeze or scoop the insides of the vegetable into a container and leave it to *ferment* for about five days.

> **DEFINITION**
>
> **Fermentation** is the anaerobic conversion of carbohydrates to alcohols and carbon dioxide (or organic acids) using bacteria, yeasts, or a combination of both.

The process may look unsavory, but it turns out that during fermentation, many diseases that would otherwise affect the next vegetable generation are killed off by the bacteria and yeast.

There are two trains of thought on the next step. Some gardeners scoop the seeds out of the fruit and put them into a water-filled container with a lid. However, gardeners in the *other* camp won't add the water in with the fruit's pulp.

In *Seed to Seed*, Suzanne Ashworth recommends skipping adding water to the pulp and juice so as not to slow down the fermenting process. She goes on to say that diluting the natural juices could also cause "premature sprouting of the seeds near the end of the process."

In any case, in three to five days, the mixture will ferment and mold will form over them. This is just fine. Fermenting actually encourages seed germination later and kills some diseases.

Take a large spoon and scoop as much of the mold-fungus off of the top of the seeds as you can. Now, you'll add a lot of water into the container and swish everything around.

If you let everything settle in the container for a moment, you notice that some of the seeds float and some of the seeds sink. It's the "sinkers" that are the keepers; these are the viable seeds. Ideally, it's easiest to use a small-holed strainer or a screen-type strainer for the rinsing. Of course, you need to be sure that the holes are smaller than the seeds you're cleaning.

The next step is to pour off the rest of the debris and most of the water, being careful to keep the sinkers. Then proceed to the straining/rinsing step. This eliminates most of the mold and bacteria.

Seeds collected from the center of vegetables have a lot of moisture in them and need more time for drying before they are stored than those gathered from pods. Ideally, these seeds should be dried as quickly as possible. That said, be careful not to dry them so fast as within a week, because if you dry them too quickly, they'll shrink and crack.

WEED!

Don't use your oven or direct sun to dry your heirloom seeds. The heat from both the sun and the oven can damage them. If you'd like to speed up the drying process, try using a ceiling fan.

You can do this by placing them in a netted bag and hanging them in an airy place to dry. You can also put them on a tray or in a container on the counter or a shady windowsill. Stir the seeds once in a while to give them a chance to dry evenly all over.

HERITAGE HINT

Excellent record-keeping is your best friend when it comes to seed-saving, especially with heirloom vegetables. Label your seed containers clearly and immediately with the name of the seeds and the date they were collected. It's amazing how easy it is to mix up seed varieties!

Dry Processing

This technique is used for those veggies whose seeds are held inside pods, husks, or any other dry casing like peas, beans, and carrots. Dry processing is even less involved than wet processing—making it so easy you could hire your 10-year-old to do it. Unless wet weather is in the forecast, these types of seeds are allowed to dry right on the plants.

Some plants let the seeds fall naturally little by little. Some gardeners make it easy on themselves and as the seeds begin to look mature, secure paper bags over the seed heads and attach them to the stems of the plants. This will catch any seeds that ripen early.

Collecting the seed from dry-process plants is done differently than those that are wet processed. The stuff you're left with after collecting these seeds is actually a mixture of seeds and what's called "chaff." Chaff is pod or husk coverings and other debris that fall in with the seeds.

Separating the seeds from the chaff is a technique called "threshing." Threshing is a process used to remove the coverings from the seeds. Commercial threshing is done by multitasking machines that can harvest, thresh, and winnow the seeds all at once. For the home gardener, a bag, pillowcase, or small sack will do just fine.

Simply put the collected seeds into the bag, secure the ends, and roll it around, lightly crushing the contents a bit. Don't get all macho on me; this isn't the job for a framing hammer. You don't want to damage the seeds. For the tinier ones, there's nothing wrong with using a flat board to gently press on the seeds to loosen the chaff.

After the seeds are collected, the next step of dry harvesting is called "winnowing." Winnowing is just a five-dollar word for getting the loosened chaff off of your seeds before you store them. In nature, this would be done by the wind. You can use the same idea by placing the seeds in a bowl and shaking the bowl around a bit. Most of the chaff is lighter than the seeds and it'll rise to the top.

Blow gently into the seeds to remove the lighter-weight chaff. Repeat this process until all (or most) of the chaff is gone. You may want to be sure you have a large sheet underneath your workspace so if any seeds are blown with the debris, you can retrieve them. Or work outdoors on a day that's not too windy.

If you do use a sheet, be sure all previous seeds are removed before you do any winnowing with other varieties. Another option is to use a screen or sifter where the holes are smaller than the chaff. You can simply sift them apart. The size of the sifter holes will depend on the size of the seeds and the chaff.

Storing Seed

You may not have thought about it, but you're creating your own seed bank. Many a casual hobbyist has collected and grown their own heirloom seeds only to find that after a couple of years they've become rather obsessive. After taking stock of your seed collection one day, you may realize that you could supply enough produce to feed a small town. This is as it should be.

For the home gardener, the simplest way to store seeds is in individual envelopes, which should be placed as a group inside an airtight container for extra protection. Many years ago I saved seeds using standard letter-size envelopes. Later I discovered manila envelopes like the ones used for mailing documents, but in a much smaller size such as coin envelopes.

You can also purchase Silica gel for the airtight container. Don't put it directly inside the envelopes *with* the seeds. The Silica gel sucks up any moisture in the container and keeps it away from the seeds.

The idea is to keep the air or atmosphere free of moisture and have as little temperature fluctuation as possible. You don't want the combination of the temperature and the humidity levels to exceed 100. For example, with a storage temperature of 60°F, the humidity should not exceed 40 percent.

Keeping seeds in canning jars (either loose or in envelopes) is ideal because, as long as they have a rubber gasket, they're moisture-proof and pretty close to airtight. I've also put the envelopes into a plastic container, which isn't airtight, but it's worked for me.

The best place to store your seed containers is somewhere cool, dark, and dry. The refrigerator is an excellent place to store them, but I'd look for guidance before tossing them into the freezer. If the water inside the seeds freezes, it can do damage in the thawing process.

If the refrigerator isn't convenient for you, consider floor-level areas such as an unused room, cellar, or mudroom. Even if you're using the refrigerator as your seed storage facility, you'll want to have a backup plan (like a cool garage or cellar) in case of a power failure. If your power is out for an extended period of time, it could mean a total seed loss!

Simple Vegetable Seeds to Save

Although anyone can learn how to save nearly every type of seed, there are some vegetables that are simpler than others. The vegetables listed here are among the easiest to start with if you'd like to begin saving your own heirloom seed.

Beans—After you've harvested beans from the vine or bush for eating, leave a few pods on the vine for three weeks or more. If you're interested in collecting seeds and you expect rain or snow, you can pull the entire plant from the soil and hang it upside down in a sheltered area. This way, you won't lose them due to the weather.

Choose a place that's cool and dry until the pods are completely dried out. They'll look brittle and brown and will completely shatter when tapped with a hammer. Of course, the hammer would only be used as a test for dryness before storing the remaining seeds. Remove the dried beans from the pod and sort out small or discolored seeds before saving them. Remember, the seeds you want to save are those that best resemble the seeds you planted. Also, you shouldn't be able to dent the surface of the bean with a fingernail if they're properly dried.

Cucumbers—When we want to harvest cukes for food, we harvest them when they're young, being careful not to let them become over-ripe. But if you want to save the seeds for future use, don't do that. Leave them there on the vine until they are way past over-ripe, to the point where the fruit is big, soft, and yellow. This is when the cucumbers are ready to be harvested for seed-saving.

You'll want to pull them off the vine before the frost comes, or any signs of rotting appear. But be sure to save seeds from the cucumbers that ripen at the very end of the harvesting season. If you let even one become over-ripe at the beginning of the season, it will send a signal to the plant to stop producing fruit. It's not the signal you want to send too early if you intend to eat them. After you've collected the seeds, use wet processing to complete the procedure.

Eggplant—You can recognize an eggplant that's ready for seed collecting in a couple of ways. One, they lose the sheen on their skin and can appear a bit wrinkled. Two, their color is different than the color they are when you're harvesting them for eating. The purple varieties will turn brown, and the ivory varieties will turn yellow.

The eggplant should be taken from its vine before a frost and the seeds scooped out. The pulp will come out with the seeds, so separate them by swirling them around in a water bath. Lay 'em out and let 'em dry.

Another way to collect the seeds from eggplant is to put the bottom ²/₃ of an eggplant into a food processor (a metal blade is fine), along with an equal amount of water or more, and process until it's mush. Pour the mush into a large container and let it set for about 10 to 15 minutes. The seeds will sink to the bottom and the "mush" on top can be spooned or poured off (into the compost pile, perhaps). The seeds are flat and slippery, so the metal blade does no damage.

Peas—After you've collected what you wanted from the pea plant, leave some pods on the vine to dry for about another month. If you think there will be a frost or wet weather coming, you can snip off the pods or pull the entire plant from the ground and hang it upside down in a cool, dry place. It's important for air to circulate around the drying pods or the seed quality will be low. Think "separate, don't stack" if you pull them up to dry. Remove the dried peas from the pod and sort before saving.

Peppers—You'll know your peppers are ready to have their seeds harvested because they turn to their mature color: red, orange, or black. Just scrape the seeds out of the pepper and put them in a colander or a screen (sieve). Rinse the seeds if you need to and air-dry.

When saving seeds from hot peppers, the same techniques are used; however, wear gloves and work in a well-ventilated area to protect your lungs.

Squash and pumpkins—With squash, you'll want to be sure that the fruit is completely mature before you harvest them for seed. When summer squashes have been left on the vine for so long that their outer skin hardens, leave them there another three weeks. That'll give their seeds time to ripen.

Harvest the seeds from pumpkins, winter squashes, and summer squashes by letting them become fully ripe (the same time that you would harvest and store them) and just chop them open. Saving the seeds is as easy as it comes.

Swirl them in a water bath, working any strings or remaining flesh free from the seeds with your fingers, then spread them out to dry. To be certain they're dry (and therefore safe to store), try to bend one in half. If it snaps cleanly in half, they're good to go.

Tomatoes—Saving seeds from tomatoes uses the same procedure as saving seed from cucumbers; use wet processing. You want to make every effort to keep the fruit from the best plants that meet the description of the variety. This helps keep the genetics of the variety strong. So if that variety is supposed to mature in 100 days, don't save a tomato for seeds that matured in 86 days, nor one that matured in 128 days.

Share the Wealth

As an heirloom gardener, you'll be compelled to share your bounty with others. If you're a seed-saver, then it'll feel like a duty! People you may want to share your vegetables with are friends, co-workers, neighbors, and most certainly your family.

Often people aren't growing heirlooms simply because they haven't been introduced to them. Here are five great opportunities to share heirloom vegetables and their seeds with others:

1. **Over-the-fence:** If you haven't collected your *own* seed, then share some that you've purchased (surely you over-bought). If you've started seeds indoors, bring some seedlings to friends, family, co-workers, church members, community gardens, and neighbors as surprise gifts. Seeds and seedlings make a perfect end-of-the-year teacher gift. A great addition to this is if you can bring the vegetable itself for them to taste. This is a none-too-subtle approach that works so well it's almost cheating.

2. **Simple teaching:** Offer to teach a one-time gardening lesson to the Girl or Boy Scouts, a 4-H club, community center, or home-schooled children. Simple teaching can be taken further by offering to teach a 4-H gardening project with your local club. 4-H members not only learn during the course of the project, but they also show their goods at the local county fairs as well as put on demonstrations. This ends up reaching a much larger number of prospective heirloom gardeners.

3. **Seed parties:** Heirloom seeds are a great excuse to throw a party—specifically, a seed exchange party. Invite every gardener you know to your home on a warm day and serve scrumptious food (preferably garden-type finger foods) and drinks. Have them bring seeds that they've collected or purchased, and everyone goes home with a garden of different varieties.

   Take this concept a step further and have gardening guests bring extra seeds. Then invite people who *don't* garden (yet) to the party. Add to your invitation list your neighbors, church group, Bunco group, book club, and co-workers. Everyone knows that the way to lure people into a new idea is to stuff them with delicious appetizers. It's an invitation they won't be able to resist.

4. **Join a seed exchange:** Seed exchanges are clubs where seed-savers have a chance to meet other seed-savers. These clubs have individuals listed and which seeds they save so that members can trade seed varieties among

themselves. Most of these organizations have a strong sense of saving endangered heirlooms and other open-pollinated vegetable and fruit varieties. Look for national organizations as well as local ones. Can't find a local club? Start you own.

Perhaps the most well-known organization today is the Seed Savers Exchange on their 890-acre Decorah, Iowa, farm. As the home to 25,000 endangered vegetable varieties, it's the largest nongovernmental seed bank in the United States. Seed Savers Exchange's 1,100 members have access to more than 20,400 open-pollinated varieties in their Seed Savers Yearbook. This big book combines what the Seed Savers Exchange has to offer as well as the seeds that other members privately offer. That's one heck of a lot of healthy.

> **HERITAGE HINT**
>
> If you present someone with a seedling as a gift, be sure to give them *two* seedlings if it's a vegetable that produces both male and female flowers such as squash, cucumbers, or melons. This will increase the chances of the female flowers becoming pollinated naturally.
>
> Also, if you're saving seeds, the vegetables benefit from being pollinated by another plant of the same variety, as it adds a healthy dose of genetic diversity.

The Least You Need to Know

- We can preserve genetic diversity, food control, and our heritage by saving heirloom seeds.
- Vegetable seeds are collected by using either the wet process or the dry process.
- Primary concerns with saving seeds are to keep moisture out of the seed container and to keep temperatures low with the least amount of fluctuation.
- Beans, cucumbers, eggplant, peas, peppers, squash, pumpkins, and tomatoes are among the easiest vegetable seeds to save.
- The goal of seed-saving with heirlooms is to preserve the integrity of the variety as much as possible for future generations.

The Heirloom Vegetable Directory

In this directory, I've included a wide variety of heirlooms. You'll find varieties that are 50 years old, as well as ones that are 100 years old or more. I've also included some popular varieties that are open-pollinated and are well on their way to becoming tomorrow's heritage vegetables.

As you peruse the directory section in search of your favorite vegetables, I encourage you to try a couple of varieties that are new to you (or your garden) because it's exciting and rewarding to make something that was old new again.

For color photos of the heirlooms mentioned in the heirloom vegetable directory, please visit the companion website to this book, www.cigheirloomvegetables.com.

Artichoke

 Artichokes are large perennial thistles that originated in the Canary Islands. They're an ancient vegetable and have been found in literature as far back as 77 C.E. Italy is responsible for developing the artichoke as an edible.

Apparently, the 14-year-old Italian princess, Catherine de Medici, is responsible for bringing her beloved artichokes from her home in Italy to her new home in France. Both French and Italian explorers had them aboard their ships, and now America has a love affair with this edible thistle.

Artichokes are most easily grown in a warm climate as a perennial or biennial. These Mediterranean plants make themselves especially at home in places like the California coastline, where they all but flourish.

If you live in USDA zones 8–11, you're in luck; artichokes will grow as the perennials they were always intended to be. They prefer a pH range of anywhere from 6.5–8.0 and want full sunshine (that's 8 hours a day). They require deep watering and are fairly heavy feeders, so compost their bed like crazy.

Green Globe

Green Globes are one of the fastest maturing artichokes around. They're full of nutty flavor and make interesting ornamentals. Keeping them as perennials requires a long growing season, so most zones will grow them as annuals (with the exception of zones 7–10). 85 days to harvest.

Imperial Star

This variety was the first artichoke that was bred to produce in one season from seeds to fruit, which is good because Imperial Star is bull-headed about over-wintering and is speedy. All gardeners to zone 7 can keep this one around as a perennial. 95 days to harvest.

Purple of Romagna

This favorite artichoke variety in Italy is tasty with purple heads that are large and round. Its leaves are extremely tender and popular with chefs. It is excellent for growing in warm climates. 85–100 days to harvest.

Violet de Provence

A French heirloom, Violet de Provence has nice flavor and attractive purple heads to boot. It makes a beautiful ornamental and is a rare find unless you're reading this in Europe. Days to harvest unavailable.

Violetta Precoce

This purple artichoke variety has been popular in Italy for hundreds of years. Violetta Precoce is very pretty so it doubles as an ornamental. Also, the purple variety of artichokes tend to be more tender than the green types. 90–100 days to harvest.

Violetto

This purple artichoke is an abundant producer. It matures a little later but has delicious heads. It's hardy to zone 6. 95 days to harvest.

Arugula

Arugula has many other aliases, such as rugula, roquette, rocket, or rucola. It's a wild Mediterranean salad and sandwich green with a nutty, peppery flavor. The seeds are often used in India as a spice and were used in ancient Rome to flavor oils. It's all the rage in Italian cuisine where it's often sautéed and used in ways other than in a salad bowl. This fast-growing, cool-season crop is hardy and self-seeds. Arugula is at its best when it's harvested young (around 2–3" tall).

Apollo

The Dutch really improved this domesticated arugula. It has large leaves that are high in vitamin C. Excellent-flavored Apollo is rarely bitter. If you keep the plant harvested, you'll get 3–5 cuttings from each plant. 40–45 days to harvest.

Even' Star Winter

Even' Star Winter was bred to grow fast while receiving very little water and in poor quality soils. That said, it does like its soil to become flooded but then drain well. It's a sturdy little variety and hardy to 6°F. 35 days to harvest.

Rocket (Wild Rocket or Sylvetta)

Sylvetta is a wild arugula with short and tasty leaves. Its flavor is more pungent than the more common arugulas, and it's slower to bolt than the others as well. 45 days to harvest.

Asparagus

Asparagus loses its flavor rapidly after it's harvested, so if you really want the full flavor-scope of asparagus, you need to grow it at home. Asparagus is also high in vitamins K, A, C, and E. The minerals it offers include calcium, folic acid, iron, fiber, protein, and magnesium. Unfortunately, while gardeners are quick to try their hand at tomatoes, potatoes, or radishes, they're sometimes hesitant when it comes to planting an asparagus patch.

Perhaps it's the rumors that asparagus is fussy or hard to grow that keep them from planting. I think it's the time that asparagus needs to mature that turns people off. Whatever the case is, you need to just ignore everything you've heard and grab yourself some asparagus crowns and get them in the ground—you'll be tickled pink that you did.

Asparagus is a perennial, and while you certainly can grow it from seed, if you do, you won't want to think about snapping off a spear for a year or more. If you plant it as crowns, however, you could take a spear here and there this first season. Don't get greedy, though. Asparagus rewards the patient gardener.

If you let all of the spears (or most) grow out and die down the first year, you can get a nice little harvest the following year and really decent spears the third year. This is why it's hard to give a "days to harvest" number for it. If you offer a little patience, asparagus pays off handsomely; it'll be in your garden for 20 years.

Asparagus is a heavy feeder and likes to be spoiled regularly with compost added to its bed. It enjoys full sun and prefers a pH level that's on the high side (6.5–7.5). It likes lots of room to spread out, and because the old-fashioned varieties may produce seed, it can overtake the garden if you're not watching.

Mary Washington

Before hybrids were introduced, this used to be the most commonly grown asparagus. Mary Washington has long, thick spears and is a strong producer. Days to harvest unavailable.

Precoce d'Argenteuil

This is an old Italian heirloom. It's a gourmet variety that has rose-colored buds and delicious spears. Very popular in Europe. Days to harvest unavailable.

Bean

Beans are the Swiss Army knives of the vegetable world and have been around since at least 7000 B.C.E. They're incredibly versatile and useful in terms of preparation, storage, flavors, and colors. There are so many different types and varieties of beans—you'll be hard pressed to pick just a few for your garden.

There are many ways to categorize beans. For this directory, I decided to have the main categories listed as bush and pole bean varieties. These two categories describe the bean's growing habits as opposed to their uses. However, I've added their traditional uses in the descriptions.

The other bean categories you'll find here are broad beans (fava), soybeans (edamame), and lima beans (butterbeans). Yes, the beans in these categories can have bush or pole habits as well. But they're different enough to warrant a place of their own in the bean section.

HERITAGE HINT

Snap beans are so called because of the way we use them for meals. They're traditionally "snapped" before being prepared and eaten. Snap beans are also referred to as green or fresh beans. The pods are harvested when they're young and tender, and the entire pod is eaten with the beans inside. Some snap beans grow on poles, and some grow on bushes. They come in every color you can imagine, including white, pink, green, black, buff, purple, and mottled.

Broad (Fava) Bean

These beans are Mediterranean natives and have the same growing requirements as peas. At maturity, they're about the same size as lima beans but taste like a cross between limas and peas. Like all beans, favas are popular as "green manures" because they fix nitrogen in their roots. They can be planted during the off season for major veggies, and after they flower you can turn them under the soil, which makes them release the nitrogen they're holding. This adds some nitrogen punch to the garden bed.

Fava or broad beans can be eaten fresh or dried. They're huge beans and can be ground into a meal-type staple much like cornmeal. The "skin" that covers the bean needs to be removed before you eat them, though. They're often light green, purple, and gold.

Aquadulce

This Spanish heirloom's large, white beans are a good protein source. It grows well in cool climates. 85 days to harvest.

Broad Windsor Long-Pod

This is an old English favorite with 6–8" long gourmet pods. 75–80 days to harvest.

Crimson Flowered

This is a shorter-growing fava with brilliant red flowers, which are also edible and can be tossed into salads to add color. Excellent as a green manure. 95 days to harvest.

Bush Bean

Bush beans are compact vegetables, making them well suited for small gardens. The beans mature nearly all at once, so you may want to direct seed them at three-week intervals to keep them coming all season. While pole beans usually outproduce bush beans, the bush varieties bear earlier in the season.

Appaloosa

This southwestern heirloom has quite a range of usually mottled color: white and black, lavender, pink, brown, and tan. It's predominately used as a drying bean, but can be eaten fresh as a snap bean if it's harvested young. 100 days to harvest.

Arikara Yellow

From North Dakota's Arikara tribe, this yellowish-tan bean is excellent for drying. It's also drought-tolerant. 80–90 days to harvest.

Beurre de Rocquencourt

This wax bean was named for a French farming area called Rocquencourt. This plant produces high yields of yellow, delicious pods. It's an early producer and does well in most climates. 61–70 days to harvest.

Black Valentine

These shiny, stringless, green pods contain black beans that are excellent for eating fresh (when harvested young) as well as for drying (they make a fantastic soup). Peter Henderson & Co. first introduced them in 1867. The plants are prolific and reliable. 52 days to harvest.

Blue Lake 274

This bush bean was developed from the Blue Lake pole bean in 1961. It's a reliable and bountiful producer of pods that are tender and tasty. Perfect for canning and freezing. 60 days to harvest.

Blue Ribbon

This variety is a heavy producer of a terrific snap bean that pulls double duty as a beautiful, purple-streaked dry bean. Hard to find, but Sustainable Seed Company has it. 55 days to harvest.

Bolita

This variety is *really* old; it was one of the first brought to New Mexico by the Spanish. It has a reputation of having a very creamy texture and is considered tastier than the pinto bean. It produces creamy tan beans very early in the season. Bolita is thought to be easier on the stomach than other varieties. 90 days to harvest (as a dry bean).

Bountiful

This bush bean produces tons of high-quality, stringless pods whose tan beans, at maturity, are wonderful for freezing. It tends to be resistant against beetles, rust, and mildew. 49 days to harvest.

Bumble Bee

These pods produce three to five large beans that are white with a maroon-black splash at the eye of the bean. Bumble Bee is used as a drying bean and is high in vitamins and minerals. 85–98 days to harvest.

Burpee's Stringless

In 1864, this snap bean was touted as the only truly stringless pod around. It's a prolific producer of dark brown, waxy beans for drying. It is also drought-tolerant and heat-resistant. 46–50 days to harvest.

Calypso

These dry beans are black and white with a contrasting eye and are nice for soups and baking. Very productive and adaptable bush. 70–90 days to harvest.

Calypso Red

These beans can be harvested while they are young to be eaten fresh and their seeds harvested later as a drying bean. They have a nice texture and are great for baking. They're also a pretty dried bean: maroon-red and white with maroon dots on the white parts. 70–90 days to harvest.

Cannellini

This is an old Italian heirloom with a smooth texture and a nutty flavor that arrived in America somewhere in the early 1800s. It's an Italian favorite in minestrone soup and can be used as a dry bean as well. When cooked, the off-white Cannellini beans increase to two and a half times their dried size. 80 days to harvest.

Cherokee Wax

These beans are black inside long, waxy, yellow pods. The pods are terrific used fresh, frozen, or canned. A heavy-yielding and vigorous bush, they also tend to be disease-resistant. 58 days to harvest.

Contender (Buff Valentine)

Introduced in 1949, this is a warm-season favorite of many gardeners. It offers super-high yields of delicious, disease-resistant green pods. 42–50 days to harvest.

Cranberry (Speckled Bays, Dwarf Horticulture Taylor Bean)

A popular New England 1800s heirloom, these buff and cranberry mottled beans can be used as *shelly beans* and as dry beans. They have a light, sweet flavor as compared to pinto beans. Popular in Italian, Portuguese, and Spanish dishes. 70 days to harvest.

DEFINITION

Shelly beans are beans that are harvested as "green-shelled" varieties. Shellies are harvested when the bean seeds are fully mature inside the pod, yet before they're dry.

Dragon Tongue

Dragon Tongue is a Dutch wax bean heirloom. The pods are a creamy yellow with thin, purple streaks. They're not just another pretty face, however. Dragon Tongue is known for its superb flavor, which makes it popular with chefs. It's stringless, a great producer, and makes a tasty shelled bean, too. 55–60 days to harvest.

Dwarf Bees

Introduced in 1853, this short bush is ornamental with its beautiful scarlet flowers that attract hummingbirds. The beans are used as a snap bean when harvested young and later used like a shelly bean, a lima bean, and a dry bean. 75 days to harvest.

Empress

These snap beans have stupendous flavor, and can be eaten fresh or used for canning and freezing. Empress produces heavy yields of stringless beans. Offered originally by Guerneys as Experimental Bean 121, the name then changed to Empress in 1979. 55 days to harvest.

Everbearing Brand Joy

This hardy bush will provide you with a continuous harvest of delicious 5" bean pods. 57 days to harvest.

EZ Pick

This is a common commercial snap bean variety. It's very productive and has a sweet flavor. The pods are easy to pick because they grow above the foliage. 55 days to harvest.

Fin de Bagnol

Fin de Bagnol is a delicious French gourmet string bean. Its flavor is best when picked every other day while the pods are young. Grows well in cool soils. 49–57 days to harvest.

Goldcrop

Goldcrop's 5–7" long, waxy seed pods are formed high on this bushy plant, so harvesting is a snap. The pods are stringless and bright yellow in color, while the seeds themselves are smooth and white. It's heat-resistant, and resists diseases such as curly top virus, common bean mosaic virus, and blossom drop. 55 days to harvest.

Great Northern

Rumor has it that Oscar H. Will received the Great Northern bean from a Hidatsa Indian and brought it to market in 1937. It's particularly adaptable to northern gardens and is a heavy producer. It's a common household dried bean that's used in myriad soups and stews, and an easy bean to cook with that cooks faster than Navy beans. 91 days to harvest.

Harvester

Succulent 6" pods are formed on this hardy bush. It's resistant to common bean mosaic virus, bean rust, and root rot. 53 days to harvest.

Hidatsa Red

Hidatsa Red is a Native American heirloom shelling bean or dry bean. The seeds are dark red. It is perfect for arid growing zones. 80–90 days to harvest.

Hutterite Soup

This dry bean was grown and preserved by the Hutterite Christian Group. Seeds are a creamy, green-yellow color with a dark ring around the eye. It's an excellent variety for soup making (soup ends up creamy white). 85–90 days to harvest.

Ireland Creek Annie

This 1930s English heirloom is a reliable, high-yielding bush. The buff-yellow beans have superb flavor and make for a thick sauce. Used as a dry bean for soups. 70–75 days to harvest.

Jacob's Cattle (Trout, Forellen)

This early variety, old dry bean from New England has white and maroon mottling. It's a nice soup or baking bean and is good as a snap bean, too. Some seed sources claim that Trout is the same as Jacob's Cattle Bean and Anasazi; some claim that just isn't so. We'll put them as one for this directory. 90 days to harvest.

Jacob's Cattle Gold

This dry bean is a stable cross between Jacob's Cattle and Paint. The vigorous plants are loaded with brown and white mottled 5" pods that have great flavor. 80 days to harvest.

Kenearly Yellow Eye

Kenearly Yellow Eye offers early harvesting with high yields. The beans are white with yellowish-brown eyes and are excellent for baking and easy to shell. 80–95 days to harvest.

Kentucky Wonder Bush (Commodore)

Kentucky Wonder was introduced as a bush bean during the late 1800s. It's a heavy producer of stringless 6–8" flavorful pods of excellent quality. 65 days to harvest.

Landreth Stringless

Landreth Seed Company introduced this early bush bean in 1885. It produces 5" pods that are brittle—easy to snap as well as juicy and flavorful. 54 days to harvest.

Lina Sisco's Bird Egg

This dry bean was brought to Missouri during the 1880s in covered wagons. This *horticultural*-type bean has excellent flavor. 85 days to harvest.

> **DEFINITION**
>
> **Horticultural beans** are large-seeded beans used in the green-shell/shelly stage. A young horticultural bean is not generally used as a snap bean because the pod's fiber is too tough.

Montezuma Red (Mexican Red)

This was a popular heirloom in California for many years from the mid-1800s, but you don't see it around much anymore. The bushes have a tendency to ramble, and the dry beans are a medium-size dark red, and rather flat. 95 days to harvest.

Montpellier

This is a French filet snap bean that produces thin, 5–6" pods. They're best when harvested at ¼" in diameter. 55 days to harvest.

Nance

This thin, green snap bean was introduced by Underwood Gardens in 2004 from seeds sent by a woman in Tennessee whose family has grown it since the Civil War. It has classic, sweet bean flavor. The seeds are an off-white color flecked with black. Lovely pink flowers allow it to double as an ornamental, and it's a heavy producer. 64 days to harvest.

Nickel Bush

Nickel is a 4" long, French baby gourmet filet. It is high quality, stringless, and delicious. It's a long-holding pod that's resistant to white mold and brown spot. 52 days to harvest.

October

This Native American heirloom can be traced back to the Cherchei Nation in Tennessee during the 1830s. It's a prolific bush and a good dried winter staple. 85–90 days to harvest.

Painted Pony

This is a stringless, dual-purpose bean that's great as a snap, but is also excellent as a dried bean for soups. The beans are a lovely white and brown color. Its markings stay true after cooking. 60 days to harvest if used as a snap bean. 80 days if used as a drying bean.

Pencil Pod Black Wax

Dating back to 1900, this bush bean was created by crossing Improved Black Wax and Black Eyed Wax. Its yellow, stringless, 5½–6" long curved pods are perfect for eating fresh, as well as for canning. It's an early and continuous producer and it adapts to a wide range of environments. 52 days to harvest.

Pencil Pod Golden Wax

An old-fashioned favorite that was introduced in 1900, this is a wax bean of superb quality and rich flavor. The stringless, 5–7" yellow pods are formed on vigorous bushes and are excellent for canning or freezing. 50–65 days to harvest.

Pinto III

Pinto III is a vigorous plant that produces 3–4" green, flat pods. They make good snap beans when they're harvested young, but are usually grown for their seeds, which make a good dry bean. The beans are beige with red-brown splashes. 95 days to harvest.

Promise

This is an 1898 half-runner bean that was first grown in Promise, Oregon, by an original settler, John Phillips. Promise was a particularly hard area to homestead, but these small, white bean seeds produced plants that proved to be both hardy and prolific and the family persevered. Promise beans only became available to the public in 2004. They're good eaten fresh or canned. 60 days to harvest.

Provider

Introduced in 1965, Provider is a very dependable early snap bean. The bushes are prolific and often hold longer than most snap beans. It germinates in cool soil and is disease-resistant. An excellent bean for canning and freezing. 48–54 days to harvest.

Purple Kidney (Norberg or Wanda)

While Purple Kidney resembles a regular kidney bean, the flavor is supposed to outshine its plain cousin. It's a large, meaty, dark maroon-purple bean that turns brown when it's cooked and tends to stay moist. 90 days to harvest.

Purple Queen

The pods start out a lovely deep purple that changes to a dark green while they're cooking. They are known for their delicious, fresh flavor and are good for canning and freezing. 55 days to harvest.

Red Nightfall

These lovely little dry beans are mottled red and pinkish-grey. and have a slightly sweet flavor. The smart cook would use it in dishes like salads and relishes to show off its beautiful color. 80 days to harvest.

Red Swan

This snap bean is a stabilized cross between a purple snap and a pinto bean. It has 4–5" long dusty-rose pods that have great flavor. It's also harvested as a shelly bean. 52–58 days to harvest.

Roma II

Roma II is an improved Romano bean. It's a prolific producer of 6–7" wide, flavorful pods. It is resistant to common mosaic virus. 55 days to harvest.

Romanette Italian White

This is an excellent white-seeded bean variety for the home garden. Its green pods are 5" long and they freeze very well. 65 days to harvest.

Romano 14

This bush version of Romano Pole Bean is good for fresh eating, as well as canning and freezing. It has a reputation for great flavor. The pods are flat, thick, and stringless. Excellent rust resistance makes it a favorite for planting in the fall. 54 days to harvest.

Royal Burgundy

Royal Burgundy is a stringless, tender bean with pods that change from purple to dark green while cooking. 55–60 days to harvest.

Royalty Purple Pod

This bean was introduced in 1957 by the Billy Hepler Seed Company. A wonderful variety for the home garden, Royalty Purple Pod blooms in purple flowers letting it double as an ornamental in the garden. The 5" stringless purple pods turn green when they're cooked and the seeds are buff-colored. It germinates well in cool soil. An excellent bean for veggie soup. 55 days to harvest.

Saint-Esprit à Oeil Rouge (Soldier Bean, Beans of the Religious, Holy Spirit in Red Eye, Navel of Good Sister)

I'm not sure I've ever heard of a bean that's had so many names. When dry, its markings are supposed to resemble an angel, soldier, dove, or nun depending on exactly how many glasses of wine you've had. It's a wonderful dry bean for soups or baking. 100 days to harvest.

Slenderette

These gourmet-quality 5" pods are dark green and stringless. The bush is resistant to common bean mosaic virus, pod mottle, and curly top virus. 53 days to harvest.

State Half Runner

This high-yielding, semi-runner plant grows to about 3' tall, so staking isn't an issue. It produces 4", very flavorful pods. This variety is used both as a fresh green bean and a dry bean. Great for canning and freezing. 60 days to harvest.

Steuben Yellow Eye (Molasses Face)

This bean is a heavy producer and very hardy. It's wonderful for baking and drying for soups. It's a lovely cream color and has a splash of yellow over the eye. 90 days to harvest.

Swedish Brown

A Swedish immigrant family brought this shelling bean to Montana during the nineteenth century. It grows well in colder climates and is a prolific bush. The small, oval, brown beans have a tender, light, nutty flavor. 90 days to harvest.

Tanya's Pink Pod

This plant produces Romanolike, flat pods that are mottled pink and green color. The pink fades when they're cooked. 60 days to harvest.

Tavera

This is a wonderful gourmet French filet green bean. Extremely flavorful, fine, and tender 4–5" pods. 54 days to harvest.

Taylor Dwarf

This is a horticultural bean from the early 1800s. It's thought that this semi-runner bean (14–18" tall) was introduced to the United States via the Italians. Taylor Dwarf grows well in cool climates and is primarily used as a shelling bean, although it's also used as an early snap bean. 68 days to harvest.

Tendercrop

Tendercrop is a perfect snap bean for the northern midwest and west. The bush is a heavy producer of 6" pods. 55 days to harvest.

Tenderette

This plant produces well even in hot weather. The 6" pods are fiberless and stringless. 55 days to harvest.

Tendergreen

Introduced in 1922, Tendergreen is heat-tolerant and disease-resistant. The 6" pods are stringless and the plant offers high yields. Nice for fresh eating. Great for canning and freezing. 55 days to harvest.

Tiger's Eye

Tiger's Eye is a productive bush that produces a rich bean with smooth flavor. The skins are said to be so tender that they nearly disappear when they're cooked. This bean is an orange color with maroon swirls that will remind you of the eye of a tiger. It's used for shelling, chili, and refried beans. 80–90 days to harvest.

Tongue of Fire (Borlotto Lingua di Fuoco)

This Italian heirloom is a horticultural bean whose seed starts as a tan color and acquires red streaks and spots as it matures. The large round beans have fantastic flavor and are deliciously versatile as they can be eaten fresh or frozen, canned or dried. 70 days to harvest.

Top Crop

This heavy-producing bush offers meaty, round, and stringless 6" pods. 52 days to harvest.

Top Notch Golden Wax Improved

This is a heavy-yielding variety that's perfect for the home garden. It produces 5", thick, flat, golden pods that are stringless. The tender beans inside are white with brown marks on the eyes. Used as a fresh snap bean or as a dry bean. 50 days to harvest.

White Half-Runner

These plants are a bush type that have really short runners (24–36") so I put them in the bush beans section. White Half-Runner has a wonderful flavor, and is super heat- and drought-tolerant. They are heavy producers with 4" pods. A stringless snap bean whose contents are also used as shelly beans.

White Rice

Although these small ivory beans are only about ⅓" long, they have a rich flavor that enhances casserole and rice dishes nicely.

Lima Bean (Butterbean)

Lima beans, also known as butterbeans, can be large or small and may be colored white, black, red, or purple. They can be borne on bush or pole varieties. Lima beans come in large-seed and small-seed varieties. They need a long growing season and perish in a hard frost.

Lima beans like their soil a little warmer than traditional snap beans and they like it well-drained. They can be eaten fresh like snap beans when you see the pod is filled and plump. Or they can be left on the plant until they're dry and harvested for storing as a dry bean. Following, I've listed both the bush and pole limas together, but have labeled each in the variety descriptions.

Black Knight Butterbean

This pole bean is both vigorous and prolific. It produces maroon-black beans with good flavor; usually used as a dried bean. 83 days to harvest.

Burpee Improved Christmas Pole (Large Speckled Calico, Giant Butter, Giant Florida Pole)

This dependable bean with good flavor can be traced back to the 1840s. It's heat-resistant and is extremely prolific in areas that are hot and humid. Inside 5–6" pods are quarter-size, cream-colored beans with red stripes or swirls and a rich flavor. Young pods can be used as a snap but can also be harvested as a shelly and dried bean, too. 90 days to harvest.

Dixie Speckled Butterpea

Dixie Speckled Butterpea is a highly productive bush that grows well in hot climates. The tasty baby limas are pea-size and red-speckled. 76 days to harvest.

Dr. Martin

This is a long-vined lima bean that trails to 10' on average. It produces 5" pods containing three or four lima beans. They're very tasty fresh and are good dried as well. 90 days to harvest.

Fordhook 242

This bush lima is heat-tolerant and drought-resistant. It produces thick 4" pods with three to five flat, greenish-white beans that have a nutty flavor. 72 days to harvest.

Henderson Bush (Henderson's Dwarf or Baby Bush)

This bush lima is an old favorite. The story goes that this bush was found growing wild on a roadside in Virginia. It was introduced in 1888 by Peter Henderson & Co. Henderson Bush is prolific and adapts to many climates. The beans are tender, small, creamy white, and mature early. They're eaten fresh, frozen, or canned. 72 days to harvest.

Hopi Yellow

Hopi Yellow pole produces beautiful limas that range from deep yellow to dark orange with dark brown speckling. There are about three beans per pod. 80 days to harvest.

Illinois Giant

Introduced in 1992, this pole lima was created by crossing Christmas with Dr. Martin which produced this drought- and heat-tolerant, heavy-yielding, large-seeded lima variety. The beans are a lovely light green splashed with maroon-red. This is an easy-shelling bean. 86 days to harvest.

Jackson Wonder Butterbean

Introduced by David Landreth & Sons in 1888, this is a common southern variety bush butterbean (lima) because it enjoys heat and humidity. But it grows well in northern climates, too. The pods hold three to five buff-colored seeds with purplish-black mottling when they're dry. They're used as a fresh bean when harvested young, or as a dried bean when mature. 66–75 days to harvest as a shelly bean.

King of the Garden

King of the Garden may be the most popular pole lima heirloom out there. It's an old-fashioned favorite due to its excellent quality. Introduced in 1883 by Frank Platt, it's a heavy producer of 4–7" pods. The large, creamy white beans have a honey flavor. 88 days to harvest.

Sieva (Carolina or Southern Pole)

Sieva is a pole lima that grows very well in the south but can also be grown in the north. It's cold-resistant and is wonderful for the home garden as well as a market variety. It produces flat, medium green pods that have terrific flavor. 60–75 days to harvest.

Violet's Multi-Colored Butterbeans

This is a pole variety that's both disease- and drought-resistant and produces 3–5" pods. The beans come in multiple colors of beige, cream, violet-purple, and reddish-brown with swirls and speckles. They're small seeds, but they have excellent flavor. Great as a fresh lima or dried. 80–90 days to harvest.

White Christmas

This reliable butterbean with a pole habit was created through an accidental cross-breeding of Christmas and Sieva and introduced in 2000 by Southern Exposure Seed Exchange. The beans are large and white with a purple that looks like it's been air-brushed on. It's prolific, easy to shell, and good in hot areas. 80–90 days to harvest.

Willow-Leaf White

Introduced in 1891, this pole bean has incredible heat and drought resistance. It's a high-yielding plant in the hotter zones, but still performs well (maybe less prolifically) in northern climates. The leaves are willow-shape and it has 3" pods that hold small, white limas. The vines are very attractive, and some gardeners will plant them as ornamentals. 86 days to harvest.

Worcester Indian Red Pole

Introduced in 1990 by Southern Exposure Seed Exchange, this is a seriously hardy pole lima. Its history is said to have pre-1868 Native American roots. Worcester Indian Red is prolific and heat- and drought-resistant. It has dull red to dull maroon seeds. This lima reverts back to its wild cousins by shattering (sort of exploding open) its pods when they're thoroughly dry. 85 days to harvest.

Pole Bean and Runner Bean

Runner or pole beans grow exactly the way their name implies—on vines up to 20' tall. Many gardeners enjoy growing them because they double as ornamental plants in the garden and save space by using vertical growing areas. They also have a reputation for having better flavor than the bush varieties of green bean and produce a higher yield. They can produce flowers in white and red, white, and purple. Runner beans are either harvested while they're young as snap beans or dried and stored.

I like growing both pole and bush beans because although the pole beans usually produce later than their bushy cousins, they offer a higher yield in terms of productivity. You can be harvesting pole beans for more than six weeks during the season. For your pole beans, try to use a support that's at least 8' high.

Asian Winged

This bean is beautiful and extremely useful. The pods are delicious, the roots have a nutty flavor, and the leaves can be cooked just like spinach. There's just no waste with this bean. The pods have four winged edges for a very unique look. This variety needs regions that have good heat and humidity to grow well. Days to harvest unavailable.

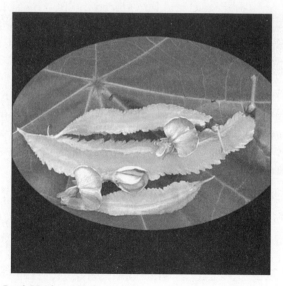

Photo by Baker Creek Heirloom Seeds

Black-Seeded Kentucky Wonder

This is an Ohio heirloom snap bean that germinates well in cool soil. The 6–8" pods are stringless and have good flavor and texture. 84 days to harvest.

Blue Coco

Blue Coco is a pre-1775 French heirloom that has green leaves with a hint of purple. The pods are a purple-blue color and the beans are chocolate, hence its name. The 6–7½" pods are rather flat and curved with a hearty flavor. This snap variety performs admirably in the heat. 79 days to harvest.

Blue Lake Stringless

Here's a stringless version of the wonderful Blue Lake green bean. Blue Lake features 6" long pods that are smooth, crisp, and have a full-bodied flavor. They never go limp on you. They're prolific producers setting pods from the top of the plant all the way to the very bottom. 63 days to harvest.

Brockton Horticultural

Brockton Horticultural was introduced in 1885 by Aaron Lowe Seed Co. It bears gorgeous red-striped pods but is used only as a dry bean. This buff and dark brown–flecked pole bean has excellent flavor. 85 days to harvest.

Cascade Giant Stringless

Cascade Giant was bred with the West Coast in mind. Created by utilizing the Oregon Giant Pole bean, it grows extremely well in cool environments and damp areas. It's a prolific plant that produces a ton of 8–10" dark green pods with purple mottling. They're terrific for eating as a snap bean or for canning. 65 days to harvest.

Cherokee Cornfield

This is a pole bean that's been popular for planting in the cornfield. It grows well in hot growing zones. It was grown by the Iroquois as a dried bean for corn soup and bean bread. Its pods are 7" long and the seeds are a gray-brown color with brown mottling. The pods can be eaten fresh or saved as a dry bean. 70 days to harvest.

Cherokee Greasy

This is a Cherokee heirloom bean that's still grown on the reservation at Cherokee, North Carolina. It produces 4" pods with 7 to 10 white beans inside each one. They're best used as a shelling or dry bean. 75 days to harvest.

Cherokee Trail of Tears

This is a story to remember. These beans were given to the Southern Seed Exchange by the late Dr. John Wyche, whose ancestors carried the bean with them during the death march of the Trail of Tears from 1831 to 1839.

The American Indians were forced to leave their home by the Federal Government and trek through the Smoky Mountains, ending up in Oklahoma on March 26, 1839. It's said there are 5,500 Indians buried along the way.

The shiny black beans are formed inside 6" pods that are green with a purple overlay. They're good harvested young as a snap bean or as a dried bean when mature. 85 days to harvest.

Chinese Red Noodle Bean

This yard-long snap bean is a stunning and unique addition to the veggie garden. Its pods are a gorgeous dark red and average 18" long. They also keep most of that color even after preparing (i.e., sautéed). They're a prolific producer all summer long and have a terrific reputation for having tremendous flavor as well as being loaded with nutrients. 80 days to harvest.

Photo by Baker Creek Heirloom Seeds

Climbing French

Introduced in the 1930s, Climbing French was supposed to be the most widely popular climbing French bean in England. Its flowers are lilac and have 4–7" pods that are stringless and have excellent flavor. 65–75 days to harvest.

Dean's Purple Pole

This snap bean variety is not only prolific and hardy, it's beautiful to boot. It's a Tennessee family heirloom that becomes covered with brilliant purple bean pods. It's also bean beetle–resistant. 75 days to harvest.

Genuine Cornfield (Scotia or Striped Crease-Black)

This is one of the oldest beans cultivated by the Iroquois. It's heat-tolerant, and also takes some shade. To use as snap beans, the 5–7" pods should be harvested before the seeds fill the pods. The dried seeds are buff-brown mottled with dark brown. 70 days to harvest.

Gold of Bacau

Romania is responsible for this high-yielding, stringless pole bean. The pods are a flattened Romano type and are 6–10" long. A very sweet and tender snap bean. Great for freezing as well. 60–70 days to harvest.

Good Mother Stellard

This is a prolific, well-loved family heirloom. It has a hearty, rich flavor that makes it a perfect dry bean for soups. 85–95 days to harvest.

Grady Bailly

This North Carolina heirloom is a prolific and very tender green bean. It's very similar to Lazy Housewife. 80 days to harvest.

Grandma Nellie's Yellow Mushroom

Marge Mozelisky was given this yellow-pod bean by her grandmother. This plant is prolific and the pods are very tender if picked at 5" instead of 7". Some say it has a mushroomlike flavor when cooked. 70 days to harvest.

Greasy Grits

This is an old heirloom from the Appalachian Mountains that was commonly grown in the midwest and the south. Greasy Grits has been hard to find, but a couple of companies are carrying it. The beans acquired their name because the smooth, shiny appearance of the pods, compared to other beans, gives them a greasy look. This is a very productive vine and the beans are versatile. Use them as a snap bean when young or as a dry bean for soups when mature. Easy to shell. Days to harvest unavailable.

Henderson's Black Valentine

Introduced in 1897 by Peter Henderson & Co., this pole bean offers good yields and delicious pods. This is an excellent choice for an all-purpose bean variety as it makes a great dry bean for soups, too. 53 days to harvest.

Hidatsa Shield Figure

This is a bean from the Hidatsa Indians in the Missouri River Valley of North Dakota. It is a hugely productive dry bean. 90 days to harvest.

Ideal Market (Black Creaseback)

Originally introduced in 1914 by the Seed Store of Mobile, Alabama. Years later Reuter's Seed Company renamed it Reuter's Ideal Market. This is a productive, hardy pole bean and an early producer. Its pods are high quality, stringless, and fine-textured. 65–70 days to harvest.

Kentucky Wonder Pole (Old Homestead)

This bean was introduced in 1864 with the name Texas Pole but then reintroduced in 1877 by James J.H. Gregory & Sons as Kentucky Wonder. It was an extremely popular variety in 1901 and is still widely planted today. The plants are vigorous vines that produce flat, oval, and stringless 7–10" pods. Wonderful flavor eaten fresh, but can be canned or dried, too. 58–65 days to harvest.

Lazy Housewife

This is an exceptionally old bean variety. Around 1810, Lazy Housewife was introduced and claimed to be the very first stringless bean. Very productive plant with white bean seeds. It's good harvested as a young snap, as well as a shelly or dry bean. 75–80 days to harvest.

Louisiana Purple Pod

This lovely southern heirloom is drought-resistant but can be grown in the north, too. The vines are a purplish-green color with bright purple stems and flowers. It's a high-yielding plant that produces (you guessed it) purple stringless 7" pods that turn green while cooking. The bean seeds are a light to medium brown color. The pods have great flavor, especially when cooked lightly. Louisiana Purple Pod tastes best as a snap bean when harvested young. 75–80 days to harvest as a snap bean.

Mayflower

Like its name suggests, this all-purpose bean is thought to have come to America with the pilgrims via the Mayflower. It has been a long-time favorite in the Carolinas. This green bean is flavorful as a snap bean while it's young. The red and white bean seeds are great dried for soups. 90 days to harvest as a dry bean.

McCaslan 42

The McCaslan family of Georgia began growing these beans before 1900, and they were introduced to the public by the Corneli Seed Co in 1962. It's a hardy and productive plant with stringless, dark green pods. The bean seeds are white and are good for drying, too. 62–65 days to harvest.

Missouri Wonder

This bean was introduced in 1931 and was grown in the cornfields because the corn stalks made a great vine support. The pods have good flavor and make good snap beans, and the pinto-looking beans can be dried, too. 70 days to harvest.

Mostoller Wild Goose Bean

The Mostoller family of Pennsylvania has been growing these beans for over 100 years, which was when John Mostoller was said to have shot the goose that had these beans in its craw. The vine produces white flowers and 5" pods that contain four to five beans. The dried beans are buff with a brown patch over the eye. 60 days to harvest.

Oriental Yard-Long (Chinese Long Bean, Snake Bean, Asparagus Bean)

This is an annual climbing yard-long whose vines easily reach 10' and above. Their long pods grow from 14–30" and hang in pairs from the vine. This is quite a sight in a typical garden setting. The green beans are tender and crisp and have fantastic flavor. They're usually cut into shorter pieces before cooking. This pole bean grows exceptionally fast in hot climates, but matures much slower in cooler environments. 60–80 days to harvest.

Painted Lady Improved

A beautiful flowering pole bean, Painted Lady blooms are lovely red and white, attracting hummingbirds and hummingbird (Sphinx) moths alike into the garden. This English variety has been around since 1596 and produces 10" long pods. Painted Lady is harvested and eaten fresh when young, but mottled chocolate beans are useful dried, too. 80 days to harvest.

Papa de Rola (Dove's Breast)

This rare heirloom comes from Portugal. These plants only get to 4' tall, but because they require a little support, I put them in the pole category. Papa de Rola makes a tasty green bean, and the plump beans are great for drying as a delicious soup bean. The beans are half white and half beige with streaks of red. 90 days to harvest.

Pretzel

This is a pole bean/cowpea used as a snap, shelly, and dried bean. It was introduced by Underwood Gardens in 2006 from seeds sent by William Woys Weaver. It has an excellent bean flavor and an unusual shape—it curls around like a pretzel. Not bothered by bean beetles, it's also successful in extreme environments like high temperatures, drought, and poor soils. 52 days to harvest.

Purple Podded Pole

Henry Field first found this variety growing in a garden in the Ozarks during the 1930s. It's a high-yielding pole bean that bears 5–7" quality pods. The pods are stringless, tender, and deep purple. Very ornamental. 68 days to harvest.

HERITAGE HINT

Shelling or dry beans are so called because they're harvested when the beans are fully mature and their pods are swollen and dry. After they're shelled and dried, they can be stored for later use for steaming, baking, or cooking.

Rattlesnake Pole (Rattlesnake Snap)

These plants are drought-resistant and will grow to 10' tall. They're especially good for gardeners with sandy soils. They're excellent for hot growing zones and bear 7–10" dark green pods that have purple streaks. The sweet, rich dried beans are a light buff color with brown splashes. Excellent flavor. 73–90 days to harvest in both stages.

Romano Pole (Italian)

This old-world Italian flat bean is a reliable gourmet variety. The pods are thick, tender, and stringless. They're also resistant to mosaic virus. 70 days to harvest.

Ruth Bible

This Kentucky heirloom was grown in 1832 by the Buoys family and was introduced in 1984 by Seed Savers Exchange. It's a cornfield type and drought-resistant. It's a heavy-yielding variety with 3½" pods that may have slight strings. They're best harvested when they're small and tender as a snap bean. The seeds are a brown-tan and can be harvested when mature for storing as a dry bean. 75 days to harvest.

Scarlet Runner (Scarlet Runner Emperor)

Scarlet Runner beans have vibrant red flowers—super ornamental for the vegetable garden. The vines grow over 10' tall and are hardy but really prefer cooler weather than most pole bean varieties. The bean seeds are violet-purple with black mottling. This variety produces good snap, shell, and dry beans. 80 days to harvest.

Snow Cap

Snow Cap is one of the largest of the dried bean varieties. It's an excellent producer of reddish-tan beans with a white cap. They've been touted as one of the best soup beans because of their extremely creamy texture. When the beans are cooked, they increase to two and a half times their size. 100 days or less to harvest.

Speckled Cranberry

This bean was brought to America courtesy of England around 1825. Considered to be the best pole horticultural bean, it's a heavy producer of thin, stringless 7–9" pods. It continues to produce until the first frost. Some gardeners will harvest Speckled Cranberry at 80 days as a shelling bean, others will let it mature to 90 days and harvest as a dry bean.

Succotash

This cool-looking shelly and dry bean is deep purple and looks just like a corn kernel. You have to do a double-take to be sure it's a bean. It produces late, but has wonderful flavor. Days to harvest unavailable.

Sultan's Golden Crescent

Seed Savers Exchange is reintroducing this rare and nearly extinct snap bean. It's a heavy producer with stringless yellow pods that are early—and curly—and have excellent flavor. 75 days to harvest.

Sultan's Green Crescent

This variety is exactly the same plant as the Sultan's Golden Crescent except that the pods are green. 75 days to harvest.

Sunset Runner

Sunset Runner has some gorgeous peachy-pink-colored blooms to add some femininity to the garden. It produces flavorful green beans early and continuously. The black seeds are terrific for canning and freezing as well. 75 days to harvest.

Trionfo Violetto Pole

This stringless pole bean is ornamental as well as a snap bean. It has beautiful lavender blossoms and leaves with attractive purple veining. The lightly nutty and sweet purple pods turn green during cooking. This variety is dependable and early. 60 days to harvest.

Turkey Craw

The story handed down about this variety is that a hunter shot a turkey and found a bean in its craw, which he kept and planted. Turkey Craw is often planted in cornfields and can be used as a snap or dry bean. The pods are 1½–4" long and stringless. It has lovely green-colored beans. Days to harvest unavailable.

Soybean (Edamame)

Edamame has been grown in Asia for thousands of years and is just as easy to grow as bush beans. Like other beans, soybeans can be directly planted in the garden bed. They reach about 2–5' tall at maturity. Soybeans are harvested at the shelly stage, so collect the pods when they are about 80–90 percent filled out.

Asmara

These short, 2' determinate plants bear large beans and were bred for flavor and nutritional value. Moderately resistant to beetles. Days to harvest unavailable.

Kuro Mame (Kuromame)

This black soybean is used to flavor many dishes in Japan. It's famous for its tastiness. Days to harvest unavailable.

Envy

Envy has great flavor perfect for shelling or as a dried bean. Good variety for the northern zones. 80 days to harvest.

Lanco

Lanco's large green beans have a nutty, sweet flavor. These beans never fill out all the way, so don't rely on that sign for harvesting. Instead, harvest when the tops of the plants lose their deep green color. 120 days to harvest.

Moon Cake

These large soybeans were bred for flavor and nutrition. The stalks can reach 5–6' tall. 120 days to harvest.

Owen

Owen is compact and grows to just 2'. This dark soy's flavor is described as hearty. 120 days to harvest.

Beet

 People have been eating beets since prehistoric times—at least the tops. The Romans were the ones who decided to give the roots a try and decided they enjoyed that part of the plant, too. Beets enjoyed popularity in the sixteenth century and were referred to as "blood turnips." Beets are actually in the same plant family as Swiss Chard.

There's nothing tricky about growing beets, but you have to respect the fact that they thrive in cool environments. They'll grow best in an early spring or fall garden as they'll take some hard frosts in stride. And while they can survive in clay soils, they'll grow infinitely better in a sandy-loam one. All veggies dig compost, but don't add too much in the way of rich nutrients or they'll go to seed quickly.

If you're interested in harvesting the tops for salads or cooking, you'll want to cut those off the top of the beets when the roots reach about half their mature size (this depends on the variety). If you need to thin beets, you can cook up or toss the little beets into salads. Most beets have the best (sweetest) flavor when they're harvested young. If you let your fall beets go through several light frosts, they'll taste and store better as well.

Albino

Here's a beet of a different color—it's pure white. Got kids? No staining the hands here. It's round, is mostly smooth, and has delicious flesh. Its greens can also be eaten. Albino is a nice beet for sugar-making. 55 days to harvest.

Bull's Blood

This beet produces gorgeous deep red-purple tops that are lovely in salads when harvested young. Bull's Blood roots are ringed on the inside, incredibly sweet, and the juice is used to make food coloring. 35 days to harvest the baby leaf tops; 55 days to harvest the root.

Burpee's Golden

This is a pre-1828 globe-shaped beet that's also used for its tender roots and sweet greens. The roots are orange but turn a golden yellow while cooking. Because their color doesn't bleed, they're terrific in salads. 55–60 days to harvest.

Chioggia (Candystripe, Bassano, Dolce di Chioggia)

This is a pre-1840 heirloom from the Chioggia region of northeastern Italy. This early producer has a bright red skin and the inside is marked with alternating white and cherry-colored rings (like a bull's-eye). Its root is wonderfully sweet and it has mildly sweet and tender greens, too. 55–60 days to harvest.

Crapaudine

This beet has been touted as quite possibly the oldest beet variety on the planet. Foodie experts say that they can trace it back as far as 1,000 years ago. These beets have rough, carrot-shaped roots and dark skin. While the skin looks like bark and, well … like it just might be 1,000 years old, it's actually one of the most flavorful beet varieties. Chefs who are after fine flavor enjoy this beet. 70–80 days to harvest.

Crosby's Egyptian

Although "Egyptian" is in the name, this variety didn't come from Egypt at all; it's actually from Germany. This variety made its way to America in 1869 and was recommended in 1871 by Peter Henderson. The root basically grows on the soil's surface. This tender beet is early and has a fine flavor, so it's a favorite among chefs. 55–60 days to harvest.

Cylindra (Formanova)

This beet came from Denmark and is shaped remarkably like a dark red carrot. If you have a small space to grow beets in, Cylindra is one to consider because the roots grow down instead of out. It slices up nicely as the slices are very uniform compared to traditional round beet roots, and is very sweet and easy to peel. 46–80 days to harvest.

Detroit Dark Red

Introduced in 1892, Detroit Dark Red's shape is nearly a perfect 3″ globe. The sweet roots are perfect for eating fresh, as well as canning. This variety keeps well. 55–65 days to harvest.

Early Blood Turnip

This beet has been traced back to the year 1825. It's terrific for the home garden and as a market variety. It's good for canning as well as fresh, but hard to find (try Seed Savers Exchange). 48–68 days to harvest.

Early Wonder Tall Top

This pre-1811 heirloom is a smooth, very round beet that harvests early. The greens are tender and the fast-growing, uniform roots are good for pickling, borscht, cooking, or just fresh. 50 days to harvest.

Flat of Egypt

This variety produces 3″ flattened roots that are crimson in color. It's an early one that has an excellent kitchen reputation. 50 days to harvest.

Giant Yellow Eckendorf

This variety produces giant roots that can weigh up to 20 pounds. They're yellow-skinned with white flesh. They're highly nutritious, so this beet was used primarily in the 1800s as an animal feed. Days to harvest unavailable.

Golden Beet

Golden Beet has been traced back to the 1820s—maybe earlier. Being a deep, golden yellow, this beet doesn't bleed like the deep red ones do. It's not only lovely, but very sweet as well. The greens are also used in salads. 55 days to harvest.

Lutz Green Leaf (Winter Keeper)

This excellent keeper also happens to be one of the sweetest varieties. Even when large and mature, it retains its sugar-sweetness. The leaves are good for salads, too. One of the best for a fall harvest and for storing all winter. 76 days to harvest.

McGregor's Favorite

I'm tempted to grow this beet on the merits of its name alone. This is an heirloom from Scotland that has long and sweet roots and awesome-looking, purple metallic leaves that are shaped like spears. These greens really dress up a salad on top of having good flavor. 60 days to harvest.

Ruby Queen

This is an exceptional beet variety both for eating fresh and for canning. Its fine qualities are a buttery-smooth texture and top-notch flavor. Its roots are red and produce early. 60 days to harvest.

Broccoli

 Broccoli is just one of the members of the largest vegetable family, *brassica*. Others veggies that belong to this family include Brussels sprouts, collards, cauliflower, cabbage, kale, kohlrabi, mustards, turnip, and rutabaga. Broccoli is almost exactly like cauliflower, except it's green and won't tolerate the heat the way cauliflower will.

Broccoli is a cold-weather lover, but it's also fairly easy to grow. For broccoli, 20°F and frost is easy to live through. If you notice the weather warming up, mulch broccoli heavily to keep the moisture in the soil. In fact, broccoli appreciates rich and heavy mulch at any time.

If you have a broccoli that's not finished producing when the head is harvested, it's called a sprouting broccoli. The side shoots continue to sprout more florets and they're harvested throughout the season. Sprouting types should be harvested as often as possible because the more sprouts you harvest, the more you'll get.

When harvesting heads of broccoli, cut off the heads with a sharp knife while the buds are still tight. Because what you're actually going to eat are the unopened flower buds of the plant, you'll want to harvest before you see any yellow on them. Yellow means the flowers are opening and you're harvesting too late. Once they open, they'll signal to the plant to stop producing the delicious florets. Also, after blooming the florets and stalk turn bitter.

Broccoli is an excellent source of vitamins and minerals no matter how it's served. In fact, it has nearly the same amount of vitamin C as oranges do and as much calcium as a glass of milk.

Calabrese Green Sprouting

This variety provides delicious 5–8" heads. The heirloom was brought to America from Italy in the 1880s. It makes a great sprouting broccoli (hence its name) as it continues to produce many side shoots during the growing season. Heat will cause Calabrese to bolt in a hurry. 60–90 days to harvest.

De Cicco

Another old Italian heirloom that was introduced to the United States in 1890, De Cicco is reputed to be one of the best-tasting open-pollinated broccoli varieties out there. It is a compact (2–3' plants) and dependable plant that produces very early and keeps producing side shoots after the main 4" head is harvested. Its blue and green speckled heads are tender and sweet and freeze beautifully. It's also a nice canning broccoli. 50–70 days to harvest.

Early Purple Sprouting

Early Purple Sprouting broccoli quickly produces delicious purple heads. It's a large broccoli and offers many side shoots for the season. While it's a lovely purple in the garden, making it gorgeous as a raw garnish in salads, it turns green when cooked. It's extremely cold-hardy because the English bred this heirloom for over-wintering. 59 days to harvest.

Green Goliath

This broccoli's claim to fame is that it outproduces every other broccoli variety. Its giant, blue-green heads have fantastic flavor—fresh or frozen. It offers a longer harvest by producing early and growing a lot of side shoots after the main head is cut. 56 days to harvest.

Nutri-Bud

Developed by plant breeder Alan Kapular, Nutri-Bud is an early maturing broccoli that produces 4–6" heads. It's high in free glutamines, which is one of the building blocks of protein—hence the "Nutri" part of its name. It's high producing and has moderate side shoots throughout the season. 55–70 days to harvest.

Purple Peacock

This is a beautiful broccoli that produces a purple head nestled in scalloped leaves with pink veining, perfect as an ornamental while you're waiting to harvest as they resemble a peacock's tail.

There's no waste with Purple Peacock, either. It's a cross between a broccoli and a kale, so after you've harvested the broccoli heads, the leaves can be treated like kale or a raab. The leaves and stems can be cut after (or along with) the heads and cooked all together.

This variety is extremely tender when harvested young. Purple Peacock is a delicious variety and continues to produce side shoots for harvesting all season.

I've seen this variety as a hybrid, too, so watch that you're purchasing the open-pollinated seeds. The color fades while cooking. 70 days to harvest.

Romanesco Italia

Chefs go gaga over this variety. This Italian prize of tremendous flavor is one of the favorites and has been widely grown throughout Italy since the sixteenth century. This variety not only has nice production, but its flavor is touted to be head and shoulders above the rest of the broccoli varieties. Its buds are formed like raised spirals and are bright green—the ultimate in garden drama. 75–100 days to harvest.

Thompson

Tim Peters brought us this fine-flavored broccoli with its medium to dark green heads—which can be medium size or large. Thompson is the total package. It's a vigorous broccoli with an extended harvest period. It has excellent flavor and is great for the home garden. 70 days to harvest.

Waltham 29

The University of Massachusetts introduced the tasty Waltham 29 around 1950. This compact broccoli produces high yields of 4–8" bluish-green heads and side shoots that produce steadily after you've harvested the main crop. 74 days to harvest.

Broccoli Raab or Rabe (Rapini)

 Broccoli raab (sometimes spelled "rabe" but pronounced "rob") is known as rapini in Italy where it's extremely popular, so you may also hear it referred to as "Italian Broccoli." Although raab is in the broccoli family, it differs from broccoli in nearly every way. Broccoli raab isn't grown for its pre-blossoming florets, but rather its tender stalks, leaves, and flowers.

In fact, broccoli raab is actually a turnip that's grown for its greens. Its flavor has been described as tangy, peppery, and as having a little bite. Its flavor is best when harvested as a young plant; after it ages, it can become quite bitter and the stems will get woody.

This plant has earned its place on the healthy dinner table as it's loaded with vitamin C, vitamin A, calcium, potassium, and iron. It thrives in cool, short days and doesn't grow well in warm climates. Because it matures quickly, gardeners are often able to get several crops in a year.

It needs plenty of water, and like its *brassica* cousins will bolt quickly in the heat. Broccoli raab is ready for harvest just as the florets begin to open.

A Foglia di Olivo Brocoletti

This raab has a leaf shaped like an olive leaf and is a difficult variety to find. It's also grown for its leaves and shoots. It grows to about 14–15" tall and has a nice flavor. 70 days to harvest.

Rapini (Raab Rapini)

Because of the tender stems that are harvested for cooking, Rapini is known in Italy as "Broccolo asparago" (asparagus broccoli). The slightly bitter stems and leaves are often tossed into salads or used as a side dish to liven up a bland main course. 45 days to harvest.

Sorrento

Sorrento's florets are very uniform and dark green with a mild broccoli flavor. It has a mustard look, and bluish-green leaves. Harvest time for Sorrento is the spring and fall; it is the fastest maturing broccoli raab. 40 days to harvest.

Spigariello (Minestra Nera)

This broccoli raab variety has all the flavor of traditional broccoli without the typical broccoli heads. Spigariello greens have a sweet flavor as opposed to the bite that many other raabs do. They also have a great crunchy texture. Planted in midsummer, Spigariello can be harvested all the way up until the next hard frost if you constantly harvest leaves from the plant. Chefs and gourmet cooks are starting to request it. 65 days to harvest.

Zamboni

Zamboni resembles an asparagus. Another Italian heirloom, it has blue-green, turnip-like leaves and is a heavy producer. It can be planted from spring to late summer, and produces large spring buds and plenty of side shoots which are all are excellent in stir-frys, sautéed veggie mixes, or salads. 45 days to harvest.

Brussels Sprouts

Brussels sprouts were discovered in the fourteenth century near Brussels, Belgium, and look like teeny-tiny cabbages on a stalk, although, botanically, they're not. Brussels sprouts have a rather poor reputation as far as tasty vegetables go, and there's a reason for that: bad cooks.

Brussels sprouts can be seriously unpleasant (to the tongue as well as the nose) if they're overcooked. When they're gently steamed and topped with a garlic butter or other sauce such as a hollandaise, their sweet, nutty flavor comes through.

Brussels sprouts are very frost-tolerant. In fact, the cooler the temperatures, the sweeter the sprouts. In your fall garden, Brussels sprouts will be among the survivors like kale, broccoli, and collard greens. They need to be given a generous amount of time to mature (about 100 days).

Don't forget to pinch the tip off of the plant when you see sprouts beginning to form on the stalk—it'll encourage the little Brussels to swell. On top of being good growers when most vegetables are nowhere in sight, they can be harvested as needed from the veggie garden.

Catskill

This Brussels sprouts variety was developed by plant breeder Arthur White of New York in 1941. Catskill produces numerous 2" sprouts on strong stalks. They're dwarfed plants, but are hardy, easy to pick, and have good flavor. It's an exceptional variety for freezing. 100 days to harvest.

Long Island Improved

This is the most well-known Brussels sprouts variety. It's sometimes mistaken for Catskill, but Long Island Improved is a much older variety. This is a semi-dwarf (20–24" tall) and is a big producer of 1–2" sprouts. Anywhere from 50–100 dark green sprouts can be found on this plant. They also freeze well. 100 days to harvest.

Mezzo Nano

This mid-early producer's name means "half tall." Its sprouts are tender and compact. When it's given the fertile, loamy soil it craves, the plant is highly productive. It holds its own in yield against any hybrid variety. Harvest after the early frosts hit your zone. 110 days to harvest.

Cabbage

 While they aren't talked about nearly as much as tomatoes or peppers, cabbages are extremely popular in home gardens. They aren't demanding, but they do have some cultivation preferences. The first thing to note about them is that they thrive in cool weather. In fact, they really need it if you'd like them to produce nicely formed heads. Cabbages can take a light frost, but a hard one could do them in. Because they're shallow-rooted they also need constant moisture. They don't fare well if they're subjected to long dry periods with irregular watering, and may end up with split heads.

One of the best things you can do for cabbages is give them some compost-amended soil and mulch them after they're planted to hold in the moisture. In addition to being good eating, cabbages are lovely in the garden. They come in all ranges of green, green-blue, and purple hues. Cabbage heads can be round, oval, pointed, or flat.

Because cabbages are usually started indoors about eight weeks before the last frost date, the days to harvest will start "from transplant."

Bacalan de Rennes

Listed in 1867, this French heirloom forms green, oxheart-shaped heads and likes cool weather in mild and coastal climates. It is flavorful and an early variety. I found it at Baker Creek Seeds. Days to harvest unavailable.

Brunswick

This drumhead German variety was introduced in 1924 and is becoming rare. It's a fall and winter cabbage that's extremely cold-hardy and stores well. It's perfect for making sauerkraut. 90 days to harvest.

Charleston Wakefield (Henderson's Charleston Wakefield)

Peter Henderson & Co. developed this variety in 1892. Among the Wakefield cabbages, this is the one that produces the largest head at 4–6 pounds. It's a short-season variety, so it's a good one for growing in the cool-weather seasons of the west and south. It over-winters and stores well. 70 days to harvest.

Chieftain Savoy

The Savoy cabbages are known worldwide as the sweetest of all the cabbage types. This heirloom variety is an old favorite and is highly adaptable to zones with extremely different temperatures. It tolerates anything from heat to frost. The heads are round and flattened with savoyed (wrinkled) blue-green leaves wrapped around the outside. The leaves inside the 6–8-pound heads are white. 83 days to harvest.

Copenhagen Market

This cabbage was introduced by H. Hartman & Co. in 1909 and has been a favorite of home gardeners as well as market growers everywhere. It produces medium-size, 4–5-pound heads early in the season. This ball-type cabbage is tender and flavorful. Copenhagen Market is compact, so it's a perfect variety for home gardens. This large cabbage is great for fresh eating or cooking. 63–100 days to harvest.

Coeur de Boeuf Des Vertus

This is a French cabbage that's been around since before 1856. It has tender, tasty leaves that can be harvested early and is great for market. This is another cabbage variety that I've so far found only at Baker Creek Heirloom Seeds. Days to harvest unavailable.

Photo by Baker Creek Heirloom Seeds

Cuor di Bue

Cuor di Bue is Italian for "Bull's Heart." This old Italian heirloom produces oxheart-shaped (conical) heads. The 3–4-pound light green cabbages are of fine quality and mature early. It's a nice all-purpose cabbage that was very popular about 150 years ago. 70 days to harvest.

Danish Ballhead

This dependable cabbage, introduced in 1887 by W. Atlee Burpee, is a standard variety used for storage. The 6-pound, blue-green heads are tender and have a mild flavor. It's both bolt- and split-resistant and grows well in cool areas with short seasons. 110 days to harvest.

Early Jersey Wakefield

Early Jersey Wakefield was introduced around 1840 and has dark green, conical 5" heads that weigh about 2–3 pounds each. Its core is small with nice yellow outer wrapper leaves—perfect for home gardens and for the market. This frost-resistant variety is considered to be one of the best-tasting cabbages and is a good candidate for succession planting. Excellent for gardeners that live in the west. 70–80 days to harvest.

HERITAGE HINT

Succession planting can mean different things to different gardeners. But it's all based on the same premise: to get as much harvest as possible before the season ends.

Rather than planting all your seeds at once, plant smaller amounts at intervals. This can establish a continuous harvest as long as the season lasts. Of course, to be successful you'll need to know how many days of the season your area has and plan to grow crops that mature well before your season ends. Cabbages and lettuces lend themselves beautifully to this practice.

Glory of Enkhuizen

This large, globe-shaped cabbage has been on the scene since 1899, when it was introduced by Sluis & Groot in Enkhuizen, Holland. It excels in early production of its 10-pound solid heads. They're deep green with fine-ribbed leaves and they keep well. Perfect for coleslaw, sauerkraut, and cabbage rolls. 90 days to harvest.

Golden Acre

Here's a superior cabbage variety that's known for its tender and sweet 3–4-pound heads. Golden Acre cabbage is an early variety that has tight, ball-shaped heads that are wonderful for coleslaw and stir-fry. It matures about a week earlier than Copenhagen Market and is said to be unsurpassed for both the home garden and the market. 64 days to harvest.

Mammoth Red Rock (Red Danish)

Mammoth Red Rock was introduced in 1889 and produces 4–7-pound, solid, dark red heads with great flavor. It's used for cooking, pickling, and salads. 90 days to harvest.

Michihli Chinese

This tender, sweet variety is happiest in the cool-weather seasons in mild climates. Michihili has cylindrical heads that are around 17" tall and 6" wide. They are light green and tasty, making it an excellent choice for pickling and stir-frys. 70 days to harvest.

Nero di Toscana (Black Palm Tree)

This cabbage is often loosely referred to as a kale. I have to admit, it doesn't look very cabbagelike, but botanically it's a cabbage. Nero di Toscana can be traced back to the early 1800s for sure. It has dark green (almost black), savoyed (wrinkled) leaves that resemble kale. This is a popular cabbage in Italy and is often used for soups and stews. 60 days to harvest.

Pak Choi (Bok Choy)

Pak Choi is a very popular Asian nonheading leaf cabbage. Its large, round heads are glossy green on white stalks. It's crisp with a mild flavor that's excellent for any Asian cooking. The leaves reach 8–10 inches long and are cold-hardy. You can harvest the entire head at once or just pull off the outer leaves as needed—they'll continue to reproduce. 45 days to harvest.

Perfection Drumhead Savoy

Perfection Drumhead Savoy goes back at least as far as 1888. If you like the taste of cabbage but can't stand the smell of it cooking, this may be the one for you. This cabbage variety doesn't have that sulfur smell while it's being prepared. It has fantastic flavor that's both mild and sweet. It's a compact plant with savoyed (wrinkled), grayish-green leaves. It keeps very well. 92 days to harvest.

Premium Early Flat Dutch

This is a nice variety for cool-weather periods in both coastal and southern growing zones. It's heat- and split-resistant, and great for storing. The large, flat, 6–10-pound heads make an excellent sauerkraut. 85 days to harvest.

Premium Late Flat Dutch

German immigrants introduced Premium Late Flat Dutch in the 1860s. Its 10–15-pound heads resent hot weather, but will make a comeback if cool weather swings around again. A good choice for the west coast. This variety has good flavor, and is a good keeper. 100 days to harvest.

Red Acre

Red Acre is a superb all-around cabbage, and if you only choose one variety to grow, this may just be the right one. Gardeners swear by its flavor and reliability. It adds vibrant color to the garden with its round-headed, brilliant reddish-purple color. It weighs about 3 pounds and is 6–7" wide. It's an early producer, slow to bolt or split, and stores better than most of the early cabbages out there. Because it takes up little space, Red Acre is especially suited for small or home gardens. Makes a beautiful addition to salads, or as a coleslaw. 76 days to harvest.

Tete Noir

This is a French variety that's grown in the fall in its native France. It has deep red heads and is rare unless you're reading this in Europe. Days to harvest unavailable.

Winningstadt

In 1866, Winningstadt was listed in America by J. J. H. Gregory & Sons and is another favorite with gardeners everywhere. It is an early producer of medium, very solid, blue-green heads that are about 6–7" in diameter. They have hard, pointy heads that are relatively resistant to cabbage worms. It's a very hardy variety and a good keeper with mild flavor. Very nice for sauerkraut. 80–90 days to harvest.

Carrots

Carrots have been a useful food staple since as early as the 900s when yellow carrots were first noted in Turkey. All over the Mediterranean, carrots grow wild and historian-foodies believe that they may have originated somewhere around Afghanistan, although those carrots came in colors of red, white, and purple. It was the Dutch in the 1600s who brought us the traditional orange carrots of today.

Carrots' idea of the perfect soil is loam—that is, light and fluffy. But they're troopers and will tolerate a wide variety of soils. Gardeners with clay soil may want to consider staying clear of the long, tapered heirloom carrot varieties and planting ball-type or "baby" carrots instead.

Because they're a root crop, the best way to grow carrots is to direct seed them into the garden bed. You want nicely amended soil, but don't plant them where fresh manure (not yet composted) has been planted as fresh manure encourages forked roots.

Carrots are cool-weather lovers and can be planted all the way through spring and seeded again in the late summer for a fall and winter harvest. In some growing zones, heavy mulch will allow carrot harvesting through the entire winter.

Carrots and radishes make good bedfellows because the radishes germinate quickly and carrots take their own sweet time to make an appearance. The radishes become markers for where carrot seeds lie so the gardener is careful in planting and weed-pulling. The speedy radishes are ready to harvest just as the carrot seedlings are ready for thinning.

Amarillo

A beautiful lemon-yellow carrot, Amarillo has bright yellow flesh and promises extra crunch and juice. The roots are 8" long. Great summer to fall crop. 75 days to harvest.

Atomic Red

Now, here's an interesting twist. Lycopene, which is normally associated with tomatoes, is high in the Atomic Red carrot, giving it a wonderfully intense red color as well as extra health points. Atomic Red's color becomes more vivid as it's cooked—which is the best way to eat these guys. The root is 9" and tapered. 65 days to harvest.

Belgian White (Lunar White, Blanche a Collet Vert)

This is an old variety that was introduced by Henri Vilmorin in 1839. It has quite heavy white roots that are 12–24" long with green shoulders. The white color makes it a good variety for people who don't tolerate carotene. Historically, White Belgian was grown in farm fields across Europe as a feed for horses and cattle as well as for the kitchen. It's highly vigorous, but won't tolerate frost to make it through the winter. 75 days to harvest.

Berlicum 2

Berlicum's roots grow to 8" and are extra smooth with a blunt end. They have a nice habit of staying tender instead of getting woody as some varieties can. They're deep orange in color and have good flavor. Very popular in Europe. 72 days to harvest.

Chantenay (Rouge Demi-Longue de Chantenay)

Chantenay was introduced by France in the 1830s. It's a terrific bright orange carrot that's perfect for canning, juicing, freezing, and storing. It's a good producer of large and super flavorful sweet carrots. It doesn't even mind heavy soils. 70 days to harvest.

Chantenay Red Core

In 1929, France brought us Chantenay Red Core. Its 5½" root is a dark orange, with a blunt tip. This is a sweet variety that is highly adaptable to many soils. 65 days to harvest.

Cosmic Purple

This variety was recorded sometime in the tenth century in Asia Minor. While 7" Cosmic Purple's skin is indeed purple, its flesh is orange and yellow. The surprising flesh color isn't Cosmic Purple's only surprise. Turns out while it's sweet, it has a little bite, too. Spicier than most carrots, it also brings great color to the salad bowl or stir-fry recipes. 70 days to harvest.

Danvers 126

Here's a wonderful all-around carrot that actually outperforms many hybrids. Eastern States Farmers Exchange introduced it in 1947. It's reliable, and offers high yields and uniformity. It's a highly adaptable variety that produces well even in clay soils. The 6–7" root is heat-tolerant and resists splitting and cracking. Danvers 126 is especially loved for its storage ability. 75 days to harvest.

Dragon

Dragon is carrot royalty, the crème de la crème of all purple carrots. When you bite into it, you'll be surprised to find a yellow-orange flesh. The other pleasant surprise is the little bit of spice inside this predominately sweet carrot. 90 days to harvest.

Early Scarlet Horn

This short carrot (2–6") has been hanging around since before 1610 and is said to be the oldest cultivated carrot variety. That's reason enough to grow Early Scarlet Horn, but it also has an excellent flavor. 65–70 days to harvest.

WEED!

If you want tasty roots, lay off the heavy nitrogen while growing carrots. Excessive nitrogen will make the green growth above the soil tastier than the part you're going to eat. Too much nitrogen can also cause root forking.

Gold King

Red-orange Gold King is about 6" long with a stumpy, semi-tapered root. It's very sweet and grows well in heavy soils. 70 days to harvest.

Healthmaster

Beefy Healthmaster weighs in at a whopping 1½ pounds and can grow as long as 10". It has excellent flavor and is touted as containing 35 percent more vitamin A than Danvers. It's crack-resistant and is a perfect juicing carrot. It takes a little longer to grow, but it's worth the wait. 140 days to harvest.

Imperator 58

This is the carrot you'll find in grocery stores because it's so reliable. Imperator 58 is a Danvers type with smooth, tapered roots. The 9" long root is fine-grained, tender, and sweet. It offers excellent performance if you give it loamy, friable soil. 68 days to harvest.

Jaune Obtuse du Doubs

France has records of this carrot variety as far back as 1894. Originally, it was grown to feed livestock. Its roots are thick, extremely sweet, and a bright lemon-yellow color that so far hasn't been duplicated in other modern carrots. Chefs are falling in love with it. Days to harvest unavailable.

Kuroda Long 8"

This variety has a sweet and mild flavor. It is short with stubby roots and is excellent for juicing. It grows well in a variety of climates and soils. 75 days to harvest.

Little Finger

These are little 3" snacking carrots. This deep orange, baby-type carrot is also nice for pickling and canning. 55 days to harvest.

Long Orange Improved

Long Orange Improved was introduced by the Dutch before 1700. Its long, tapered roots come in scarlet to orange shades. The flesh has lighter tones. It has excellent flavor and is a good storage carrot. 85 days to harvest.

Long Red Surrey

These carrots have roots as long as 12" and are drought-tolerant. Their orange flesh and yellow core make a delicious snack. This is a sturdy carrot that over-winters well if you pile on the mulch. 70 days to harvest.

Oxheart (Guerande)

Here's a stout carrot that could use some extra space when planted. Oxheart (introduced in 1884) may be stubby, but it can weigh in at 1 pound. It has good flavor and stores well. 73–80 days to harvest.

Muscade

This variety hails from North Africa and has exceptional flavor and texture with a sound crunch. The orange roots grow in at a blocky 7". Muscade rarely bolts and remains fresh at the market. It's a rare carrot to find, but Baker Creek Heirloom Seeds carries it. 62 days to harvest.

Nantes Fancy (Nantes Coreless)

Nantes Fancy is deep orange and has a wonderful crispy-fresh flavor. It stores well. 68 days to harvest.

Paris Market

If you're a chef, pay attention to this one; gourmet restaurants are always on the lookout for Paris Market carrots. These uniform, 1–2", red-orange carrots are early harvesters. They are perfect for container growing and perform well in shallow and rocky soil. 50–68 days to harvest (that's fast for a carrot).

Parisian Rondo

A very popular variety in France, Parisian Rondo is a small, round carrot about 1–1½" in diameter. It is orange-red and has a very tender and sweet flavor. 75 days to harvest.

Parisienne

Very popular in France, these small, ball-shaped carrots are excellent when lightly steamed. The round shape makes them perfect candidates for heavy clay soils. 50–68 days to harvest.

Red Samurai

Although Red Samuri is good in salads, it really comes alive as a cooked carrot. It is bold red and slender with 10" roots. Its crisp flesh is sweet and it keeps its true color when steamed. 75 days to harvest.

Royal Chantenay

Northrup King & Co. released Royal Chantenay in 1952. Its red-orange, 5–7" roots are cylindrical with a stumped tip. It grows well in heavy or shallow soils, and the green tops can grow to 15" tall. This versatile carrot is good for freezing, canning, or drying. 70 days to harvest.

Scarlet Nantes (Early Coreless, Nantes Half Long)

Introduced in 1870, gardeners compare the flavor of 7" Scarlet Nantes to a baby carrot. This bright orange, almost coreless variety is well known for its sweet flavor, but it also stores well. Gardeners who mulch it well are often rewarded with a harvest all winter. 70 days to harvest.

Shin Kuroda 5"

This is Japan's baby carrot variety. They're short (3–5") and have a fine flavor. 75 days to harvest.

Snow White

A white carrot variety that's as attractive as it is delicious. Snow White is mild and sweet with a good crunch. Its roots grow 7–8" long and are tasty whether eaten raw or cooked. 75 days to harvest.

Solar Yellow

Solar Yellow is a 6" Danvers type and will add festive color to your salads, especially if you mix in some purple and red carrots, too. 60 days to harvest.

St. Valery

St. Valery is a rare French heirloom that was introduced in 1885, though the French claim it has been around for a lot longer. This is a pretty carrot with 8–12" roots that are a dark red-orange. It's productive, tender, sweet, and good for storing. 70 days to harvest.

Sweetness II

Sweetness II is a newcomer to the open-pollinated scene and is touted as possibly the best tasting of the newer varieties. Its roots are 8" long with smooth and bright orange skin. It matures in early to mid-season. 66 days to harvest.

Tendersweet

Tendersweet is a reliable producer of long, 9–10", tapered, deep orange roots that are uniform in size. It's coreless and sweet—perfect for the home garden. 75 days to harvest.

Thumbelina

Thumbelina may have small, round, 1½" roots, but it's also full of crisp, sweet flavor and never needs to be peeled. This is an excellent variety for containers and clay soils. Chefs enjoy using Thumbelina in gourmet dishes. 60 days to harvest.

Tonda di Parigi

An excellent round carrot from nineteenth-century Paris, these beauties are harvested at 1–2". Their deep orange roots are uniform and exceptionally sweet. A popular marketing carrot. 60 days to harvest.

Photo by Baker Creek Heirloom Seeds

Cauliflower

Cauliflower has been around for at least 2,000 years, as far as human cultivation is concerned. But it wasn't until the 1800s that cauliflower became popular in the United States. Some cauliflowers enjoy the cool weather and some are heat-tolerant, but it is best to avoid fluctuating temperatures. The timing will depend on your growing zone and the cauliflower variety.

Cauliflower's cultivation is very similar to broccoli or cabbage. The heads or curds are usually white, but there are varieties that produce purple, orange, and green curds as well. Harvesting the heads is the same as broccoli with the exception that cauliflower doesn't continue to produce the side shoots that broccoli does.

These plants like to be kept evenly watered, and they're heavy feeders. They enjoy some fertilizing during the growing season in the way of kelp fertilizers, compost teas, and the like. You could also choose a commercial vegetable fertilizer.

If you're interested in keeping the curds white, for most varieties, you'll need to pull the leaves around them and secure them together (using rubber bands or twine) so that their heads aren't exposed to the sun, which will turn them yellow.

Because cauliflower is usually started indoors before being transplanted into their permanent beds, the days to harvest are based on this assumption.

Brocoverde (Broccoflower)

This is a heat-tolerant cauliflower that produces semi-domed green heads that are a cross between broccoli and cauliflower. It's a rare variety; I found it at D. Landreth Seed Company. 68 days to harvest.

Early Snowball

Peter Henderson introduced this early and compact cauliflower in 1888. White, 6" heads are formed on this dwarf cauliflower. It's an excellent performer and is perfect for over-wintering in warm climates. 60–80 days to harvest (from transplant).

Giant of Naples

This is a wonderful Italian heirloom that's hard to find. It produces 3-pound white heads and is a vigorous plant. 88 days to harvest.

Green Macerata

An Italian heirloom that produces 2-pound, bright green heads. This variety is excellent in salads or cooked. 60–85 days to harvest.

Igloo

Igloo is a late season variety that produces heavy heads that are about 7" wide with dense, upright leaves. Terrific for eating fresh and an excellent variety if you're interested in freezing or processing. 70 days to harvest.

Lemington English Winter

This is a delicious, old cauliflower variety from Lemington Spa, England, that was nearly extinct. These hardy plants produce giant heads that over-winter then mature in May. You can find them at Sustainable Seed Company. 80 days to harvest.

Purple Cape

This winter-heading variety was brought from South Africa in 1808. It produces delicious purple heads that mature in late winter or early spring. Purple Cape grows best if it's planted in the late fall and over-wintered in a cold frame. 200 days to harvest (from transplant).

Snowball Self-Blanching

This variety has leaves that wrap around the head, which protects the white head from heat and sun. You won't need to tie the leaves over the head unless it grows larger than 6" wide. 68 days to harvest.

Snowbally

Introduced in 1947, Snowbally produces smooth, large, and white heads. It's best as a fall crop and is highly adaptable to its environment. 80 days to harvest.

Violetto di Sicilia (Violetta Italia, Violet of Sicily)

This is a nice Italian cauliflower that has a beautiful purple head that turns bright green when cooked. It is pest-resistant and has excellent flavor. 80–85 days to harvest.

Celery

Originally, celery was a highly ignored food crop because of its bitter taste. Then the Italians and the French got a hold of it in the 1500s and worked some breeding magic.

Celery is a biennial that is grown as an annual for harvesting as a food crop. Celery will tolerate a variety of soils, from growing well in richly organic soils to thriving in marshlike, murky ones. Celery plants like the cool seasons and need to have their feet wet. Moisture is important to celery, and mulching can go a long way in this case.

Golden Pascal

Golden Pascal grows thick, 18–20", yellowish-green stalks. It's a self-blanching variety that's tender with good flavor. 110 days to harvest.

Golden Self-Blanching

Introduced in 1886, Golden Self-Blanching grow medium green, stringless stalks that turn yellow after they've blanched. It's an old heavy-yielding variety, with fat hearts of good quality. 90 days to harvest.

Tendercrisp

This is an extra-tall celery that grows to 36". It's crunchy and delicious with very tasty green leaves at the top. 112 days to harvest.

Utah 52/70 Tall Improved

Introduced in 1953, Utah 52/70 Tall Improved is head and shoulders tastier than what you'll find in the produce section of the supermarket. The medium green stalks grow to about 30". It's crisp and delicious. 110–120 days to harvest.

Zwolsche

This Dutch heirloom celery is hardy and can reach 3" tall. It's a leaf-type celery with curly leaves that will remind you of a curly parsley. Its flavor is stronger than most celery varieties and it's good as an ornamental and as a food crop. Days to harvest unavailable.

Collard Greens

Gardeners differ on whether collards are actually just kale. Botanically speaking, they're pretty much the same. But don't say that in front of a true southerner. They'll tell you that the two are very different plants.

Although collard greens are predominantly a cool-weather crop, they can be successfully grown in the southern United States, while kale loses quality in hot weather. Collard greens grow in most soils, from average to rich and fertile, but don't overdo the fertilizing. They'll grow very well in average soil, too. Collard greens are chock-full of nutritional value; they're rich in vitamins A and C and also have good amounts of calcium and potassium.

Champion

Champion is a nonheading variety with dark blue leaves that produces well. It's resistant to bolting and is winter-hardy. 75 days to harvest.

Even' Star Land Race

This variety produces small, tender, sweet leaves that can be tossed into a mesclun mix. It's winter-hardy and isn't susceptible to powdery mildew. It's highly adaptable to a variety of soils and is best planted in the fall. Days to harvest unavailable.

Georgia Green (Georgia Southern, Creole)

Georgia Southern was introduced before 1880. Due to its resistance to heat, it grows well in the south (but it does fine in the north, too). It tolerates sandy and poor soils well. It's a huge producer and the heads grow loosely and taste sweet and tender. 70–80 days to harvest.

Green Glaze

Old-fashioned Green Glaze was introduced in 1820 by David Landreth. It's a unique garden variety with its smooth, bright green, 30–34" tall leaves. It's a nonheading type that's slow to bolt, as well as disease- and cabbage worm–resistant. Perfect for southern and warm coastal growing zones. 79 days to harvest.

Morris Heading

Old-timers refer to Morris Heading as "cabbage collards." This variety produces dark green, heavy heads that are loose and slightly savoyed. It's a long-time favorite with tasty, tender leaves. 70 days to harvest.

Vates

Vates is slow to bolt and quite suited for southern areas and the mid-Atlantic states. Its leaves are blue-green, large, and frost-resistant. 68 days to harvest.

White Mountain Cabbage Collard

This is a family heirloom from South Carolina. It's a heading variety that produces dark green, savoyed leaves that can reach up to 3' high. 70 days to harvest.

Corn

Corn falls into several different categories: dent or flint corn, sweet corn, and popcorn. The dent or flint corn categories contain those corns that are high in starch that are best used for roasting, corn bread, hominy, and grinding into flour.

Sweet corn, with its high sugar content, is usually what the home gardener is after for the dinner table. Popcorn is another popular home garden corn and, aside from its obvious use as a snack, it can also be ground into flour like the dent varieties.

If you'd like to grow some sweet corn for the kitchen, remember that corn loves the brilliant sun and moist soil. It's also an extremely heavy feeder. It often sucks every last nutritional drop out of the ground its grown in, so feed it something high in everything—nitrogen, phosphorus, and potassium—every two weeks. At the end of the season, replace the spent corn with a nitrogen-fixing cover crop (such as a legume).

Ashworth

Ashworth is an early maturing, yellow sweet corn that's not only great tasting but is very dependable, too. The stalks grow to 5' tall and produce one to two ears per stalk. 69 days to harvest.

Black Aztec

This is a corn that can be traced back to the Aztecs some 2,000 years ago. It was introduced and made available to growers in the 1860s. It's a versatile variety that can be used as a fresh eating corn as well as for grinding into cornmeal and as an ornamental. The 6' stalks produce the perfect old-fashioned corn taste and are drought-tolerant, too. 70–100 days to harvest.

Black Mexican (Mexican Sweet, Black Iroquois)

Black Mexican is a sweet corn that originated in upstate New York and was introduced in 1864. The stalks grow to 5½' tall and produce ears that are 7½"×1½". The kernels are white at the milk stage (which is when you would eat them) and in the late milk stage turn bluish-black. 76 days to harvest.

Bloody Butcher

This Virginia heirloom was introduced in 1845. It grows 10–12' stalks that produce two ears on each stalk. The corn kernels are blood-red with even darker stripes. Sometimes a blue or white one will pop up here and there. It's used for making flour, cereal, and roasting ears. 120 days to harvest.

Buhl

This is a yellow sweet corn that has stalks that grow to 6–7' tall and produce super-sweet kernels of fantastic quality. 81 days to harvest.

Cherokee Long Ear Small

This small-kernelled popcorn was one of the corns that made its way with the American Indians over the Trail of Tears. It has great popcorn flavor and is very ornamental. The 5–7" ears have shiny kernels in many colors, including orange, white, red, blue, and yellow. 100 days to harvest.

Cherokee Popcorn

This is a variety introduced by Underwood Gardens in 1999 to assist the Cherokee tribe in Georgia. This is a blend of Cherokee popcorns brought west over the Trail of Tears. Vigorous seed. Fertility and soil moisture will determine if the 9' plants have two, three, or four ears. Considerable tolerance to heat and drought. 100–110 days to harvest.

Cherokee White Eagle

Here's a striking dent corn with blue and white kernels and a red cob. It was introduced by Underwood Gardens in 1999, in conjunction with the USDA Natural Resources Conservation Service of Georgia, to assist the Cherokee tribe with the reestablishment of "Trail of Tears" corn and other crops. Once in a while an all-blue ear will make an appearance on the 8–10' tall stalks. It's said that the image of a white eagle can be seen in the kernels. 110 days to harvest.

Chires

This is a variety that produces those teeny-tiny mini ears of corn that you see in salads and stir-frys. It can also be frozen or dried for popcorn. The plants are multi-stalked and can produce 20 little ears on each stalk. 75–85 days to harvest.

Chocolate Cherry

This variety was introduced in 1998 and has the flavor of good yellow popcorn. The red-brown ears have bright pink silks, and the cobs have 16–18 rows of kernels. It has good drought and earworm resistance. 120 days to harvest.

Country Gentleman (Shoepeg)

This is an 1891 sweet corn with white, tightly packed kernels that grow in an irregular pattern instead of in typical rows. The kernels tend to stay in the milk stage longer than most. This is a good variety for freezing and cream-style corn. 93 days to harvest.

Dakota Black

This popcorn variety grows 6' stalks and produces beautiful maroon-purple kernels. There's only one ear per stalk, but it has a higher than average resistance to pests. 90 days to harvest.

Floriani Red Flint

This Italian family heirloom grows 7–10' tall and produces slightly pointed, medium-to dark red kernels. Cornmeal made from this lovely dent variety has a pink cast and the polenta made with it has a wonderfully rich flavor. It matures a little faster than many varieties. 100 days to harvest.

Golden Bantam 8 Row

Burpee introduced this sweet heirloom in 1902. It grows 5–6' stalks that you can plant closer than you normally would. You'll need to pick the ears as soon as they are ready because this variety doesn't stay in the milk stage for long. 78 days to harvest.

Hickory King

This pre-1875 heirloom is considered to be the best type for hominy, as the kernel's skin is removed easily when soaked. It's a nice variety for cornmeal, flour, grits, and roasting. Hickory King grows 12' tall and produces two ears of corn per stalk. Kernels are large, flat, and white. This dent corn has good heat tolerance and is resistant to northern leaf blight and southern leaf blight. 85–110 days to harvest.

Longfellow

This truly old variety is said to have not changed since the Native Americans grew it in New England. The stalks reach to 10' tall and the ears are 10–13" long with bright, deep yellow-orange kernels. Traditionally, the ears have been harvested in the green stage, like any sweet corn. But Longfellow makes a terrific cornmeal, too. 115 days to harvest.

Luther Hill

A 1902 heirloom, Luther Hill is a sweet, white corn that produces two ears on its 5½' stalks. It has excellent flavor. 82 days to harvest.

Neal's Paymaster

This pre-1915 variety was the first reliable two-eared dent corn. It's heat-tolerant and will perform in subpar soils. Produces high yields in moderately fertile soil. 100–120 days to harvest.

Pencil Cob

This dent corn produces long, thin cobs, hence the "pencil" in its name. The 6' stalks produce two to three ears each. It can be picked young as a roasting corn or you could use the white kernels for cornmeal. 75–100 days to harvest.

Pennsylvania Butter-Flavored

This pre-1885 heirloom popcorn is maintained by the Pennsylvania Dutch and was introduced by Southern Exposure Seed Exchange in 1988. The superior-flavor white-kernelled corn average two ears per stalk. Ears are 4–6" long. 102 days to harvest.

Pungo Creek Butcher

This dent variety has been grown by farmers in Pungo Creek, Virginia, for 165 years. The stalks reach 11' tall and produce corn that has multi-colored kernels in red, yellow, brown, and purple. It's a good flock feed when milled rough, but can also be ground into a delicious meal for corn bread or muffins. 120 days to harvest.

Rainbow Sweet Inca

This variety produces gorgeous multi-colored corn kernels that are delicious when picked while the colors are very pale on the cob. Once the ears are fully mature, they're perfect for grinding into a flour with terrific flavor. 80–95 days to harvest.

Reid's Yellow Dent

This is an 1840s heirloom that's the beginning line for many yellow dent varieties. It's very reliable in the heat and soils of the south. Reid's is considered to be one of the most prolific and hardy corns ever developed. The stalks are 7' tall and produce two ears of corn that have 16 rows of deep and moderately flat kernels. 85–110 days to harvest.

Seneca Red Stalker

This variety is originally from the Seneca Nation. Its beautiful purple-red stalks and husks make it the perfect ornamental corn. The ears are 8–9" and have multi-colored kernels. 100 days to harvest.

Stowell's Evergreen

This is one of the oldest known sweet corns, dating back to 1848, although it was introduced in 1856. Stalks are 8' tall and the corn stays in the milk stage for a long time, hence "evergreen." 95 days to harvest.

Strawberry

Strawberry is a well-known popcorn that has ears shaped like large, dark red strawberries. The lovely mahogany-red kernels make this variety highly ornamental as well as good for popping. Stalks grow to 8' high and produce 4–6" ears, averaging three ears per stalk. Strawberry has high earworm resistance because it produces a naturally occurring anti-feedant called maysin. 98 days to harvest.

Photo by Southern Exposure Seed Exchange

Tennessee Red Cob

This is a pre-1900 heirloom dent that bears medium to large ears but only one per stalk. It makes terrific corn bread. 120 days to harvest.

Texas Honey June

Like its name implies, Texas Honey June's white kernels have good corn flavor and a sweetness that will remind you of honey. This heirloom is very adaptable and can be grown in both northern and southern growing zones. The 8' stalks produce two to three ears each. 97 days to harvest.

Thompson Prolific

This is a pale yellow, dent variety that produces two ears per stalk. It's an excellent variety to grow in the middle south. Days to harvest unavailable.

Tom Thumb Popcorn

This is a cute little popcorn that kids will enjoy growing. The stalks grow to a short $3\frac{1}{2}'$ and produce ears that are 3–4" long. 85–90 days to harvest.

True Gold

This is a nice home and market sweet corn variety. The yellow kernels are very flavorful. 75 days to harvest.

Wade's Giant Indian

This is a terrific Indian flint corn with ears that average an amazing 12". It comes in a rainbow of colors such as yellow, purple, white, orange, red, and blue. It's used for animal feed, cornmeal, and decoration. Days to harvest unavailable.

Wisconsin Black

This Mennonite heirloom has 6' stalks that produce two ornamental dark maroon and black ears per stalk. The kernels pop well and have great flavor. When the kernels are popped, they are bright white with black accents. 80 days to harvest.

Cucumber

The prolific cucumber was brought to America by the European explorers. Before that, they enjoyed a wonderfully long heyday with the ancient Romans and Greeks. But before *that*—3,000 years before—they were growing in India and China.

Cucumbers are an accommodating vegetable that allows us to grow it upward and use the real estate over our gardens, but is just as happy sprawling across the garden bed producing little cukes faster than rabbits.

Personally, I think the cucumbers prefer the airspace. I'm basing this on their inherent nature to use their slender tendrils to grab on to anything around and pull themselves up onto it. Also, when cukes are allowed to grow on a trellis, they tend to avoid some things that are unpleasant to gardeners like insects munching them or diseases shriveling them. Fewer cucumbers end up rotting because they are more likely to be seen—and therefore picked at the right time. Trellising your cucumbers also saves garden space. And space, for many urban and suburban gardeners, is worth its weight in gold.

Remember to harvest your cucumbers often and take the time to find all of the ripened fruit. It only takes one over-ripe fruit to trigger the plant to stop production. This is because mature fruits (with their mature seeds) are now on the vine. A signal is sent to the plant that it has done its job—to reproduce itself.

If you'd like to save the seeds, let the fruits near the end of the season mature fully so that you can harvest as many cucumbers as possible for the kitchen.

A & C Pickling (Ace)

This super-productive pickling cucumber was introduced in 1928 by Abbot & Cobb of Philadelphia. It produces 8–10" fruits that are excellent for home and market. 50–55 days to harvest.

Ashley

Ashley was introduced in 1956 and is a popular variety in the southeast. The prolific vines produce deep green, slicing cucumbers that are 7–8" long. 66 days to harvest.

Beit Alpha

This is a popular variety in the Mediterranean. Its sweet and delicious flavor and high yields are making it popular in America now. They also store well and are burpless. 56 days to harvest.

Boothby's Blonde

The Boothby family of Livermore, Maine, brought this heirloom to the gardening world's attention. It produces oval-shaped fruits that are a creamy yellow color with black spines and warts. The cucumber can grow from 6–8", but is best when harvested at 4". This heritage cucumber has an excellent, sweet flavor—you don't even need to peel it. This is a perfect variety for making bread and butter pickles. 55–60 days to harvest.

Boston Pickling

This 1880 heirloom is medium green, very productive, and exactly the right size for pickling. The fruits are mild and crisp. It has been a very popular and reliable variety. 58 days to harvest.

Bushy

Seed Savers Exchange introduced Bushy to gardeners in 1992. It originally came from the southern regions of Russia, where it had been well known for decades. This is a compact plant with fruits that are 3–5" long. It's a high yielder and great for fresh eating and pickling. 46–49 days to harvest.

Chinese Yellow

This gorgeous cucumber becomes a yellow-orange when it's ripe. This apple-crisp, 10" fruit comes from China. It's a rare, very productive variety that's great for both pickles and slicing. 60 days to harvest.

Crystal Apple

This 3" variety is from New Zealand and has an apple shape and mild flavor. It's a creamy white color, tender, and very prolific. It's good for pickling or for fresh eating. Like most cucumbers, it's best when harvested small. 65 days to harvest.

De Bourbonne

This is an old French heirloom that's popular for making 2" long cornichon pickles. These are very productive vines. 50 days to harvest.

Delikatesse

This German variety is a big producer of delicious cucumbers that are exactly right for pickling or slicing. The 10" long fruits are pale green with small warts. 60 days to harvest.

Double Yield

Joseph Harris & Company introduced this variety in 1924 in New York, but it was actually developed by a home gardener. The cucumber's claim to fame is that it's extremely productive. It's said that for every cuke you harvest, two or three will show up to take its place. The 5–6" slender fruits are perfect pickling cucumbers. 50–60 days to harvest.

Early Fortune

This cucumber was created by the skin of its teeth. George Starr of Michigan found this single plant variety in a crop of the now-extinct Davis Perfect and continued to breed it. The Jerome B. Rice Seed Company of New York introduced Early Fortune in 1910. It's a very early maturing, white-spined cuke that's 7–8" long and 2" in diameter. 55–60 days to harvest.

Early Russian

Early Russian is an 1854 heirloom variety that produces a ton of short, medium green cukes that have sweet flavor. The plant is hardy and a good choice for northern gardeners who have short seasons. Use it to make pickles or toss into salads. 55 days to harvest.

Edmonson

This was a Kansas family heirloom from as far back as 1913; Southern Exposure Seed Exchange introduced it in 1987. This is a super hardy pickling cucumber. It has a terrific buttery flavor with a tender and crisp texture. The plant has good insect, drought, and disease resistance. The fruits are 4" long and white-green in color. 70 days to harvest.

Ellen's Family White

This is a small, compact vine that produces a little, white pickling cucumber. Its skin has enough tenderness to be eaten raw on a veggie plate. 35–60 days to harvest.

Empereur Alexandre

This is a hugely productive variety of dark green fruit with a mild flavor. Harvest them when they are 6" long for slicing. 60 days to harvest.

Everbearing SMR58

The vines of this variety are disease-resistant and produce cukes over and over as long as you can keep up the harvest. The cucumbers are crisp and have excellent flavor. 55 days to harvest.

Fin de Meaux

This variety is popular in France but can be hard to find. It produces a cuke that's darker green than most. The fruits are little, slender, and best eaten at 2" long. Days to harvest unavailable.

Fuzzy White Italian

This is a rare Italian cucumber variety that's small, fuzzy, white, and will remind you of a tennis ball. The fruits are slightly sweet and crisp and can be harvested when they are the size of a golf ball for snacking, or left to mature longer. The vines produce a ton of fruit and the more you pick them, the more you'll get. 50 days to harvest.

Himangi

These 6", cream-colored fruits were developed by M.P.K.V. University in India in 1992. They're a crisp cuke with sweet flavor. Himangi is one of the preferred types of cucumber in India and should prove to be a good market variety in America. 35–40 days to harvest.

Hmong Red

This heirloom cucumber's seed was collected from a Hmong immigrant. The cukes start out white to pale green and are unusual in the fact that they become a gold-orange as they mature. They have a mild flavor even when they are quite large. Days to harvest unavailable.

Homemade Pickles

Medium-size, green fruits grow on vigorous plants that have good resistance to disease. The fruits are solid, crisp, and up to 6" long, making for a nice, big, juicy pickle. 55 days to harvest.

Japanese Climbing

This cucumber variety was introduced to American gardeners in 1892 by Japan. The cukes are 7–9" long and 3" in diameter. Excellent for pickling or slicing. 58–65 days to harvest.

Japanese Long

This is a productive variety that's both delicious and easy to digest. The fruits are long, slim, and crisp. 68 days to harvest. 75 days to harvest.

Jaune Dickfleischige

This extremely rare variety originated in Germany but has long been grown in France as well. The fruits are huge and can weigh up to 5 pounds. They're a yellow-green color that turns lemon-yellow at maturity. The variety tastes crisp and flavorful. Days to harvest unavailable.

Jelly Melon (Kiwano, African Horned Cucumber)

These oval, thorny cukes were imported from New Zealand to sell at specialty markets for over 25 years. Now you can grow them and sell them to specialty markets. They're filled with a greenish-gold gel and are very seedy. Jelly Melon's flavor is said to be like a pomegranate and citrus cross. They're generally used as a decorative fruit or as a garnish. 120 days to harvest.

Lemon (True Lemon)

This is a fun variety because the 7' vines produce a round, yellow, and crunchy cucumber. The flavor is never bitter and has a good cucumber taste with just a smidge of nuttiness. For pickling, the cukes are best when they're harvested at 1½". Harvest at 2" for salads. Both gardeners and chefs love this little cuke. 67 days to harvest.

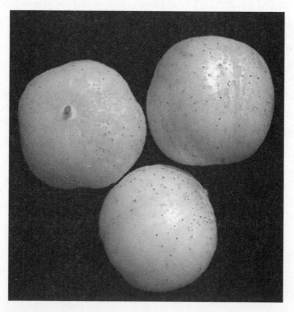

Photo by Baker Creek Heirloom Seeds

Little Leaf H-19

This compact vine produces medium-size, blocky cukes that are perfect for pickling but can easily be used for slicing. It's a white-spined variety that's also disease-resistant. 55 days to harvest.

Long Anglais

This is an old English variety by way of France. It has a 12", slender fruit that is great as a slicing cuke because it's mild and not bitter. It takes well to trellising and climbing. Days to harvest unavailable.

Long de Chine

This variety is grown commercially in Europe and is a terrific producer. It has long, bright green fruit that has a mild and tasty flavor. 65–70 days to harvest.

Longfellow

Market growers prefer these 12–14" fruits not only for their attractiveness, but because they're perfect for the straight pack that specialty markets use for shipment. 62–80 days to harvest.

Marketmore 76

This is a dependable market cuke that grows well in the mid-Atlantic as well as the north. The fruits are 8" and bitter-resistant. It's a wonderful eating cuke. 70 days to harvest.

Marketmore 80

This is a rare slicing cucumber variety that has resistance to many diseases. It's a recommended variety for the north but also grows well in the south. The fruits are 8–9" long, green, and not bitter. 61 days to harvest.

Mexican Sour Gherkin

This is an heirloom that has been recently rediscovered. The fruits are 1–2" and look like little watermelons that fall off their vines when they mature. Although they have sweet cucumber flavor, there's also a surprising sourness that makes it seem as if they've been naturally pickled. This is a good trellis-climbing variety. 60–70 days to harvest.

Miniature White

This very popular mini cucumber has vines that rarely get longer than 3'. The fruit is a yellow-white color with mild, sweet flavor and no peeling needed. They're great for eating raw and best eaten when they're under 3" long. 50–55 days to harvest.

Parade

This cucumber is a popular Russian variety that produces a big yield of fruits that mature almost all at the same time, which is nice if you're planning on processing them—or having a really big summer party. The cucumbers grow to 5"×2" and are extremely weather-resistant. 50–60 days to harvest.

Parisian Pickling (Improved Bourbonne)

Parisian Pickling was first listed in America in 1892 by J. J. H. Gregory. This variety is very hard to find and can be eaten fresh when young or used as a slicing cucumber when mature. 70–80 days to harvest (for slicing).

Poinsett 76

Poinsett 76 is the improved variety of Poinsett as it has resistance to multiple diseases. The fruit is deep green, 7–8" long and 2½" in diameter. It's the perfect variety for the southeast and mid-Atlantic coastal zones. 67 days to harvest.

Poona Kherra

This heirloom from India starts out white, turns yellow, and ends up golden brown when it's mature. The fruit is 4"×2", delicious, and never bitter. It's a hardy plant that is disease-resistant. 60 days to harvest.

Richmond (River) Green Apple

This heirloom is from Australia and produces lemon-size fruits that have a refreshing, mild, and sweet flavor. This is a compact variety well suited to the small garden. The cukes are green and oval and have a white, crispy flesh. 55–70 days to harvest.

Ruby Wallace's Old Time White

Mrs. Ruby Wallace grew this white cucumber for over 50 years in her North Carolina garden. Her family has used it for both slicing and pickling (remember to use white vinegar to make white pickles). 65 days to harvest.

Snow's Fancy Pickling

Vaughn's Seed House of Chicago introduced this pickling cucumber in 1905. At that time, this cuke was considered too short and fat to be a good dill pickle, but it was used in the small pickle niche of the market. These are slender, 5–6" long and 1½–2" in diameter. 50–60 days to harvest.

Spacemaster

Spacemaster is wonderful at adapting to different climates and soil types. It's a bushy plant that produces 7½" long cucumbers for pickling or slicing. If you remember to harvest routinely, this variety will reward you with nonstop cukes. It's a perfect choice for small gardens or containers. 60 days to harvest.

Straight Eight

Straight Eight was introduced in 1935 and is a good slicing cucumber. The plants are prolific and produce deep green, blunt-end, 7–8" long cukes. 63 days to harvest.

Suyo Longs

This is a nice burpless cucumber for both pickling and slicing. It's a hardy variety from China that's widely adaptable and very tolerant of hot weather. It has nice flavor and is very productive. 61 days to harvest.

Photo by Baker Creek Heirloom Seeds

Telegraph Improved

This 1897 English heirloom produces 18" long, smooth, straight, deep green fruit with a tender and crisp flesh. It has super flavor and produces very little seed. 60 days to harvest.

Thai Green

This 7" cucumber is a popular variety in Thailand. It is medium green and heat-tolerant. This variety is hard to find outside of Thailand. Days to harvest unavailable.

West Indian Gherkin

West Indian Gherkin can be traced back to at least the early 1790s. The large, prolific vine has leaves that look more like watermelon leaves than cucumber leaves. The fruits are 2–3" long and are an oval shape. It's super drought-tolerant and is good for making relish or small pickles. 60–65 days to harvest.

White Wonder

Here's a cucumber of a different color—white, to be specific. W. Atlee Burpee introduced this variety in 1893. It's an old southern heirloom with fruits that are 7" long and a creamy white color. Super delicious for both slicing and pickling. 58–60 days to harvest.

Yamato

Yamato is very similar to Suyo Long, but it actually outperforms it both in flavor and performance. Yamato is a white-spined green cuke with yellow stripes that grows 12–16" long. The fruit has a rather buttery, sweet, and crisp flavor. The plant is reliable and tolerates heat and humidity. 60 days to harvest.

Yok Kao

Yok Kao is a 5", green-yellow fruit that's crisp and has good cucumber flavor. It's an easy variety to grow and wonderful for fresh eating or preserving. Days to harvest unavailable.

Eggplant

When people think of eggplant, they think of a dark purple, egg-shaped variety, which is usually what is found in the produce section of the grocery stores in the United States. But eggplants are much more popular in the eastern and southern parts of Europe, where they come in a wide variety of colors, shapes, and sizes. They can be dark purple, pale purple, white, yellow, green, or striped. Their shapes range from elongated or egg, to short, long, round, and globular.

Eggplants are originally from China and India and grow best in a tropical or sub-tropical climate. They need steady warmth to produce fruit correctly. Also note that you should harvest them while they're young for the best flavor. This usually means when they reach about half of their mature size.

Most eggplants are started indoors before the last frost. So where harvest dates are given, it refers to the date after transplanting them to the garden.

Applegreen

This variety with apple-size fruit is a 1964 heirloom that's early maturing and has tender skin that you don't need to peel. Because they mature early, Applegreen is nice for northern gardens. 62 days to harvest.

Black Beauty

Black Beauty is a 1902 heirloom eggplant that's had a reputation as a dependable producer for decades. It's one that adapts well to its environment and is great for mid-Atlantic, southern, and northern gardens. The fruits are deep purple and can weigh up to 3 pounds—but you'll want to harvest them well before that. They have excellent flavor. 74 days to harvest.

Blush Eggplant

This little beauty is creamy white with a light lavender blush when it's ripe. It is long and cylindrical, which is wonderful for slicing or stuffing. 85 days to harvest.

Casper

This is a wonderful eggplant that's nice for fresh eating in the early part of summer. The plants are compact and the 6"×2" fruit is snow-white and has a mild-tasting flesh. If you harvest them small, there's no need to peel this variety. 70 days to harvest.

Diamond

This heirloom from the Ukraine is an excellent eggplant with dark purple fruits that are 6–9" long and 2–3" in diameter. It has wonderful flavor and texture and is never bitter. 65–95 days to harvest.

Early Black Egg

This Japanese eggplant is a small, early maturing variety with an egg shape. It's a nice one for mid-Atlantic gardens and does well in areas with short growing seasons. It's also more tolerant of the flea beetle than other varieties. 65 days to harvest.

Florida High Bush

This plant is disease- and drought-resistant, as well as ever-bearing. The fruits are large, purple on the outside, and pure white on the inside. It's a hardy, upright plant that produces the fruit high off the ground. 76–80 days to harvest.

Goyo Kumba

This highly prolific plant produces bright red, 2–3" fruit that's slightly flattened. It's a nice ornamental variety, as the fruits last for a long time on the plant. 90–100 days to harvest.

Japanese White Egg

These eggplants offer heavy yields of white eggplant all season long. They're 2–3" and have a full, rich flavor that's perfect for stir-frying. 65 days to harvest.

Lao Green Stripe (Green Tiger)

This is a productive variety that bears 2", round eggplants with green stripes on the upper part of the fruit. It has a nice eggplant flavor and is best when harvested young. 90 days to harvest.

Lao Purple Stripe (Purple Tiger)

Nearly exactly the same as the green stripe version but a different color. Both are perfect for containers and small gardens. Great for cooking while the fruits are small. 90 days to harvest.

Lista de Gandia

This egg-shaped, Italian heirloom came from France around 1850. It produces 5–6" purple fruits that have irregular white striping and don't need to be peeled. It grows well in high heat and is drought-tolerant. In fact, it grows best in areas with a long growing season. 75–80 days to harvest.

Long Purple (Long Purple Italian)

A variety from the 1850s, this is a deep purple fruit that can be sliced just like a cucumber. It's long and has a slightly bulbous end. Harvest these when they're about 1" in diameter. 75 days to harvest.

Louisiana Long Green

This eggplant produces a spineless, 7", banana-shaped fruit that is light green with creamy green stripes. 100 days to harvest.

Pingtung Long

This is a beautiful, shiny, deep lavender variety that originally came from Pingtung, Taiwan. The fruits grow to 18" or longer. It's a high-yielding plant that's also disease-resistant. 62 days to harvest.

Purple Pickling

This is a traditional Italian eggplant that is eaten fresh or used for an eggplant relish. The beautiful, thorn-free plants bear smooth, bell-shaped fruits. 90 days to harvest.

Red Ruffled (Hmong Red, Pumpkin Tree)

This eggplant looks absolutely unreal. The leaves have spines along the midribs and the eggplants look like shiny little 3" pumpkins formed on black branches. The bitter fruits are popular in Asian stir-fry dishes. You can cut the branches with the eggplants and let them dry to use in fall arrangements. They're super ornamental in the garden. 65–70 days to harvest.

Rosa Bianca

The Italian Rosa Bianca has a group of loyal followers that swear by its superb sweet and mild flavor and beautiful creamy color with pink-purple striping. It's perfect for eggplant parmesiana. 83 days to harvest.

Rosita

Rosita is a Puerto Rican heirloom variety that grows teardrop-shaped, lavender-pink fruits with white shoulders. The flesh has a sweet, tender flavor with no sign of bitterness. It's more productive than and considered generally a superior plant to Rosa Bianca. 70–80 days to harvest.

Round Mauve

China brings us this tennis ball–size variety. The fruits are a lovely lavender and white. This is a good choice for container planting or small gardens. 80–90 days to harvest.

Striped Toga

This beautiful eggplant variety produces fruits that start as a striped green color and change to a striped orange. The tennis ball–size eggplants taste strong but not bitter. They hold their shape well in fresh or dried flower arrangements. 70–85 days to harvest.

Sweet African Orange

This is a nice variety for gardeners who like rare fruits. It produces fat, round, or oval eggplants that change from white to a bright, shiny orange when mature. You can harvest these sweet fruits young or mature, but the young ones have the mildest flavor. 70–90 days to harvest.

Thai Long Green (Thai Green)

This heirloom from Thailand has good-quality fruits with a 10"×1½" elongated shape and a light green color. The plants are short, nearly spineless, and drought-resistant. 80 days to harvest.

Photo by Baker Creek Heirloom Seeds

Turkish Italian Orange

This Italian heirloom was originally from Turkey and introduced to American gardeners in 1990 by Southern Exposure Seed Exchange. The plant is spineless and very attractive with the fruit hanging from it. The 2-ounce eggplants start out orange and mature to red. The little tomato look-alikes should be harvested before they turn red so the fruits aren't bitter. 65–85 days to harvest.

Udumalapet

This Indian heirloom's fruits are teardrop-shaped and green with bright lavender stripes. When this variety matures, it turns to yellow. The fruits are best if they're harvested small, at about 3" long. This is a prolific producer. 80–90 days to harvest.

Ukrainian Beauty

This variety is a big producer of large fruits that are colored deep purple with a slight green cast. 75 days to harvest.

Endive and Escarole

 Endive and escarole are the same species of chicory—only the leaves are different. The differences are slight (as far as growing and eating are concerned) and mostly visual. Endive's leaves are curly or crinkly and grow as a loose head. Its flavor is bitter and sharp. The leaves of escarole grow as a tighter head and are thick and flat. Escarole's flavor is less bitter than endive.

You'll want to grow both in the spring or fall, as they will become extremely bitter if temperatures are too warm. If you direct seed them in the early spring, you can usually do a couple of succession plantings three weeks apart before the weather warms up too much.

Barese Escarole (Cardoncella Barese)

This lovely Italian heirloom is from the Puglia region. It has long, thick stems and grows beautifully in the fall garden. Let it over-winter in a cold frame or hoop house and harvest in early spring. Days to harvest unavailable.

Batavian Broad-Leaf Escarole (Batavian Full Heart Escarole)

This variety produces curled leaves that grow thick and broad into 12–16" round heads. The heart blanches to white and is buttery. It's an excellent choice for salads. 90 days to harvest.

De Louviers Endive

This heirloom grows curled leaves that are deeply notched and produces a curled, yellow, and tasty heart. Days to harvest unavailable.

De Meaux Endive

This pre-1885 French heirloom produces dark green, broad, deeply notched heads that have blanched, creamy white hearts. Absolutely delicious in salads. Days to harvest unavailable.

Florida Deep-Hearted Endive

This is a southern broad-leaf variety that has dark green, thick, and crumpled leaves. 85 days to harvest.

Green Curled Ruffec Endive

As you might imagine, the leaves of this variety are deeply ruffled with thick, white midribs. It blanches to white and resists cold weather and bolting. 85 days to harvest.

Salad King Green Curled Endive

This variety produces heads that reach 32" tall and has ribbed, white leaves. Bolt-resistant and early frost–tolerant. 100 days to harvest.

Garlic and Rocambole

Garlic is a perennial bulb that belongs to the onion family. It's one of the oldest known culinary seasonings, and the Egyptian pyramid builders ate it every day because it was thought to strengthen the body. The Romans swore by the sustenance-giving properties of garlic and ate it to help them stay healthy during long marches. Today, we mostly grow garlic to improve the flavor of countless dishes.

While the general look and flavor of all garlic types are the same, there are some subtle differences. There are three main garlic types grown for culinary purposes: softneck, hardneck, and Elephant garlic.

The softneck type derived from the hardnecks through domestication, which prevents them from producing topsets, so their necks and leaf blades are quite braidable. The softnecks are considered the more productive type of garlic and are more adaptable to different growing conditions. They're also easier to grow than other types but are a little less cold-hardy in deep northern areas.

The hardneck garlics are also known as rocombole or topsetting garlic. Rocambole sends up a flower stalk called a scape that coils 360 degrees and then straightens out once again to grow a little cluster of bulblets (topsets) at the very top. This is a really cool visual.

Another garlic type that you've probably seen before is the monstrous Elephant garlic. To be fair, Elephant garlic isn't a true garlic at all. It's a leek cousin that's disguised quite effectively as a garlic. It offers the same garlic flavor, but milder. The cloves are really big compared to the others, but it isn't usually as hardy as true garlics.

Garlic is generally planted in the fall and then harvested the following summer. The days needed for garlic to mature has everything to do with which month in the fall you plant them, as well as where you are in the country and when your spring hits that year. Garlic is ready to be harvested when two thirds of the leaves have died back and turned brown. The garlic should be left out in a cool, dry area to "cure" for about two weeks before storing. The softneck varieties have a longer storage life than the hardneck varieties.

Bogatyr

This is a large hardneck variety originally from Moscow. It has lovely coloring with marbled purple or brown stripes. Bogatyr produces five to seven cloves per bulb and stores well.

Broadleaf Czech

This softneck variety has large, tan cloves with a touch of red. When eaten raw, the flavor is described as hot. However, the flavor becomes full and mild when it's cooked. It produces 10–14 cloves per bulb.

Brown Tempest

This hardneck is nicely shaped and produces cloves that are brown with a rose tint. When eaten raw, it has a rather intensely hot flavor at first, then mellows. It keeps well and produces six cloves per bulb.

Chesnok Red (Shvelisi)

This hardneck variety is touted as one of the best baking and roasting varieties. The bulbs are a creamy white blushed with red. The bulbs peel easily, and the flavor remains even after cooking. It produces 8–10 cloves per bulb.

Chet's Italian Red

This softneck is productive and adaptable to varying conditions. The flavor is not overpowering at all, which makes it a nice choice for eating raw. It produces 12–14 cloves per bulb.

Elephant Garlic

Once again, Elephant garlic isn't really a garlic, but rather a leek imitating a garlic. It produces monstrous cloves that are actually very mild compared to true garlic. It's possible for the cloves to reach 3–5" in diameter and weigh up to 1 pound when they're dry. Produces four to six cloves per bulb.

Georgian Crystal (Cichisdzhvari)

This is a hardneck that produces gorgeous bulbs and stores very well. The flavor is mild when eaten raw, but has a soft, buttery texture and flavor when roasted. It produces four to six cloves per bulb.

Georgian Fire

The taste of this variety is said to be strong and hot—but not unpleasantly so— making it the perfect choice for salsa and salads. Produces four to six cloves per bulb.

German Extra-Hardy

This is an extremely large hardneck variety that has a very high sugar content. It's a perfect choice for roasting. The skin of the clove is dark red-purple, but the outside skin is ivory. A very winter-hardy variety. Produces four to six cloves per bulb.

German Porcelain (Northern White)

This hardneck produces bulbs that can grow to about half the size of Elephant garlic. It's a cold-hardy variety that's popular for baking because of its large size and good flavor. The cloves' color is blushed red with white wrapping on the outside. It produces five to seven cloves per bulb.

Inchelium Red

This softneck was found growing on the Colville Indian Reservation in Inchelium, Washington. In 1990, the Rodale Institute touted it as the best-tasting variety. The large bulbs sport some light purple blotching. These bulbs are compound, with 10–15 small to medium cloves at the center of the bulb surrounded by 8–10 larger ones.

Italian Softneck

Brought to New York in 1882, this softneck Italian heirloom produces large bulbs with excellent flavor. If stored well, it'll keep for up to 10 months.

Loiacono

This softneck has great flavor and, as a plus, is easy to peel. It's perfect for long storage.

Mild French Silverskin

This softneck grows well in hot, dry areas, so it's perfect for gardeners living in the south. It is a popular braiding garlic and its flavor is best shown off when cooked. It's an easy variety to store and has around 14 cloves per bulb.

Music

This is an Italian hardneck variety that's a reliable producer of 2½–3" bulbs. It's white with a touch of pink and has a sweet, pungent flavor. Produces four to seven cloves per bulb.

Persian Star (Samarkand)

Here's a hardneck variety collected from Uzbekistan that has mild flavor with a little spicy zip. It's a nice, reliable, all-purpose variety. It produces 8–12 cloves per bulb.

Pskem River

Another hardneck from Uzbekistan that has lovely purple-striped cloves and a full flavor. It produces four to five large cloves per bulb.

Red Toch

This softneck is a nice garlic for eating raw. It has perfect, multidimensional flavor and a spicy scent. It produces large cloves with pink and red striping.

Siberian

Siberian is one of the most popular hardneck varieties. The bulbs look white with a pink blush, but as you peel away the outer wrappers, the clove becomes nearly pure purple. The bulbs are large and have good flavor but they're not overpowering. It produces four to seven cloves per bulb.

Silver Rose

Silver Rose is a good braiding softneck with rose-colored cloves and a white outer skin. It has delicious, mild flavor and is a good choice for southern gardens. This variety can be stored for up to a year.

Silverwhite Silverskin

This is the softneck you may have seen in the grocery store. It produces very pretty, big cloves with a mild flavor. If it's cured well, it'll store easily for a year.

Gourd

 Gourds have been used for bowls, bottles, and other utilitarian containers; for birdhouses; and as the resonating chamber in many musical instruments. Typically today, gourds are used for decoration or crafting purposes. There are a few gourd varieties that are edible, however. Whatever your reason for growing them, they're fun, unusual, and very interesting.

Harvest gourds when the fruit stem changes from green to yellow or a yellow-brown and be sure to leave about a 4" stem. Wash off your gourds with some soapy water and dry them well. After that, it's all about letting them cure (dry thoroughly) so they can be crafted.

Apple Gourd

These 4-pound gourds look like big apples and are a medium green color speckled with a darker green. The 6–8" tall and 4–6" wide gourds are unusual and really attractive for fall decorating. They can also be dried and painted. 110 days to harvest.

Birdhouse Gourd

This is one of the best-known craft gourds. This variety has a large ball-shaped bottom and a long-handled neck, or sometimes a smaller ball shape at the top. They're usually hollowed out and made into birdhouses or dipping gourds. 95 days to harvest.

Bule

This is a hard-shell French gourd that's dried to make crafts. It's 6–8" tall and 5–6" across with small warts or bumps covering the entire outside of its skin. 100–120 days to harvest.

Bushel Gourd

It's not unheard of for this fruit to grow past the size of a bushel basket. If they're trimmed to one fruit per plant, you'll have a better chance of getting the great size. These slate gray gourds with super-strong shells are perfect to use as baskets after they've dried. 130 days to harvest.

Chinese Miniature

Seed from this variety was brought to America in 1982. These are small gourds—about 3" across. Great for holiday decorating when matured or as miniature roasting squash when young. 100 days to harvest.

Corsica Flat

These gourds were introduced in 1992 by Southern Exposure Seed Exchange. They were traditionally used in Peru as carved decorative bowls. These good-looking round, flattened gourds are 3½–5" deep and 6–12" around. 130 days to harvest.

Dancing (Spinning)

This variety is super hard-shelled when it's dry. Years ago kids would bring them to school and spin them on their desks. 90–100 days to harvest.

Dinosaur

This variety was traditionally used as decoration for sweat lodges. The fruits are solid green and have curved necks. The bowl is 8" around with interesting serpentine projections on the sides. Great for craft-making. 125 days to harvest.

Luffa (Chinese Vining Okra, Vegetable Sponge, Dishcloth Gourd)

Luffa looks like big okra pods when left to mature on the vine. If you want to eat them, harvest this gourd while it's young—and treat it like okra. If you'd like to make a Luffa sponge, take a mature gourd and let it soak in water to soften the tissue. Then clean it to use in the bathtub. 150 days to harvest.

Sweet Honey Sponge Gourd

This gourd variety produces lovely vines and flowers. It's long, smooth, and green. Its flavor resembles a cross between a squash and an okra. You may know it as a luffa gourd, which is dried and then used in the bath. But when it's harvested under 10", it's delicious baked or in soups. Days to harvest unavailable.

Photo by Baker Creek Heirloom Seeds

Ten Commandments

These gourds are about the size of a softball and have prongs that point toward the blossom end of the fruit. The colors vary, with a mix of mottled, striped, and multi-colored gourds. 95 days to harvest.

Kale

For some reason, kale is often overlooked by gardeners and cooks. It's hard to imagine why, because kale is the total package. From a nutritional standpoint, it's a wise choice, as it's high in vitamins and minerals (kale has been called a superfood).

Unassuming kale is also a handsome plant. Though you may not have noticed it in a vegetable garden, the entire garden is embellished by kale's leaf texture and deep color.

Last, kale has great flavor and is accommodating. Kale can be steamed, baked, sautéed, roasted, or tossed into soups. Its flavor is best when it grows quickly, so you'll want to be certain that you have lots of compost worked into the bed.

Kale is part of the cabbage family, so it stands to reason that it enjoys the cooler temperatures just like its family members. Spring, fall, and winter are all good seasons to grow kale because the soils are cool. In fact, a light frost only enhances kale's flavor. This is a hardy vegetable that can over-winter in many climates.

Dwarf Blue Curled Scotch

This low-growing plant (12–15" tall) contains oodles of vitamin A. It's best to harvest just after a light frost as this improves the flavor. 53–65 days to harvest.

Dwarf Siberian

This Russian variety has good flavor and is winter-hardy and prolific. The leaves only have a slight frill. 50 days to harvest.

Hanover Salad

This Siberian kale variety is an early maturing plant that has large, smooth leaves. You'll be able to harvest it while it's young and add it to your spring salads before anything else is ready. 30 days to harvest.

Lacinato

This kale dates back to Tuscany in the eighteenth century. Its 3"x10" leaves are blue-green and straplike in shape. They're also heavily savoyed. You'll want to harvest Lacinato while it's young and tender, but time it right after a light frost to enhance its flavor. 60–90 days to harvest.

Premier

This variety has smooth, dark green leaves with scalloped edges. It can be over-wintered, which lets the plant develop new growing points on the main stem, giving you more leaves to harvest in the spring. 60 days to harvest.

Red Russian (Ragged Jack)

This is a pre-1885 heirloom with oak-type, red-tinged leaves and purple-pink veining. It's a beautiful kale that has tender leaves and great flavor. 50–65 days to harvest.

Vates

This Scotch-type variety can be planted in the spring or the fall and it over-winters in the mid-Atlantic region. Its blue-green leaves are finely curled and it's slow to bolt. 50–80 days to harvest.

Kohlrabi

 Kohlrabi belongs to the *brassica* family and is a cousin to broccoli, ruta-baga, cabbage, cauliflower, Brussels sprouts, kale, and turnip.

This is a seriously unique and alien-looking veggie for your garden that can be tender and flavorful—plus it stores pretty darn well. The edible part of kohlrabi is the swollen area of the stem.

Kohlrabi's name translates to "cabbage turnip" in German but it was first recorded in 1554 in Italy. Like its *brassica* cousins, it likes the cooler temperatures and matures in the fall. It needs continuous moisture and should be harvested when the bulbous part of the stem is about 2" in diameter. Kohlrabi's flesh is cabbage-sweet when it's harvested young.

Early Purple Vienna

A pre-1860 heirloom, Early Purple Vienna is a little larger than White Vienna and more flavorful. The flesh is white under purple skin. 60 days to harvest.

Early White Vienna

This mild variety has nice flavor with white flesh and light green skin. 55–60 days to harvest.

Gigant Winter 60

This is a Czechoslovakian heirloom that was introduced by Southern Exposure Seed Exchange in 1989. This large kohlrabi can grow to 8–10" in diameter and still manage to stay tender. It's root maggot–resistant, stores very well, and in milder regions can stay in the ground all winter when protected by mulch. The leaves can be eaten the same way as kale. 130 days to harvest.

Peking Green

This is a medium-size, Chinese kohlrabi variety. The bulbs are light green with a fine-quality white flesh. 50 days to harvest.

Leeks

Think of leeks as scallions that pump iron. They are biennial onion family members that have a more delicate onion flavor than their cousins. This makes them popular for soups and salads. They don't develop a bulb the way garlic and onions do; their underground stem is nearly the same width as the top stems of the plant. The "bulbous" part is white and it becomes greener up the stem into the leaves.

They like soil that's loamy and fertile and enjoy having some fish emulsion or meal fed to them every couple of weeks during the growing season. You can blanch the stalks by hilling the soil up around them. Depending on what growing zone you're in, you'll have a choice of short-season and long-season varieties.

American Flag (Broad London)

This is the standard variety for most home gardens. It has a delicate flavor and stems that are about 8–10" tall. 95 days to harvest.

Blue Solaize (Blu of Solaise)

This French heirloom is truly stunning in a garden. It has blue leaves that turn violet after a cold snap. The stalks are tall (15–20") and quite hardy. They have a sweet flavor and are good for short-season growing zones. 100–120 days to harvest.

Bulgarian Giant Leek

This thin leek is a European favorite. It has light green leaves and a fine quality. 110 days to harvest.

Carentan Leek

This is an old European variety that has white stems and is very productive. Great for fall and winter use. 100 days to harvest.

Giant Musselburgh (Scotch Flag)

This monstrous 1800s Scottish variety can grow up to 36" tall and 2–3" in diameter. The stalks are white with medium blue-green leaves that are fan-shaped. It has a mild flavor that's very nice and it tolerates the winter quite well. 80–150 days to harvest.

King Richard

This is an early leek variety that grows best in summer and early fall. It's 12"×1" (slender) and should be harvested before temperatures reach below 20°F. 75 days to harvest.

King Sieg

King Sieg has blue-green leaves that are short and thick, about 3"×6". It's a good over-wintering variety. 84 days to harvest.

Prizetaker (The Lyon)

This English heirloom showed up in American catalogs at the end of the 1880s. It has thick, white stalks that can reach up to 36" tall. Prizetaker may be huge, but it keeps its tender texture and mild taste. 110–135 days to harvest.

Lettuce

If we left it up to the produce department to show us what lettuce is all about, we'd be very bored indeed. But iceberg lettuce is just the tip of the, well … iceberg. There are literally hundreds of lettuces that come in all shapes, colors, textures, and flavors.

Another great reason to try your hand at heirloom lettuces is that they are easy to grow—we're talking *ridiculously easy*. They're also a crop that matures fast, so there's some instant veggie gratification. The one thing to keep in mind is that they won't fare well in a heat wave. Lettuce is a cool-weather worshipper, although a little bit of sun can be tolerated.

I usually start my first spring crop of lettuce indoors about four weeks before the last frost. The next sowing I do is in late spring, when I just seed them directly into the garden beds. We don't have hard winters here, but we do have hard frosts regularly. So during the winter, I plant them in a cold frame that lets me take advantage of what sun I have (for growing) but keep the freezing temps from killing the tender leaves.

There are four general lettuce categories. Romaine or cos lettuce produces long, thick, and crinkly leaves. It's an upright type with succulent leaves that will tolerate a fair amount of heat. It's also the healthiest of the lettuces.

Butterhead or Bibb lettuce has short, loose-leaf heads and yellow interiors. The leaves are thin and soft and this lettuce is fairly good at tolerating heat. It's the runner-up to romaine in nutrition. You'll find the widest selection of heirlooms in this lettuce category.

The last groups of lettuces are the crispheads or icebergs and Batavian lettuces. They're the most popular type of lettuce, and you'll recognize the tightly layered leaves that form a nice head. While they're thought of as having the least nutritional value, icebergs are a good source of choline and vitamin K. They need cool weather to form proper heads.

Amish Deer Tongue

This loose-leaf lettuce is a heavy-producing variety that has sharp, triangular leaves with straight edges. It's rugged and thick with good texture. The flavor is sharp but good. 45–55 days to harvest.

Anuenue

Anuenue (pronounced *ah-nu-ee-nu-ee*) means "rainbow" in Hawaiian. It's both heat-tolerant and bolt-resistant, so it's a nice lettuce to grow in any season. This Batavian's leaves are a bright glossy green, resembling an iceberg lettuce. 50 days to harvest.

Australian Yellow (Australian Yellowleaf)

This Australian heirloom is a loose-leaf lettuce that has a tender texture with a good, slightly sweet flavor. It has light yellow-green leaves that end up crinkled and grow 12–16". It's a terrific spring lettuce. 54 days to harvest.

Baby Oakleaf

Just like it sounds, Baby Oakleaf is the dwarf (compact) version of its loose-leaf big brother Oakleaf or Green Oakleaf. The oak-shaped leaves are a medium green color that hold for an extended period. 50 days to harvest.

Black-Seeded Simpson

This standard loose leaf has been hanging around since before 1850. It's one of the earliest varieties to mature but won't take the heat. 49 days to harvest.

Bronze Arrow (Bronze Arrowhead)

Here's a California heirloom that is a big producer and is slow to bolt. The leaves are an attractive oakleaf shape tipped with a red-brown color. It's a cut-and-come-again lettuce, so the more leaves you take, the more leaves grow back in. It has delicious flavor. 50–60 days to harvest.

Buttercrunch

Buttercrunch produces dark green leaves and a compact head. It's heat- and stress-tolerant with good bolt resistance as well. It's a flavorful, reliable variety for both the home garden and market. 55 days to harvest.

Capitan

This butterhead variety has light green leaves that have a nice, buttery flavor. It's heat-, cold-, and mosaic virus–resistant. In Rodale's 1983 trials it was voted the best Boston-type lettuce. 62 days to harvest.

Cimarron (Little Leprechaun)

This is an eighteenth-century heirloom romaine that's 10–12" tall, deep red, and lovely. Its center is a creamy yellow-bronze that's tender and delicious. It resists bolting and is both heat- and cold-tolerant. 60–70 days to harvest.

Cosmo

This romaine lettuce has broad, savoyed leaves that are bright green, crisp, and sweet. The heads grow to 12" tall and don't turn bitter as fast as some romaines. 55 days to harvest.

Cracoviensis

This is a fast-growing, loose-leaf, European heirloom that produces open heads of maroon-tipped, buttery leaves. It can be quick to bolt, but the leaves are tender the whole time without any bitterness. 65 days to harvest.

Crisp Mint

These romaine leaves are unique in that they're almost serrated in form. The compact heads grow almost vertical to 10" and have excellent flavor. Crisp Mint really stands out in the garden. 45–55 days to harvest.

Deer Tongue (Matchless)

The leaves on this variety are triangular, slightly savoyed, and round-tipped. They grow as an upright, loose-head lettuce that has sweet flavor and a crisp texture. 54 days to harvest.

Devil's Tongue

Devil's Tongue has thick leaves that are deep, dark red-purple in color. They have a buttery texture and loose heads. 55 days to harvest.

Drunken Woman Lettuce (Drunken Woman Frizzy Headed)

I just had to grow this loose-leaf variety for the name. Drunken Woman has gorgeous, bright green leaves with edges that are ruffled—almost to a fringe. It's a lovely, crisp lettuce with sweet taste. 55 days to harvest.

Flame

This loose-leaf variety was introduced to gardeners in 1988. The leaves are shiny red and slow to bolt. Not many seed companies offer this variety. 60 days to harvest.

Forellenschluss

This Austrian romaine's name translates to "speckled trout" for good reason. The plant is beautiful with its green leaves and maroon speckling. It has thick midribs, crispy leaves, and excellent flavor. Watch as it grows fast while the weather is cool, but once it warms up, it'll bolt. 58 days to harvest.

Gold Rush

This loose-leaf variety adds a little something extra to a salad—fantastic texture. Its lime-green leaves are extremely frilled, crinkled, and curly. The flavor is clean and mild and it's slow to bolt compared to others like it (such as Tango). 50–60 days to harvest.

Grandpa Admire's

George Admire (born 1822) was a Civil War veteran. His granddaughter, Cloe Lowrey, gave this seed to Seed Savers Exchange in 1977 when she was 90 years old. It's a butterhead lettuce with bronze leaves that's slow to bolt. This variety stays tender longer than most, even when it's super hot. The flavor is fine and mild. 60 days to harvest.

Jericho (Super Jericho)

Due to its Israeli heritage, Jericho was bred for the heat. This heavy romaine thrives in hot summers and has light green, sweet leaves that keep their sweetness longer than the other varieties. 60 days to harvest.

Landis Winter

William Woys Weaver sent seeds for this unusual lettuce to Underwood Gardens in 1998. It's a loose butterhead type that reaches 11–12" in diameter. The sweet, tender, flavorful green heads are very resistant to hard frosts. They succeed well enough in cold frames that, when well established by mid-October, it can be picked and enjoyed at Christmas. Listed in the 1878 seed list and 1785 agricultural treatise by Abbe Rozier. 45 days to harvest.

Lollo Rossa

Lollo Rossa has gorgeous loose-leaf, frilly, magenta heads with a light green base. The heads are small (5–8") and it makes a nice cut-and-come-again variety. It makes a perfect baby lettuce. 55 days to harvest.

Mascara

Imagine frilly, dark red, oakleaf-shaped leaves that form a curly rosette—this is the beautiful Mascara. It's just fabulous with a nice, mild flavor; plus it's quite slow to bolt. 60–65 days to harvest.

May Queen (Regina di Maggio)

This was a famous butterhead in the early 1800s. Its medium-size, pale green leaves tinged in red give way to a creamy yellow heart with a blushed center. It's the ultimate butterhead for the market or gourmet chefs. You'd be hard-pressed to find a finer variety. 45–60 days to harvest.

Merlot

This is a beautiful leaf lettuce with deep, wine-red frills. The leaves taste full-bodied and smooth. It's a good candidate for the cut-and-come-again technique. 50–60 days to harvest.

Merveille Des Quatre Saisons (Marvel of Four Seasons)

This is a lovely butterhead variety that produces reddish rosettes with crispy, wonderful flavor. Cool weather will encourage the leaves to show their deepest red. 60 days to harvest.

Oakleaf (Green Oakleaf)

This one dates back to before 1771. This old, standard loose-leaf is overlooked as of late, but it's a proven performer and great for early summer growing. Its oakleaf-shaped leaves form a tight cluster. It is bolt-resistant and bitter-free for a long time compared to other varieties. 45 days to harvest.

Pablo Batavian (Pablo)

This loose-leaf lettuce is so pretty that you could use it as an ornamental alone. The leaves are wine-red with a bit of dark green and have a sweet flavor. 60 days to harvest.

Parris Island Cos

This slow-to-bolt romaine was introduced in 1952. It's becoming a popular variety with its 10–12" heads, barely savoyed leaves, and creamy white heart. It is mosaic virus–tolerant and resistant to tipburn. 68 days to harvest.

Red Coral

When compared to other red loose-leaf varieties, Red Coral's frilly leaves are more pink. This variety is useful for harvesting leaf by leaf over the entire season. 55 days to harvest.

Red Deer Tongue

This variety has the same great quality that the regular Deer Tongue has, but with red-tinged leaves. 58 days to harvest.

Red Iceberg

If you're tired of the same old green iceberg, try this red variety. It's nearly as beautiful as the loose-leafs with a medium-large head (16" wide) that holds well and is slow to bolt. It has a nice, mild flavor. 70–80 days to harvest.

Red Leprechaun

This romaine has paddle-shaped leaves that are a shiny, dark purple and have smooth edges with large bumps. The center rib is pink and it grows upright. The hearts are crisp and clean. It has good flavor with a nice little bite. 60 days to harvest.

Red Romaine

This romaine grows 12" tall and 10–12" wide. It's big, colorful, and tangy—perfect for salads. It shows its deepest red when grown in cool weather. 70 days to harvest.

Red Sails

Red Sails was introduced in 1985 and has crinkled, maroon-red leaves with color that gets deeper as it matures. It's an early producer and slow to bitterness compared to other red varieties. 45 days to harvest.

Red Salad Bowl

This loose-leaf variety has large, wine-red leaves. It's exactly like the regular Salad Bowl, but red instead of green. 55 days to harvest.

Red Velvet

This is one of the darkest red loose-leaf lettuces you'll find. Its striking color brings wonderful contrast to the garden bed. The heads grow 6–8" tall, 10–12" wide, and are slow to bolt. 55 days to harvest.

Reine des Glaces (Ice Queen)

This crisphead lettuce's name translates to "Queen of the Ices" in French, which is appropriate as the outer wrapper leaves are long and spiky-looking, resembling a crown. The leaves are beautifully frilly and the heart is light green and crisp. This variety makes a great baby lettuce. It continues to grow in the cold when other varieties have called it quits, and it's very slow to bolt. 60–65 days to harvest.

Rossa di Trento

From Milan, Italy, we have this lovely loose-leaf with red-brown, savoyed leaves. It's a widely adaptable variety that resists bolting. 45–60 days to harvest.

Rossimo

This loose-leaf grows 6" tall and 12" wide and has beautiful bright red leaves. The leaves are frilled, blistered, and have super texture. 45–50 days to harvest.

Rouge d'Hiver (Red Winter)

This is an 1840 French heirloom romaine that has red and green leaves with dark red tips. It grows semi-open and has good flavor. It prefers the cooler weather. 62 days to harvest.

Rubin

Rubin is a wonderfully colorful, dark red loose-leaf with frilled edges. It's a very showy lettuce in the garden and when its crinkled leaves are tossed into salads. 55 days to harvest.

Salad Bowl

Salad Bowl has loose, frilly leaves that make a rosette. The leaves are crisp and deep-notched and are perfect for cut-and-come-again harvesting. Plus, it's heat-tolerant. 40–65 days to harvest.

Sanguine Ameliore

This 1906 French butterhead is hard to find. The heads are 7–9" in diameter and green with red mottling. The leaves are tender and flavor is excellent. 60 days to harvest.

Schweitzer's Mescher Bibb

This Bibb lettuce dates back to the 1700s but was introduced to American gardeners in 1986 by Southern Exposure Seed Exchange. Its crisp, green leaves trimmed with red make tight heads. It's a lovely looking lettuce with excellent flavor. 50 days to harvest.

Slobolt

This 1946 heirloom has bright green leaves. It's perfect for southern gardens as it's very heat-tolerant. 48 days to harvest.

Speckled Bibb

The 1946 Speckled Bibb has pretty light green leaves spotted with red dots. The leaves on this butterhead are crispy and great tasting. In the heat, it fares better than both Buttercrunch and Slobolt, but performs best in the cooler weather. 43 days to harvest.

Sunset

Sunset offers one of the deepest red loose-leaf varieties available to home gardeners and market growers. It grows 12" across and 5–8" tall. 45–55 days to harvest.

Susan's Red Rib

This loose-leaf is tinged with red leaves that are curled and blistered. It has a lime-green leaf center. This variety has a mild flavor. 50–60 days to harvest.

Sweet Valentine

The leaves are an intense dark red and a bit smaller than other romaines. It has an exceptionally sweet flavor and holds a long time before bolting in the heat. 55 days to harvest.

Tango

This is a widely adaptable loose-leaf that grows 12" across and 6–8" tall in tight, upright rosettes. The leaves are so deeply cut that they look like an endive. The dark green, tender lettuce has a tangy flavor. It's slow to bolt and is a great variety for the home garden and market. 45–60 days to harvest.

Tennis Ball

This is a pre-1804 crisphead lettuce that was grown by Thomas Jefferson at Monticello. It has light green leaves that are yellow-green at the base. The heads are medium-size and are best grown as a spring lettuce. 55 days to harvest.

Thai Oakleaf

This variety looks a lot like Oakleaf, but the leaves are larger and more upright. It tolerates hot conditions and is fairly slow to bolt. The leaves have an almond flavor. 39 days to harvest.

Tom Thumb

This is a pre-1850 butterhead heirloom that produces apple-size heads. Their compact size makes them perfect for growing in containers. The leaves are a medium green and very tender. 48 days to harvest.

Webb's Wonderful

This crisphead has large, crinkled, and robust heads that are slow to bolt. The leaves have good texture and fine flavor. Perfect choice for growing in the south. 65–70 days to harvest.

Winter Density

This is an interesting lettuce that's dubbed a "buttercos," which means that it has the characteristics of both a butterhead and a romaine lettuce. The heads grow upright, compact, and dense. This is a high-quality lettuce that's cold-tolerant. Wonderful for salads. 58 days to harvest.

Yu Mai Tsai Chinese (Pointed Leaf)

This is a popular cooking variety in Taiwan. It has long, crispy, bright green leaves that have a robust flavor when harvested young. Nice for stir-frys, stews, and soups. 60–85 days to harvest.

Yugoslavian Red Butterhead

Obtained from a family in Yugoslavia, this variety was introduced in 1987 by Southern Exposure Seed Exchange. The leaves toward the middle of the 10" head are a pretty, creamy yellow with red dapples. The outside leaves are red-tinged. This variety has a buttery flavor. It looks ornamental in a garden and is perfect as a garnish. 58 days to harvest.

Melon

You may want to sit down for this next bit of information: if you're living in the United States, the chances that you've eaten a *true* cantaloupe are slim. What we Americans know as "cantaloupe" is actually a muskmelon. Real cantaloupes have a hard, warty shell as opposed to the smooth and netted look of our melons of the same name. True cantaloupes are rarely grown outside of Europe.

This section will have varieties of muskmelons (or American melons), which shouldn't bother you a bit considering you've been eating these all along and just didn't know it. Watermelons will be covered in their own section.

A couple of things to remember about growing melons: they love nutrient-rich compost and resent their roots being disturbed. When they reach about half of their mature size, gently lift the melon (slightly) and slip a board underneath it to prevent any chance of rotting while it's ripening.

Melons develop their wonderful flavor in the last two weeks on the vine, so pull back with the watering—don't let them dry out entirely, but too much water will lessen the flavor. When they're ripe, melons come right off the vine if you press a bit with your thumb on the stem base. When the description says "pick on full slip," it's referring to when the fruit slips off easily.

Amish

These 4–7-pound, oval fruits come from the Amish community. The flesh is orange, sweet, and juicy. 80–90 days to harvest.

Banana Melon

This heirloom is not only banana-shaped, its heavy fragrance will remind you of banana, too! It's 16–24" long and weighs 5–8 pounds. It has yellow skin and salmon-colored flesh that tastes both sweet and spicy. Wonderful for specialty markets. 90 days to harvest.

Photo by Baker Creek Heirloom Seeds

Bidwell Casaba

This monstrous melon was grown by John Bidwell (1819–1900) in Chico, California. He was a Civil War general and a U.S. senator. Bidwell Casaba is a highly adaptable variety that produces 12–16-pound fruits with orange, sweet flesh. 90–95 days to harvest.

Boule d'Or (Golden Perfection)

This hard-skinned, lightly netted variety is a famous French melon that was listed by Vilmorin in 1885. It has a yellow rind and pale green flesh with good flavor. This variety will keep for weeks if kept in a cool, dry place. 95–110 days to harvest.

Burrell's Jumbo

This is an improved version of Hale's Best that's a delicious old variety. The flesh is orange and sweet—perfect for the home garden. 80 days to harvest.

Canoe Creek Colossal

This oblong variety is capable of reaching 20 pounds, which makes it one of the biggest muskmelons you can grow. The rind is yellow with a bit of green mottling and the flesh is orange, soft, and sweet. 90 days to harvest.

Charantais

This grapefruit-size, 2-pound melon is touted to have the most sublime and flavorful flesh of any melon in the world. They're round, smooth, and mature to gray-yellow with green stripes. The flesh is salmon in color and seriously sweet and juicy. Their ripe fragrance is described as heavenly. 95–110 days to harvest.

Crane Melon

Crane was developed by Oliver Crane in Santa Rosa, California, in the 1920s. This is a 4–7-pound, soccer ball–size melon that has a soft, buttery, orange flesh. It has exceptional and complex flavor—not simply sweet. It owes its unique flavor to the fact that it's been grown on land owned by the same family for 160 years. It's an aromatic fruit, but not in the same musky way as a cantaloupe. There are many flavor nuances in this melon—even a little banana. Even the refrigerator doesn't quell its terrific flavor. Seeds can be purchased from Sustainable Seed Company. 80 days to harvest.

Crenshaw

These large, oval-shaped melons have a green-yellow rind with salmon-pink flesh. They have a wonderfully sweet flavor and offer high yields of fruit. 105 days to harvest.

Delice de la Table

This French heirloom that translates to "Delight of the Table" was listed by Vilmorin in 1885. The 1–2-pound melons have a ribbed rind and sweet, orange flesh and are nearly extinct. 85–90 days to harvest.

Delicious 51

Here's a productive and flavorful melon for the home garden. Delicious 51 has round-oval fruits that weigh 3–4 pounds. They have medium- to lightly netted skin and salmon-orange flesh. It's tolerant to fusarium wilt (race 1). Pick on full slip. 77 days to harvest.

Early Hanover

Early Hanover is a prolific producer of 2–3-pound melons that have orange blended to green flesh that's immensely sugar-sweet. You can eat this variety right down to the rind. 70–85 days to harvest.

Early Silver Line

Here's a melon of a different texture. The small, 1–2-pound fruits have a white, crisp, refreshing, and sweet flesh. It's a high-yielding variety. 75–80 days to harvest.

Eden Gem (Rocky Ford)

This is an 1881 heirloom that's loved for its fine texture and green, sweet-flavored flesh. Its flavor is described as complex and spicy. The rind is slightly ribbed and has tons of netting. Perfect for the home garden as well as the market, it's super rust-resistant. 89 days to harvest.

Edisto 47

Edisto 47 was introduced in 1965 and is well adapted to the mid-Atlantic region as well as hot and humid growing zones. This 6–7" variety has a heavily netted rind and is well ribbed. It has super-duper disease resistance to Alternaria leaf spot, powdery mildew, and downy mildew. It keeps well. 88 days to harvest.

Emerald Gem

W. Atlee Burpee introduced this heirloom melon in 1886. The seed was sent from William Voorhees of Benzie County, Michigan. At that time, this melon was supposed to have "unapproachable flavor," as well as be "luscious beyond description." The flesh is pale orange and sweet with a little spiciness as well. This is a high-yielding plant that produces 2–3-pound melons. 70–90 days to harvest.

Far North

This 1-pound fruit with sweet, orange flesh is the perfect variety for growing in short-season areas. It's said to have been brought by settlers to Canada from the Ukraine. 65 days to harvest.

Gaucho

This is one of Brazil's favorite varieties. This melon is 14" long and 8" wide with a golden rind and deep ribbing. The flesh is creamy yellow and very juicy. Days to harvest unavailable.

Ginger's Pride

This monstrous 14–22-pound melon has an oblong shape and green skin that turns yellow when it's ripe. The flesh is high-quality, sweet, and nearly melts in your mouth. 95 days to harvest.

Golden Honeymoon

This is a rare and unique-flavored honeydew that has a bright gold rind and green, delicious flesh. It ripens two weeks earlier than most honeydews. It's also high-yielding. 92 days to harvest.

Golden Jenny

Golden Jenny has many of the same characteristics as Jenny Lind but is more compact, vigorous, and productive. This variety also has more resistance to insects. The melons weigh up to ¾ of a pound, are heavily netted, and are slightly ribbed. They have sweet, orange flesh. 85 days to harvest.

Green Nutmeg

This prolific variety has 2–3-pound fruits that have wonderful aroma and very sweet flavor with what is described as a unique spiciness. It was heralded as one of the very best varieties in 1863. 80 days to harvest.

Hales Best

This variety was introduced in 1924 and produces 4–5-pound melons. The rind is heavily netted and lightly ribbed. It resists powdery mildew, is drought-resistant, and has a very sweet flavor. 86 days to harvest.

Healy's Pride

This variety produces 10-pound, heavily netted melons that have that old-time, sweet muskmelon flavor. 80–85 days to harvest.

Hearts of Gold (HooDoo)

In the 1930s, 2–3-pound Hearts of Gold was the most popular variety grown in the midwest for the market. The high-quality flesh is firm, juicy, and super flavored. 70–90 days to harvest.

Hollybrook Luscious

This variety grows vigorous, heavy vines that produce dark green, oblong melons that weigh 8–10 pounds each. The flesh is pale orange, fine-textured, juicy, and sweet. It's a highly aromatic melon with tender skin, so handle this one gently. 90–110 days to harvest.

Honey Rock

This heirloom is an early maturing variety. The fruits are 3–4 pounds and have thick, firm, dark, salmon-colored flesh. It's a super producer. 80 days to harvest.

Honeydew—Orange Flesh

This variety has smooth, light green skin with an orange, sweet flesh. It has classic honeydew flavor. 98 days to harvest.

Honeydew—Tam Dew

This beautiful melon is an ivory-green color with a deep green, very sweet flesh. It has that classic honeydew flavor. 100 days to harvest.

Ice Cream Melon (Green Machine)

This variety with compact vines, also called Green Machine because of its huge fruit production, produces sweet, green, 2-pound melons that make the perfect bowl for a scoop of ice cream. Pick at full slip. 79 days to harvest.

Iroquois

This is a terrific melon for midwestern and northeastern gardens. It produces large, 5–7-pound fruit that has thick, dark orange flesh with great flavor. 85 days to harvest.

Jake's

This heirloom variety has a tan and orange rind with gray spots. The yellow-orange flesh is flavorful. 100 days to harvest.

Jenny Lind

This 2–2½-pound melon was known in the Philadelphia markets before 1840. The variety was named after a popular singer of that time. The fruits are slightly ribbed and have a button at the blossom end of the fruit. The flesh is white-green, sweet, and juicy. 70–80 days to harvest.

Kansas

This 4-pound, oval-shaped fruit has a ridged, heavily netted exterior and fabulously sweet, orange interior. It's a prolific plant, very hardy, and has sap beetle–resistance. 90 days to harvest.

Melon de Castillo

This is a very rare, Spanish heirloom variety that is grown in the Sierra Madres in Mexico. The flesh is pale yellow and super sweet. 91–100 days to harvest.

Minnesota Midget

These 3–4" fruits are an extra early variety that's resistant to fusarium wilt. The vines rarely exceed 3' in length, making them a good candidate for small gardens. The flesh is thick and golden-yellow and has a high sugar content. Go ahead and eat this one down to the rind. 60–75 days to harvest.

Missouri Gold

This is a Missouri family heirloom from 1840. It bears sweet, orange-flesh melons that weigh 4–5 pounds. It takes droughts well. 85 days to harvest.

Noir des Carmes

This may be one of the best melons to grow, and also happens to be one of the easiest. This variety has very dark green skin (nearly black) while it's young. It ripens to almost all orange with green mottling. The flesh is very sweet and orange. It's a super productive variety especially if it's grown on a landscape fabric or plastic mulch. 75 days to harvest.

Oka (Bizard Island Strain)

This variety was originally bred in 1912 by father Athanase of the Trappist Monastery at La Trappe, Quebec. This melon has great flavor and texture. 80–90 days to harvest.

Old Time Tennessee

Here's a variety with awesome fragrance and outstanding flavor—with a few strings attached. First, it needs to be harvested exactly on time, so don't leave town. Second, it won't keep after it's harvested. But the flavor is sublime. Some things are just worth it. It's banana-shaped and weighs 12 pounds. 95 days to harvest.

Oran's Melon

This large, 6–8-pound heirloom is from the Ozark Mountains and has been grown by the Oran Bell family for over 55 years. The rind is netted and ribbed and it has a rich, orange flesh with excellent flavor. 85 days to harvest.

Petit Gris de Rennes

This 2–3-pound, French variety was noted in the Bishop of Rennes' garden some 400 years ago. It has a gray-green rind and sweet, flavorful orange flesh. 80–85 days to harvest.

Pike

Aaron Pike (Pike & Young Seeds) introduced this variety in 1935. This orange-flesh fruit was bred especially for unirrigated, clay soils and offers fabulous flavor. The melons are oblong, heavily netted, and disease-resistant. If you're growing them in conditions they can tolerate, the melons will be 3 pounds. If you irrigate, they'll make it to 7 pounds. 85 days to harvest.

Plum Granny Melon (Queen Anne Pocket Melon)

This is a tennis ball–size heirloom from the Appalachians. It was often tucked into pockets and corsets to mask body odors. It's hugely fragrant, but the flavor is pale in comparison. The melon is yellow with maroon stripes and very high yielding when planted in the full sun. 75 days to harvest.

Prescott Fond Blanc

This French variety has been documented before 1850. This rock melon weighs 4–9 pounds and has warted skin with a dense, sweet flesh. It fills the air with an incredible scent when it's ripe. It has good tolerance to drought and is beautiful in the garden. One thing to note is that it will not slip. 85–95 days to harvest.

Pride of Wisconsin

This is an heirloom from the midwest that was originally introduced in 1937. This is a hard-shelled, 4–8-pound melon with firm, sweet flesh. This has that old-fashioned flavor that many people are looking for, so if you only have space for one variety, this may be the one you'll want to plant. 90–100 days to harvest.

Sakata's Sweet

This eastern variety is just making its way to American markets. The softball-size melon is a good variety for trellising. It has golden yellow flesh that's crisp and refreshingly sweet. 85–95 days to harvest.

Schoon's Hard Shell

This very hard-shelled variety was introduced in 1947. The melons are basically round with thick, apricot-colored flesh and weigh 5–8 pounds each. They taste flavorful and sweet and are an excellent choice for home gardens, as well as the market. It also keeps well. 88–95 days to harvest.

Sleeping Beauty

This sweet-flavored melon was named Sleeping Beauty because the orange-yellow fruits with orange flesh tend to nestle together in groups. The vines are compact and produce ½-pound, smooth, round fruits that turn light green before they ripen. 85 days to harvest.

Sweet Passion

This is an Ohio heirloom from the 1920s. This drought-resistant plant produces 3–4-pound melons that have orange, sweet, and juicy flesh. The grower, Merlyn Neidens, passed along the local legend that eating the ripe melon straight from the garden on a moonlit night produces a state of passion. 85 days to harvest.

Tigger

Baker Creek Heirloom Seeds brought this little Armenian gem to the spotlight. These 1-pound melons are stunning, vibrant yellow fruits with dark, zig-zag orange stripes on the rind. The white flesh is semi-sweet and the fragrance is wonderful. A must-have in a children's garden. 85 days to harvest.

Okra

No one does Okra like cooks in the south. They are the masters at preparing okra pods (this is actually the part we eat) for the dinner table. Okra is often deep-fried, sautéed, boiled, and cooked with a tomato sauce (like a gumbo). The nice thing about okra is that it's easy and fast to grow.

Okra is at its most tender and delicious when the pods are 2" long. You'll also enjoy its flavor the most if it's eaten as close as possible to the time it was harvested. If you live in a short-season zone, don't worry—that doesn't bother okra one bit.

Alabama Red

This is a high-yielding heirloom variety from Alabama. Large, blocky, red and green pods are formed on plants that reach 5-7' tall. Fabulous flavor as a fried dish, but also toss really young ones into a salad for a little color and different flavor. 69 days to harvest.

Beck's Big Buck (Snapping Okra)

This German heirloom was introduced by Underwood Gardens in 2004 after seeds were sent by Malcolm Beck of San Antonio, Texas. He relates the story of its being smuggled from Germany and eventually being given to the builder of the Buck Horn Saloon in Texas during the 1920s. It is sometimes called Snapping Okra because it snaps easily off the plant at harvest time. The pods are fat, tender, and fluted and are formed on 5' plants. 75 days to harvest.

Burgundy (Red Burgundy)

These plants are only about 4' tall and produce pods that stay tender almost to the point of full maturity (7½"). The plant's stems, pods, and leaf veining are maroon. Burgundy is an earlier maturing variety than other red okras. It's an attractive plant, but it doesn't handle disease or bear fruit as long as some of the other red varieties. 50 days to harvest.

Burmese

This variety's 10" long pods are slightly curved, spineless, sweet, and so tender that they can be eaten raw. They start out light green in color and ripen to a creamy yellow-green. The plants are 18" tall and have monstrous 16" leaves. A nice thing about Burmese is that it's less gooey than many other okra varieties. 58 days to harvest.

Cajun Jewel

Introduced in 1989 by Southern Exposure Seed Exchange, Cajun Jewel has been around since the 1950s. This is a good-flavored, dwarf okra that grows to 2½-4' tall. An early crop of tender pods are formed on these spineless plants. 53 days to harvest.

Choppee

This heirloom from 1850 was named for the Choppee Indians native to South Carolina. It's a heavy-producing, semi-dwarf plant—only 3½' tall. It produces tender fruit with great flavor. 69 days to harvest.

Clemson Spineless

This popular spineless variety was introduced in 1939. The plants grow 4–5' tall and bear medium-size, ribbed pods that should be harvested when they reach 3" long. 56 days to harvest.

Cow Horn

Cow Horn is a pre-1865 heirloom that grows 7–8' tall. It's a reliable plant that's also a heavy producer of pods that can reach to 10" long, but don't let them get there. Harvest them at 5–6" long. 55 days to harvest.

Eagle Pass

This okra is from a farmer in Texas. It has big, tender, and delicious pods that are less slimy than other varieties. Days to harvest unavailable.

Emerald

This smooth okra comes from the Campbell's Soup Company back in 1950. The pods are dark green, early forming, and delicious. 58 days to harvest.

Evertender

This spineless variety from India grows to 5½' tall. The pods stay tender for a long time and are easy to harvest. 50 days to harvest.

Fife Creek Cowhorn

This variety's name came about because an elderly Creek woman over 100 years ago gave this heirloom to the Fife family of Kentucky. The plants grow 6–8' tall and bear pods that stay tender longer than many other varieties. 55 days to harvest.

Hill Country Heirloom Red

This is a colorful Texas heirloom that bears 3" green pods with reddish tips and ribs. Even the stems on this 5–6' plant are red. The pods are perfect for pickling. 64 days to harvest.

Jade

Jade is an early maturing, high-yielding plant that grows 4½' tall and bears dark green pods that keep their tenderness until their mature length of 6". 55 days to harvest.

Jimmy T's

This variety has been grown in Kentucky since the 1940s. It's an excellent variety that grows to 5' tall and is a prolific producer when the plant is kept picked. Jimmy T's pods are best harvested at 4" or less. 65 days to harvest.

Silver Queen

Silver Queen okra plants grow to 6' tall and produce very unique-looking pods that are 7" long and light white-green. The pods are tender when they're harvested young and have good flavor. 80 days to harvest.

Star of David

This okra has a very strong flavor. If you're already an okra lover, this would be a great plant for you to try for variety. The plant grows 8-10' tall and produces 5–9" pods. It's a productive variety that's also tolerant of root-knot nematode. 61 days to harvest.

Stewart's Zeebest

This Louisiana heirloom is a tall plant that bears an abundant amount of long, slim, round pods that don't have ribs. The pods stay tender up to their mature 7" length when they like where they're planted. 77 days to harvest.

Onion

Onions are considered one of the main staples for any kitchen, so it makes sense to grow fresh ones for yourself. Yes, onions can be a bit picky, but if you have the right soil and match the individual variety's day length with your area, you should be successful.

Onions desire the same thing as any other veggie: loamy, friable soil that's full of nutrition. So be sure to add lots of organic matter and compost no matter what kind of soil you're dealing with.

Sandy-loam soil would be the ideal situation, but it's not necessary. Plant onions in a bed that's full of organic matter and continue to add compost and they won't complain. Equally important is good drainage—they don't like to soak.

Onion varieties are labeled as either "long day" (LD) or "short day" (SD) types. Onions that begin to form bulbs when the day length is longer than 15 or 16 hours are long-day types. Those that begin to form bulbs when the day lengths are longer than 11 or 12 hours are short-day types. Generally, northern gardeners will want the long-day onions and southern gardeners will want short-day varieties.

For the most part, gardeners start their onions before planting them in the garden, so the days to harvest will reflect this. If you're unclear about whether a particular seed source counts days to harvest from transplant or from seed, ask the seed company for clarification.

Ailsa Craig

This variety was introduced in 1887 and has a large globe shape with a solid, 2-pound bulb and a small neck. 100 days to harvest.

Bianca di Maggio

This long-day, Italian heirloom produces a small, white onion with a flat shape. The flavor is very mild and sweet and it's often used in Italy for salads, pickling, and grilling. 80–110 days to harvest.

Borettana Cipollini (Borettana Yellow)

This gourmet Italian heirloom is a traditional pickling onion when it's harvested at 2" in diameter. This variety will mature to 3–4" in diameter and will have firm, sweet flesh with a yellow-bronze skin. The flavor is deliciously sweet and well developed. 60 days to harvest.

Bronze d'Amposta

This is a good-size, intermediate-day onion that has a lovely red-bronze color. It's not hot, so it's a nice variety for fresh eating. It keeps fairly well, but it's not for long storage. Days to harvest unavailable.

Flat of Italy

Here's an old Italian heirloom that dates back to 1885. It's a beautiful, bright red, flat onion that's great for fresh eating or cooking. It's a nice market variety. 70 days to harvest.

Jaune Paille Des Vertus

This old heirloom was introduced around 1793 and was a standard onion in Europe for over 200 years. It's a flat, brown-yellow onion that can't be beat for its storing ability. It also has good flavor. Days to harvest unavailable.

Long Red Florence (Red of Florence)

This Italian heirloom has a wonderfully mild flavor, but is hard to find. The bright red bulbs are bottle-shaped and are perfect for using fresh, for salads, or for pickling. 100–120 days to harvest.

Red Wethersfield

This was an onion variety said to be grown by Thomas Jefferson at Monticello. It's a large, long-day type that's slightly flattened with a dark purple-red skin. The flesh is white tinged with pink, has a great pungent flavor, and keeps well. 100 days to harvest.

Rossa di Milano

This Italian onion is an intermediate- to long-day type that has a flat top and barrel-shaped bottom. It has gorgeous, glossy red skin and a high sugar content. The flavor is actually medium hot. It'll tolerate cool climates and is an excellent keeper. 110–120 days to harvest.

Stuttgarter

This is a yellow, medium-large onion that has a wonderful and pungent flavor. It's a good producer as well as a good keeper. It can be planted for winter eating and will store all the way to the next spring. Days to harvest unavailable.

Texas Early Grano

This 1933 Texas heirloom is a short-day variety that's a nice choice for southern gardeners. The best time to start Texas Early Grano is in the fall or winter, and then transplant in spring. It has soft, white flesh with a good, mild flavor. It resists splitting, but doesn't keep long. 110 days to harvest.

Tropena/Tropeana Lunga (Torpedo)

This long, tall bulb is an heirloom from Tropea, Italy, and is popular with chefs across the Mediterranean. It's a beautiful onion with a lovely red color that sells for top dollar at market. Days to harvest unavailable.

Yellow Ebenezer (Japanese)

Japan introduced this long-day variety in 1906. It matures early and keeps well. It's a medium-size onion with brown skin and yellow-white flesh. Good choice for mid-Atlantic and northern gardeners. 100 days to harvest.

Yellow of Parma

This rare Italian onion is a good-looking, late-maturing variety. Its 1-pound bulbs are globe-shaped with golden skin. It's a terrific storing variety. 110 days to harvest.

Yellow Sweet Spanish

These globe-shaped bulbs are large and deep yellow with white flesh that has mild flavor. It's a long-day variety that tolerates mildew. This bulb doesn't store for very long. 110 days to harvest.

Violet di Galmi

This short-day, old variety comes from the village of Galmi, a small community in southeast Niger. It's said to have been grown for over 100 years there and its popularity has spread. This variety produces thick, flat, and pretty purple-pink bulbs. It's flavorful and keeps well. 130–140 days to harvest.

Walla Walla

Walla Walla has been called the world's best-tasting onion with its extra mild and sweet flavor. It has white flesh and light brown skin. This is a very cold-hardy, long-day variety. 100–150 days to harvest.

Parsnips

Parsnips have long been a favorite in Europe and were brought to America by the colonists in 1609. Northern gardeners tend to gravitate to them because they're a particularly cold-hardy vegetable. In fact, parsnips really develop their sweet flavor after being exposed to a good freeze.

Parsnips are best sown directly into the garden bed in early spring. They prefer a very basic soil that's loose or loamy, but they don't like it rich or super fertile. Just when you thought nothing could take longer to germinate than carrots—meet the parsnips. These seeds can take three weeks to wake up. So patience is truly a virtue here.

You can store your parsnips right in the ground to harvest all winter if you mulch them heavily with straw. They'll hang on to their sweet flavor and fine texture despite Old Man Winter.

All American

The roots of the All American grow 10–12" long and have shoulders that are 2½" wide. The sugar content is terrifically high in this variety, so the fine-grain, white flesh has a sweet flavor. Great storing variety. 130 days to harvest.

Half Long Guernsey

This popular nineteenth-century variety was introduced in the 1850s. The medium-length, white root has thick shoulders with a fine, sweet flavor. Try harvesting after a hard autumn frost—the sweet flavor is amplified. Days to harvest unavailable.

Harris Model

This is another popular parsnip variety that's an excellent producer. The white, 12" roots are tender and flavorful. Perfect for baking, frying, or boiling. 130 days to harvest.

Hollow Crown

Hollow Crown was the most popular variety of the 1920s. Its long roots are white and sweet and terrific when harvested after a frost. 75 days to harvest.

Peanuts

 Peanuts thrive in hot weather, so consider making them part of your garden plan if you live in a warm climate. There are a few different types of heirloom peanuts. The Spanish type, which produces two seeds to a pod, is the best for cooler climates as they mature early. The Virginia type has two large seeds per pod and needs a long growing season. The sweet Valencia type can have three to four small seeds per pod. Many peanut varieties will succeed in zone 5. A rough guide is that if you can grow melons in your zone, you can grow peanuts.

Carolina Black

This North Carolina heirloom was sent to Southern Exposure Seed Exchange by Derek Morris in 1999. It has black skin and is a little larger than the Spanish peanuts. Carolina Black has a sweet flavor and averages two peanuts per shell. 110 days to harvest.

Carwile's Virginia

This is a family heirloom from Virginia that's been recorded since 1910, when 8-year-old Frank Carwile was given the peanut by a traveler. He grew this variety for 75 years before it was introduced by Southern Exposure Seed Exchange in 1989. It is quite drought-tolerant and forms two to four nuts per shell. 130 days to harvest.

Georgianic

This red-skinned peanut has runners that can help suppress weed growth. It has great disease resistance and good flavor. 150 days to harvest.

Tennessee Red Valencia

This is a pre-1930 red-skinned heirloom that has rich and sweet flavor. It's an early and productive plant that's easy to grow—even in clay soils. The shells contain two to five peanuts. 110 days to harvest.

Peas

Peas are a crop that should be in every spring garden. They're one of the oldest cultivated vegetables—there is evidence of peas found throughout Egypt, Europe, Asia, and, amazingly, among the ruins of Troy. Heirlooms are descendants of those peas and preserve their heritage, adaptability, genetics, and great flavor.

General categories of peas are shelling peas (English); snap peas; sugar peas (snow peas); and southern peas, which are also known as cowpeas, field peas, and black-eyed peas depending on your location.

The shelling or English peas are those that taste best when the peas are removed from inside the shells or pods and then cooked. Snap peas have fat pods that are sweet and tender even when mature. They also have a great snap to them—just like snap beans.

The sugar peas or snow peas are those small peas that you often find in Asian or Chinese dishes. They don't split open when they're mature like the shelling peas and are harvested when they're quite young.

Southern peas can be canned, cooked, or dried. These guys perform their best in climates where they have 60 to 90 warm days and nights.

Don't forget about the amending properties of peas and all legumes. They're nitrogen-fixing plants and can be used to release nitrogen into garden soil for other crops.

Shelling Peas (English)

Alaska

This is an 1880s heirloom variety that's known as "the earliest of all." It's one of the favorites for a really early pea harvest and a perfect choice for those in short-season areas. Alaska is a prolific producer of pale green pods that hold small, smooth-skinned peas. 50–60 days to harvest.

Blue Podded Shelling

This beautiful pea variety with its blue-purple pods and lovely purple flowers dates back hundreds of years in Europe. You can harvest this one young and use it as a snow pea or let it mature and use it as a shell pea that's perfect for soups. 80–85 days to harvest.

British Wonder

This pea was originally introduced to England in 1890 and then introduced to America in 1904 by W. Atlee Burpee. It produces high yields of sweet, green peas. 50–55 days to harvest.

Green Arrow

This is a standard home and market variety that's a main crop in England. It's a reliable, prolific variety. Vines reach 24–28" tall and produce slim, pointed, 4–5" pods that are almost always formed in doubles. They have wonderful flavor when eaten fresh, but they hold up well for both canning and freezing, too. 68 days to harvest.

Lincoln

This old pea variety was introduced in 1908. Tasty, sweet peas are formed on compact, high-yielding vines and are perfect for small gardens. 60–70 days to harvest.

Little Marvel (Improved American Wonder)

This 1908 heirloom is a dwarf vine that bears fine-flavor peas. It's a heavy-yielding variety that's fusarium wilt–resistant. 60 days to harvest.

Sutton's Harbinger

This very early maturing variety was introduced in 1898 and received an Award of Merit by the Royal Horticultural Society in 1901. It produces copious amounts of quality peas. 52–60 days to harvest.

Tall Telephone

This variety was introduced in 1881 and is heat-resistant enough to do well in southern climates. The long vines may reach up to 6' tall. It produces large pea pods and peas that are sweet and tender. Days to harvest unavailable.

Tom Thumb

Tom Thumb actually refers to peas that have extreme dwarf habits. Supposed to be from back in the 1800s, they're excellent for container planting or small gardens. These great-tasting little gems are extremely frost-resistant—withstanding temperatures down to 20°F. 50–55 days to harvest.

Wando

Introduced in 1943, Wando is a great pea for southern and coastal gardens, as it's both heat- and cold-resistant. Eat the medium-size peas fresh or freeze them. 68 days to harvest.

Snap Peas (Snow Peas)

Amish Snap

This variety has tall, prolific vines that produce medium-size, dark green pods with very sweet and delicious peas. 62 days to harvest.

Cascadia

Cascadia grows 32" vines that bear sweet, juicy, 3½" pods. It's a high-yielding plant that's resistant to both powdery mildew and pea enation virus. 60 days to harvest.

Corne de Belier

This French gourmet heirloom has been around since before 1860. It blooms with creamy white flowers. Its large, delicious, flat pods taste wonderful right from the plant but are great for steaming and sautéing as well. Days to harvest unavailable.

De Grace

This pre-1836 heirloom was all but extinct in the North American seed trade for more than 20 years and is now making a comeback. These tender, medium-size pods are crisp and sweet. They're more frost-tolerant than many varieties and produce for a long season. Days to harvest unavailable.

Dwarf Gray Sugar

Introduced in 1892, Dwarf Gray Sugar blooms in beautiful purple flowers. This stringless, pale green variety has 3–4" pods formed on 24–30" vines that don't need staking or trellising. Perfect for steaming or stir-frys. 60 days to harvest.

Golden Sweet

This snap pea produces gorgeous purple, two-toned blooms that give way to bright lemon-yellow pods. The flat seeds are a tan color with purple flecks. A perfect variety for adding to soups and stir-frys, but can also be dried. 60–70 days to harvest.

Mammoth Melting Sugar

This is a 5' snow pea that's wilt-resistant and a huge yielder of sweet, delicious pods. The pods even hold their high quality when harvested a bit late. This variety needs cool weather to produce well. 70 days to harvest.

Oregon Giant

Oregon Giant is an improved selection of Oregon Sugar Pod II. The huge, 5" pods are formed on 3' vines that are extremely prolific. The pods have a sweet and mild flavor. The plant is resistant to mosaic virus, common wilt, and powdery mildew. 70 days to harvest.

Oregon Sugar Pod II

This is a prolific bush variety that stays very compact, so no need for trellising. It produces thick, 4½" pods that are tender and sweet. 70 days to harvest.

Sugar Ann

This is an extra early maturing snap that produces crisp and flavorful peas on compact 2' vines. No need to trellis this variety. It's excellent for freezing. 56 days to harvest.

Sugar Daddy

This variety was the first modern stringless snap to be developed. It produces double pods that are set at the top of the plant for easy harvest. However, they aren't as sweet as many of the other snap peas. 65 days to harvest.

Sugar Snap

These 6–8' vines produce 3" snap peas that have the best flavor. It's tolerant of pea-wilt, but not tolerant of powdery mildew. They freeze well, but you may want to try them fresh. 70 days to harvest.

Southern Peas (Cowpeas, Black-Eyed Peas)

Big Red Ripper

This heirloom variety is a nice table pea with good flavor. The pods are reddish-green and grow high on the plant for easy harvesting. Hot and dry summers don't bother it at all. Peas can be eaten fresh or dried for storing. 70 days to harvest.

Calico Crowder (Hereford Pea, Polecat Pea)

These flavorful peas are buff-colored and have maroon splashes on them when dried. 79 days to harvest.

Colossus

This variety was introduced in 1972 and is one of the best (and biggest) crowder peas. The pods are straw-colored and purple-tinted. The peas are light brown and easy to shell. 58–65 days to harvest.

Mississippi Silver

This variety is highly adaptable and not only does well in the humid mid-Atlantic and southern areas, but also in the north. The 6½" pods are a silver color that is sometimes rose-streaked. The peas are easy to shell. 64 days to harvest.

Peking Black Crowder

This is a vigorous plant that produces a ton of large, black peas that are full of flavor. The plants are disease-resistant. 80 days to harvest.

Pinkeye Purple Hill

This prolific variety produces early, white peas with pink eyes that are good for fresh eating, canning, and freezing. The semi-dwarf bushes are disease-resistant. 65 days to harvest.

Queen Ann Blackeye Pea

This black-eyed pea does well in most northern gardens. It's a dependable, heavy yielder of 7–9" pods that are perfect for freezing, canning, drying, and green shelling. 68 days to harvest.

Washday

This heirloom from the 1800s produces medium-size, tan-yellow peas that are extra quick cooking. This is a half-runner vine that's highly productive. 65 days to harvest.

Whippoorwill

Whippoorwill was brought to the Americas during the slave trade and was grown at Monticello by Thomas Jefferson. It used to be the standard for southern peas because it grows well in most soils and is drought-tolerant. The 7–8" pods are green tinged with purple. When the seeds are mature, they're light brown with black speckles. The peas are good for fresh eating and drying. 85 days to harvest.

Pepper

 Right up there with tomatoes, peppers are one of the darlings of the garden—as well as in the kitchen. They range in flavor from very mild tasting, to super sweet, to sweet with a bite, and all the way to mind-blowing hot. Most people are used to seeing the traditional green peppers in the produce department along with some red and yellow. But peppers can also be orange, brown, purple, white, and lavender.

You'll never be sorry if you find a place in your home garden for heirloom peppers. They're not only easy to grow, but for gardeners with less than acreage for space, tons of pepper varieties can be grown in small spaces including pots and other containers.

Whichever heirloom peppers you choose, try harvesting a few at their different stages of color. Depending on the variety, you'll be surprised how much difference this can make in the flavor.

Most peppers are started indoors before the last frost, so harvest dates refer to the date after transplanting them to the garden.

Bell and Sweet Peppers

Alma Paprika

This is an excellent variety for drying and grinding into paprika or eating fresh. This prolific plant's peppers start out creamy white and ripen to orange and then red when mature. They are sweet with a very slight warmth. 70–80 days to harvest.

Ashe County Pimento

This bright red, non-bell pepper has incredibly sweet flavor, and is 4"×1½" in diameter. Excellent for fresh eating, canning, roasting, or cooking. 70 days to harvest.

Bull Nose

This 1759 heirloom from India was grown by Thomas Jefferson at Monticello. Its peppers start out green and turn bright red when ripe. The flesh is quite sweet, but the ribs can be pungent. 55–80 days to harvest.

Buran

This Polish heirloom is highly productive. The 4"×3" fruits are sure to be sweet whether they're harvested green or red. 90 days to harvest.

California Wonder

Introduced in 1928, this bell pepper variety is a standard one for good reason. It is adaptable to many soils and is tobacco mosaic–resistant. It's a variety that produces big, blocky, 4"×4¾" fruits that turn red when fully mature (although they're very often harvested while they're green). Many market growers use this reliable pepper. 75 days to harvest.

Candlelight

These 1", tapered fruits are formed on plants that are 12–16" tall, so it makes a lovely container variety. The peppers change color from green to yellow, then orange, and finally to bright red when mature. Beautiful ornamental as well as food pepper. 80 days to harvest.

Carmagnola

This prolific heirloom is famous all over Italy. Its bright red and yellow fruit is sweet, meaty, and wonderfully bell-scented. 65–75 days to harvest.

Carolina Wonder

Carolina Wonder is very similar in plant and fruit to California Wonder. The fruits start green and ripen to red. This variety is nematode-resistant, which is great news for many southern gardeners who have real problems growing bell peppers. 75 days to harvest.

Charleston Belle

This is the first nematode-resistant bell pepper variety. Its fruits weigh ¼–⅓ pound and are 3¼"×3⅓" in diameter. 67–70 days to harvest.

Chervena Chushka

This Bulgarian heirloom has been traditionally used as a roasting pepper, but it's just as nice as a sweet pepper for fresh eating. The red pepper is so sweet that it's been likened to candy. 85 days to harvest.

Chocolate Beauty

This is a wonderful variety for the home garden or the market. It starts out dark green in color then ripens to a rich chocolate when mature. It's productive and has an excellent sweet flavor if you let it become fully ripe. 70–75 days to harvest.

Coban Red Pimiento

This rich, small bell pepper is from Guatemala and is delicious fresh or cooked. It's a very pretty variety. Days to harvest unavailable.

Corbaci

This super-productive and unique-looking variety produces long, 10" fruits that curve and twist. It's a rare Turkish heirloom with rich flavor. Excellent for frying or pickling. 65–70 days to harvest.

Corno di Toro

This is an Italian favorite. Its name translates to "Horn of the Bull" and it is, indeed, as thick as a bull's horn. Super-productive plants produce a golden yellow pepper that's both sweet and spicy. Nice for frying and cooking. 80 days to harvest.

Corona

This is a Dutch variety that was introduced in 1991. The fancy fruit starts out green and matures to a golden orange color. It's a sweet bell pepper, perfect for salads, that you'll find in gourmet produce markets. It is mosaic-resistant. 68 days to harvest.

Doe Hill Golden Bell

This pre-1900 Virginia family heirloom produces flattened, bright orange bell peppers that are 1"×2¼". They make a wonderful salad pepper, as the flavor is sweet and fruity. The plants are disease-resistant and high producers. 75 days to harvest.

Doux d'Espagne (Spanish Mammoth)

This is a pre-1860s heirloom pepper. The fruit is 6–7" long, cone-shaped, with sweet and flavorful flesh. They're terrific for salads and cooking and are disease-resistant. 75 days to harvest.

Early Hungarian Sweet ('TH122)

This big Hungarian wax pepper is an extra-early sweet pepper. The fruit starts out creamy white and turns red when it's ripe. 55 days to harvest.

Feherozon (Feher Ozon) Paprika

This is a Hungarian variety that's a very early producer. The large, pointed, bell-shaped fruit starts out creamy white, moves to orange, and ripens to red. The fruit is exceptionally sweet. The plants are dwarfed (about 12–15" tall), yet they produce like champs. Great choice to grow in containers. 60–80 days to harvest.

Gambo

These flattened, meaty bells ripen to a deep red color. They get sweeter as they're cooked and hold up well. Very nice choice for a stir-fry pepper. 62 days to harvest.

Garden Sunshine

This pepper's flavor is best when harvested at creamy yellow or orange, before they mature to red. It's a high-yielding 12–16" plant. 80–100 days to harvest.

Golden Cal Wonder

Golden Cal Wonder grows green and turns gold when it matures. It's very similar to California Wonder both in size and adaptability. 72 days to harvest.

Golden Marconi

This Italian yellow pepper has fantastic flavor and is popular for fresh eating or frying. It's a terrific variety for market growers. 80 days to harvest.

Golden Treasure

This Italian heirloom has sweet flesh and medium-thick skin. The large fruits are 8–9" long and ripen from green to a shiny yellow. 80 days to harvest.

Healthy

This sweet, 4–6" long, triangle-shaped pepper is a Russian heirloom. It matures early in the season, and resists disease and rotting. 65–70 days to harvest.

Hungarian Paprika

This sweet Hungarian heirloom is an ideal variety for drying and grinding into paprika. The beautifully colored, 1"×5" peppers are formed on 18" plants. It's an all-around excellent variety, although it is slightly susceptible to blossom end rot and sunscald. 70 days to harvest.

Jimmy Nardello's Italian

This pepper produces banana-shaped fruits that turn a lovely crimson when ripe and have intense and sweet flavor. It's one of the very best peppers to use for drying. It's also good for freezing, frying, relishes, and salads. Mr. Nardello's mother brought these seeds with her from the Basilicata region when she immigrated to the United States in 1887. 75–90 days to harvest.

Jupiter

Here's one of the best sweet peppers for pasta sauces or stir-frys. These are huge green peppers that ripen to red and have wonderful pepper flavor. It is an adaptable variety and is resistant to tobacco mosaic virus. 65–75 days to harvest.

Kevin's Early Orange Bell

This is a sweet, $3\frac{1}{2}$"×4" bell pepper that matures to orange. It has wonderful, fine flavor with big yields. Matures on the early side. 70–80 days to harvest.

Keystone Resistant Giant

This is another mosaic-resistant variety that resembles California Wonder in many ways. It grows well in the mid-Atlantic region but not in the deep south. 79 days to harvest.

King of the North

This is one of the very best bell pepper performers for northern gardens. The fruits are nice and blocky with excellent, sweet flavor. 70 days to harvest.

Lipstick

Lipstick has a terrific sweet flavor that's perfect for salads, salsa, cooking, and roasting. It's a 5" conical pepper that is a lovely glossy red when ripe. It's an early, dependable, and high-yielding variety. 55–75 days to harvest.

Marconi Red

This 7", horn-shaped Italian heirloom is sweet whether it's harvested green or red. It's a high-yielding, versatile pepper that works for all things pepper, holds up well during frying, and is great for salads and drying. 70–90 days to harvest.

Melrose

This Italian heirloom is known for its 4" fruits with thin skin and superb flavor that mature to a brilliant red color. A wonderful pepper that's delicious no matter when it's harvested and incredibly sweet when red. The plants are prolific. 70 days to harvest.

Mini Chocolate

This Ohio heirloom from the Cress family produces tiny miniatures of a bell pepper that begin green, then ripen to a rich chocolate. The short, full bushes are perfect for growing in containers and provide a continuous harvest. 55–90 days to harvest.

Miniature Yellow Bell

These short, stocky plants become covered in 2" peppers that have wonderfully fresh flavor. Nice in salads. 90 days to harvest.

Napoleon Sweet

These bells are 7–8" long and have a sweet but mild flavor. It's an early producer that steadily offers fruit until frost. 70–90 days to harvest.

Orange Bell

Orange Bell is a big (3½"×4"), thick-walled, sweet bell that ripens to orange. It's a later-maturing variety, but the flavor is one of the very best among the orange bells. 60 days to harvest green peppers and 90–100 days to harvest orange peppers.

Patio Red Marconi

This variety produces the sweetest little fruits anywhere. The plant is compact, making it great for small growing spaces, and it's an excellent potted plant. Beautiful red fruit and easy for anyone to grow. 75 days to harvest.

Perfection (True Heart)

Perfection is also called True Heart because it is red and heart-shaped. The 3"×2½", sweet, flavorful fruits are excellent raw, roasted, peeled, or canned. Toss them into salads or egg dishes. 80 days to harvest.

Purple Beauty

This mildly sweet pepper stays purple for quite a while before it finally gives way to its mature purple-red color. It's a tender pepper with a crisp texture. 70–75 days to harvest.

Quadrato d'Asti Giallo

This beautiful thick-walled bell pepper comes from Asti, Italy. Its fantastic flavor combination is sweet with a light, spicy touch. It begins green in color, then slowly matures to yellow. Perfect to harvest at any stage of growth, it makes a great market pepper. 70–80 days to harvest.

Red Cherry (Cherry Sweet)

These pre-1860 heirlooms are bonbon-shaped (think cherry tomatoes) and perfect to tuck into a lunch box, or for canning, pickling, and stuffing. The fruits start off green and ripen to a dark red. 70 days to harvest.

Sheepnose Pimento

This pepper is pimento-shaped and is 3" long and 4" around. It's a very attractive little fruit. Sheepnose Pimento is a very meaty variety that has super-flavorful and sweet flesh. Great canning variety. 70–80 days to harvest.

Super Shepherd

This early maturing, Italian sweet pepper produces large amounts of fruit free of any imperfections. The peppers are 3" long and 5–7" in diameter. They are terrific fresh, or try frying or pickling them. 66 days to harvest.

Sweet Banana (Long Sweet Hungarian)

These lovely peppers are 6" long and $1\frac{1}{2}$" wide. They start out a pale green and move on to yellow, then orange, and eventually crimson. Harvest these delicious peppers whenever you'd like, but they're sweetest when red. 70 days to harvest.

Sweet Chocolate (Choco)

Sweet Chocolate was introduced in 1965 and produces shiny, $2\frac{1}{2}$"×$4\frac{1}{2}$" fruit that starts green and turns to a chocolate color with maroon interior when it ripens. While they might not actually *taste* like chocolate, these bells are unique in the fact that even if they're harvested green, they don't have that "green" flavor. They're high yielding and disease-resistant. 58–86 days to harvest.

Tequila Sunrise

These delicious, 4–5", carrot-shaped fruits are so attractive that they're perfect to grow as ornamentals, as well as for eating. The peppers begin green and ripen to a golden orange. The flesh is crunchy and sweet with a slightly sharp flavor. Great for making salsa. 65–85 days to harvest.

Tolli's Sweet Italian

Here's an Italian heirloom pepper that's wonderful in tomato sauces, for canning, and for fresh eating. This is a sweet, red pepper that's large (4–5") and dependable. 75–85 days to harvest.

HERITAGE HINT

Here's one of the fastest and easiest ways to dry peppers. Wash and dry your peppers thoroughly. Place as many peppers at the bottom of a paper bag as you can without stacking them. You could also lay the bag on its side and fit even more peppers.

Next, secure the bag with a chip clip, clothespin, or string. Then let them sit in the bag for a couple of weeks. You'll know they're dry when they have a tough skin and feel uniformly dry and brittle.

Topepo Rosso

Although the plants of this Italian heirloom are short and compact, they produce heavy yields of delicious, pimento-type peppers that are super sweet. They have as many uses as you can think of for peppers whether they're eaten fresh or cooked. 85 days to harvest.

Wisconsin Lakes

This sweet and delicious pepper was developed in the 1960s at the University of Wisconsin. It's an early maturing bell pepper that's reliable and gives great yields of green peppers that ripen to red. 75–85 days to harvest.

World Beater (Ruby Giant)

This pre-1912 heirloom produces 3½"×5", sweet, red (when mature) fruits on tall plants. 72 days to harvest.

Yellow Belle

This is another California Wonder–type that starts off yellow, then becomes yellow-orange, and matures to crimson. It's 2½"×4", has thick walls, and is truly attractive. In the southernmost areas, it can develop fungus in the seed cavity when exposed to very high temperatures. But it's a top salad pepper and reliable. 65 days to harvest.

Yellow Monster

These are gigantic, yellow bell peppers that can be as big as 4"×8". They're beautiful, very sweet, and have wonderful flavor, so go ahead and eat them fresh, fried, or roasted. Days to harvest unavailable.

Hot Peppers

Aji Crystal

This waxy fruit comes from Chile and starts a light green color, turns yellow, and then ripens to a red-orange color. The fruits are 1"×3½" and have a wonderfully hot citrus flavor that you'll want to taste while the fruit is young. Perfect for salsa. 90 days to harvest.

Aji Limon (Lemon Drop)

Introduced by Underwood Gardens after William Woys Weaver sent the seeds. These 2" long by 1" wide pale yellow fruits ripen a bright lemon-yellow. Elongated flattened pods with distinctive shape and citrusy taste that have thin walls and are easily oven-dried. The heat level is 7 out of 10. 90 days to harvest.

Ammazzo (Joe's Round)

This Italian heirloom's name translates to "small bunch of flowers." This ornamental hot pepper is very attractive with an unusual appearance. The tall plant produces clusters of fruits that are ½"×¾". Southern Exposure Seed Exchange describes them as looking like a bunch of red marbles in a green bowl. 65 days to harvest.

Anaheim Chile

These vigorous and productive plants produce a mild pepper with a sweet, slightly spicy flavor. They start out green and ripen to a dark red. A very versatile pepper that's great for eating fresh, canning, or drying. 77–90 days to harvest.

Aurora

Aurora has tapered, 1½" fruits with medium heat. They start off lavender in color and turn deep purple, then orange, and finally red. The plants are only 10–12" tall so they're wonderful container plants. 60–75 days to harvest.

Balloon

This pepper is deceptive. Balloon's 2" fruits are shaped like darling little bells with wings. They start as dark green fruits and ripen to bright red. At first, you'll enjoy the sweet flesh—until you get some seeds or the center (placenta) in your mouth. This part is super-duper hot; you have been warned. 90–100 days to harvest.

Beaver Dam

This is a crunchy Hungarian heirloom that was brought to Wisconsin in 1912. It's only mildly hot and has excellent flavor. They're great for fresh eating, salsas, sauces, pickling, and stuffing. 80 days to harvest.

Black Hungarian

This variety is not only useful in the kitchen, but very ornamental for the yard or garden, too. The leaves are green with purple veins and lovely purple flowers. The peppers resemble little jalapeños, but start out a glossy black and ripen to red. They have good flavor and medium heat. 70–80 days to harvest.

Bulgarian Carrot

These 18" tall plants produce a fruit that's crunchy and has a pretty decent heat. The peppers go from green to a yellow-orange when they're mature. They can add some festive color to salsas and chutney. Bulgarian Carrot is terrific when it's roasted. 70–80 days to harvest.

Cayenne, Long Red (Long Slim)

This is a pre-1827 heritage pepper that has fiery flavor, which makes it great for using fresh, dried, in salsa, and as a hot seasoning pepper for chili. The peppers are 6"×½". 72 days to harvest.

Chile Lombak

These 5–6" long peppers from Indonesia have great flavor with a hybrid twist. The lower third is very mild and can be used as a sweet pepper. The top two thirds has bite. They start as green in color, turning orange, then red when fully mature. 90 days to harvest.

Chinese Five Color

This variety is not only fiery hot, but it's an absolutely lovely ornamental. The fruits start out purple, move to a creamy yellow, then to full yellow, then orange, and finally red. All of these colors can be on the plant at the same time. The show doesn't stop there: the plant's leaves are green with purple veining and a purple blush on some of them. 70–90 days to harvest.

Chinese Ornamental

This one should be renamed Chinese *Prolific* Ornamental. There are literally hundreds of little peppers per plant. The tiny ½" fruits will hold for weeks on the plant. They start off green and ripen to red and are pretty darn hot. It's a perfect ornamental for container planting. 90 days to harvest.

Chocolate Habanero

This is a beautiful specimen. The fruits are 2" long, chocolate-brown, and lantern-shaped. These peppers hold *massive* amounts of heat. They're *scorching*, not chocolate-sweet like their appearance or name suggests. Use them in moderation. 70–75 days to harvest.

Concho

This little pepper that's similar to the landrace varieties Chimayo or Espanola is from Arizona. The small, 2' tall plants produce a chile that has flesh of medium heat and rich flavor. The placenta and seeds are extremely hot. 80–90 days to harvest.

Cyklon

This truly hot pepper comes from Poland and has very nice flavor. The fruits are 4–5" long and are used a lot in Poland as a dried spice pepper. 80 days to harvest.

Czechoslovakian Black

These 1"×2½" Czech heirloom peppers start as green fruits, then turn to black, and finally red. It's an early variety, very adaptable to climates and soils, and mildly hot when it is most ripe. This pepper is amazing as an ornamental because there can be red fruit at the base and black fruit at the top blended with purple-green leaves and lavender flowers with white streaks. 58 days to harvest.

Fatalii

Here's one of the hottest peppers around. It has a citrusy flavor, but only for those gifted people that can taste the citrus through the fire. The peppers are a 1"×3" habanero type and are golden in color. It's a nice choice for pots. 90 days to harvest.

Fish Pepper

This pepper is so named because it shows up in many seafood dishes. This pre-1870s heirloom has mottled green leaves and is quite heat-tolerant. It's good for salsa or as a drying pepper and is very hot. Some of the fruits can have variegated colors, too, which makes Fish a wonderful plant for edible landscaping. 80 days to harvest.

Georgia Flame

This thick and crunchy variety comes from the Republic of Georgia. The 6–8" fruits are some of the hottest available and are wonderful for salsa. 90 days to harvest.

Golden Nugget

This lovely ornamental pepper has variegated leaves and hundreds of golden fruits on each plant. Perfect for pots and borders in yards. 75–85 days to harvest.

Hinkelhatz

The Pennsylvania Dutch have been growing this hot pepper for over 150 years. The 1½"×2" red (when mature) peppers are especially good for pickling and making pepper vinegars. 90 days to harvest.

Hot Portugal

These bright red peppers are at the higher end of the medium heat range. They're 6" long, prolific, and early maturing. 65–75 days to harvest.

Hungarian Wax (Hot Banana, Hungarian Hot Wax)

This spicy, long, banana-shaped pepper has medium heat and is a very reliable producer. Peppers start out green, turn yellow, then ripen to a crimson red. It can grow comfortably both in the north and the deep south. Perfect for canning, pickling, or fresh eating. 60 days to harvest.

Italian Pepperoncini

One of the very best peppers grown anywhere. This is Milan's version of an old Greek variety. The plant is a huge producer of little 2–4", lime-green fruits. The flavor changes from sweet to having a nice bite very late in the ripening cycle. Terrific for fresh eating on salads and sandwiches or for pickling and canning. Grows beautifully in cool climates that have short seasons. 62–75 days to harvest.

Jalapeño

Most people are very familiar with Jalapeño because it's the classic salsa chili. The 1"×2" peppers are hot and tasty. Usually, they're harvested at the green stage, but they can be left to mature to their red color. 72 days to harvest.

Joe's Long Cayenne

These 12" long heirlooms were brought from Italy to New York by Joe Sestito's family. These peppers can be harvested at the green or red stage and are great for eating fresh or drying to use as pepper flakes. 65 days to green harvest; 85 days to red harvest.

Joe's Round

Here's another pepper that the Sestito family put on the map. These ¾" peppers start out dark green and turn bright red when they're ripe. It's a good variety for pickling as well as in fresh salsa. They're on the fiery end of hot. Days to harvest unavailable.

Little Nubian

This prize of a pepper was introduced by Underwood Gardens in 2002, thanks to a gift of seeds from William Woys Weaver. A beautiful pepper plant that's loaded with little, shiny black fruits that ripen to a garnet red. The peppers are succulent, crunchy, and have very hot flesh. It's heat- and drought-tolerant and terrific in containers. The plant itself has purple-black leaves and lavender flowers. Little Nubian is a stunning addition to any landscape or garden. 95 days to harvest.

Maule's Red Hot

The William Maule Seed Company in Pennsylvania introduced this prolific, 6–10", cayenne-type pepper. It's devilishly hot and makes a great hot sauce. 80 days to harvest.

McMahon's Bird Pepper

Bernard McMahon of Philadelphia was given these seeds by Thomas Jefferson in the 1800s. The 14" long peppers are oval-shaped and bright red. They grow upright on the plants and look like red olives. 90 days to harvest.

Mustard Habanero

This pepper reminds me of a crinkly, nearly deflated balloon. It comes in colors ranging from gold to yellow and even green with a purple blush. Its heat is legendary—you have to be tough to eat it. 95–100 days to harvest.

Nepalese Bell

These 3–4" peppers start out green and ripen to red. They're crisp and sweet around the outer edges of their flesh. As you get closer to the seeds, you'll get the hot bite. 90–100 days to harvest.

Nosegay

This ornamental, 6" plant has teeny-tiny red peppers that hang around for a long time. It's the perfect pepper to grow as a potted plant. You can eat the peppers, but don't let their small size fool you—they're on the hotter side of medium. 70–80 days to harvest.

Orange Thai

This is a gorgeous pepper plant that makes a lovely potted ornamental. It's really quite stunning when loaded with the mature 2½" long, orange peppers. Terrific as hot pepper seasoning and for drying. Fair warning: Orange Thai is very hot. 80–90 days to harvest.

Pasilla Bajio

Here's a unique little pepper that's only mildly hot and also sweet. It has a unique taste and is one of the ingredients necessary to make a decent Mexican mole. The 8–14" peppers start out deep green then ripen to brown. 75–80 days to harvest.

Peach Habanero

This is a terrific habanero variety for containers. The plants are 16–18" and are loaded with peach-colored, blazing-hot peppers. 95–100 days to harvest.

Peter

The story behind this variety is that, in the Victorian era, their phallic shape made women blush. The peppers have medium heat and great flavor. Makes a wonderful chili powder. 90 days to harvest.

Pimiento de Padron

This is an old Spanish heirloom variety that's often used for snacks, salad toppings, and on sandwiches. They're often fried up whole and sprinkled with sea salt. Eating the olive-size fruits is like playing Spanish roulette. When they're the size of olives, only about 1 in every 5 you eat will have mind-blowing heat. 55–85 days to harvest.

Poblano (Ancho Gigantea)

This variety makes a terrific stuffing pepper and starts as a blackish-green color that ripens to reddish-brown. It's a popular variety for Mexican dishes and is often used as a Rellano chili when it's green. At that point the variety is referred to as Poblano. When dried, it's called Ancho Gigantea and has a nice earthy flavor like chili powder. 75 days to harvest.

Red Cap Mushroom (Red Squash Pepper)

This 24–30" plant is an excellent choice for potting. The peppers begin green and turn red when mature. They're another truly hot variety that's usually used for drying or pickling. 90 days to harvest.

Red Habanero

If you like your peppers extremely hot (15–20 times hotter than a jalapeño) and you have a long growing season, Habanero may be the pepper for you. This variety is slow to germinate and starts out green, maturing to an orange-red. It's very flavorful, aromatic, and has some serious fire. I've seen some places tout this one as anywhere from 20 to 120 times hotter than a jalapeño. It's often used for jerk sauces and curries. 95 days to harvest.

Red Rocoto

Red Rocoto made its way to gardeners from Peru. It enjoys cooler weather but a long season. This variety has lovely purple flowers and thrives in pots and containers. The 1" fruits are green and turn red with black seeds when mature. The flavor is described as unique and very hot. 95–130 days to harvest.

Rooster Spur

This 1½" pepper variety from Laurel, Mississippi, is rare. It has been grown in Virgil T. Ainsworth's family for more than 100 years, so it's a serious heirloom. This is the pepper that was traditionally used to make Rooster Pepper Sausage. The 24" plant is right at home planted in pots or any other container. 95 days to harvest.

Royal Black

The stems and leaves of this variety are dark purple (nearly black) with a variegated green, purple, or white leaf tip here and there. The 1" long by ¼" wide fruits are shaped like bullets and look beautiful against the purple foliage of the plant. The peppers begin as purple fruits that ripen to red with purple stripes. They're wonderful for making hot vinegars. 88 days to harvest.

Santa Fe Grande

Peto Seeds introduced this pepper in 1965. It's a high-yielding variety that produces 3½"×1½" conical peppers that have quite a bit of heat. The fruits start off yellow, changing to orange, and finally red. They're nice for salsas, pickling, and canning. 75–80 days to harvest.

Serrano Tampiqueno

This is a handsome 30" plant that produces 2¼" long by ½" wide super-duper hot peppers. The fruits are used for salsa, chili, hot pepper vinegar, and pickling. The peppers start off green, turn orange, and finally turn a red-orange color, but their flavor is fiery no matter when they're harvested. 75–80 days to harvest.

Thai Hot

Thai Hot makes a terrific little potted pepper plant and it produces 200 hot little green-to-red peppers per plant. If you harvest the peppers completely, you'll get another round of these little gems. 85 days to harvest.

Tobago Seasoning

These great container peppers have very nice, mildly hot flavor and are used predominantly as a seasoning pepper. They begin light green in color, then turn orange, and finally turn red when they're mature. 90 days to harvest.

Tomato

This pepper was introduced by Underwood Gardens from seeds sent by Todd and Sue Gronholz, market growers extraordinaire (they were featured in *Readers Digest*), from Beaver Dam, Wisconsin. This Hungarian heirloom is a perfect all-purpose pepper that has sweet flesh with just a bit of heat to make it interesting. Highly productive plants bear this round and flattened fruit. Use it for fresh eating, salsas, sauces, and pickling. 80 days to harvest.

Tri-Color Variegata

Unending displays of white, green, pink, and purple foliage with no two leaves alike. Purple stems and blooms punctuate the foliage; petite purple peppers ripen to a flaming red. The color combinations are fabulous, and the peppers are tasty and hot—good for salsas, chilis, and as garnishes. Awesome edible ornamental. 70 days to harvest.

Wenk's Yellow Hots

These 2–4" long, waxy yellow peppers ripen to bright orange and finally to red. They have medium heat and are terrific for pickling and canning. 80 days to harvest.

Potato

The potato's native home is in the mountains of Peru, where it's said that there were once 3,000 varieties grown. After potatoes made their way to Europe, their history becomes a little sketchy, although most agree that they were first grown predominantly in France, Switzerland, the Netherlands, and Russia. Of course, in these more modern times, we tend to thank Ireland for putting the potato on the map.

As with tomatoes, there's a big difference between commercial and heirloom potatoes in flavor. Once you've grown and prepared some of these guys, you'll be spoiled for life.

Another fabulous thing about growing your own heritage potatoes is the array of colors and textures available to you that most people don't even know exist.

Potatoes are an easy crop to grow. They like full sun and moderate watering. Harvesting the tubers is great fun for all ages, but I hope you'll give the kids a turn at it because then they'll want to plant them every year—and so a new gardener will be born.

HERITAGE HINT

Potatoes are grown by planting seed potatoes, which are really just tiny potato tubers that are kept as seed stock. If it's a larger tuber, it can be cut into chunks as long as each piece has two eyes on it. The eyes are those little root bumps that look like they are beginning to sprout.

The flowers that bloom on the potato plant do produce little pods that hold the true seed of the plant. The problem is that even when there's no cross-pollination, these seeds tend to produce plants (and tubers) with very different characteristics than the parent plant.

So rather than take the gamble, gardeners prefer to save some small tubers and replant them, essentially cloning the plant.

All Blue

This potato has a unique, lovely color with dark blue skin and blue flesh. When it's boiled, it turns light blue. It's wonderful for baking and frying. All Blue makes for really interesting potato chips! All Blue keeps well and has lots of minerals. 90–110 days to harvest.

All Red

This is one of the best red potatoes. It has red skin with pale pink flesh that is low in starch. It's a good producer and is perfect for salads and boiling. 90–110 days to harvest.

Austrian Crescent

This variety is popular for potato salads as well as roasting and steaming. It produces yellowish-tan fingerlings with light yellow flesh. 90–110 days to harvest.

Caribe

This beautiful variety with dark purple skin and bright white flesh can grow rather large. It's an early producer with high yields. Great for boiling, baking, or frying. 95 days to harvest.

Carola

This is a mid-season variety that is a terrific producer. It has beige skin and yellow flesh with a creamy texture. A wonderful potato for baking or frying. Most excellent when harvested young as a new potato. 95 days to harvest.

Cranberry Red

This early to mid-season variety is touted as one of the very best of the red-skinned (and -fleshed) potatoes. It has a smooth texture and low starch content, making it perfect for potato salads. It's a prolific plant. 90–100 days to harvest.

Desiree

Desiree is a red-skinned, mid-season, all-purpose cooking potato that comes from Holland. It has deep golden flesh with a moist and creamy texture. Lovely, delicate flavor, disease resistance, and reliability make this easy-to-grow potato the perfect choice for a home garden. 95–100 days to harvest.

French Fingerling

French Fingerling has a wonderful story attached to it. Word is that it was smuggled into America in a horse's feedbag in the 1800s. It has rose-colored skin and soft yellow flesh and doesn't need to be peeled. It's a versatile variety and works well for all potato dishes. 90–110 days to harvest.

German Butterball

German Butterball took first place in a taste-off by Rodale's Organic Gardening. It has russet skin and buttery-yellow flesh. This is an excellent all-purpose potato that produces and stores very well. 100–120 days to harvest.

Kerr's Pink

This variety was brought to Ireland from Scotland in 1917. It produces round tubers with light pink skin and white flesh. Another wonderful, all-around cooking potato that has excellent flavor. 100–120 days to harvest.

La Ratte

French chefs can't say enough about this fingerling's long tubers with yellow flesh. Its flavor is nutty and wonderful to cook with. It's an expensive, gourmet potato at market and restaurants. 100–120 days to harvest.

Purple Viking

Here's a purple-skinned variety that's especially terrific for mashed potatoes, although it really is wonderful for all potato dishes. Its white flesh has a great-tasting, slightly sweet flavor. Good for storing, too. 80–100 days to harvest.

Red Dale (Reddale)

Red Dale is an early maturing variety with bright red tubers and white flesh. It's versatile and used for all things potato. It's highly resistant to verticillium wilt. 70–90 days to harvest.

Red Gold

While this variety isn't recommended for long storage, it more than makes up for it in flavor. Red Gold has red-orange skin and creamy, golden yellow flesh. It's an excellent choice for mashing, frying, steaming, baking, or roasting. It's also disease-resistant. 90–100 days to harvest.

Rose Finn Apple Fingerling

This is a reliable fingerling that has a lovely rose color and dry, yellow flesh with a very waxy texture. It's a high producer, very reliable, and a good keeper. 80–100 days to harvest.

Rose Gold

This is a mid-season variety with rose-red skin and dry, deep yellow flesh that makes it nice for baking or steaming. The flavor is creamy and delicious. It's also disease-resistant. 90–110 days to harvest.

Russian Banana Fingerling

Here's a gourmet variety that's a rare Russian heirloom. The crescent-shaped, finger-size, yellow potatoes have exquisite flavor and can be prepared as baked, boiled, or salad potatoes. 105–135 days to harvest.

Yellow Finn

Yellow Finn is one of the classic gourmet potatoes from Europe. It has super buttery and sweet flavor, making it perfect for any type of potato dish. It also keeps very well. 95–100 days to harvest.

Yukon Gold

Yukon Gold has long been a gardener's favorite. It's an early maturing variety that is drier than most of its yellow-fleshed counterparts. It has a reputation for being one of the best flavored of the yellows and is excellent for baking and mashing. It's a good keeper and a prolific producer. 80–90 days to harvest.

Pumpkins and Winter Squash

Pumpkins are recognized as a squash that's round, smooth, and usually orange. They're the squash we carve as Jack O' Lanterns for our porches on Halloween night. But pumpkins can also be dark green, pale green, orange-yellow, white, red, or gray.

While pumpkins and winter squash are in the same family *botanically*, for culinary purposes their flavor and texture is different. Pumpkins are predominantly orange in color, have a stronger flavor, and have rather coarse flesh. Winter squash are milder in flavor and have a finer texture than pumpkins.

Although we refer to this group as "winter" squash, they're actually a warm-weather crop. Winter squashes all develop a thick, hard shell that's especially useful for winter storage.

Anna Swartz Hubbard

In the 1950s, Anna Swartz's friend gave her this family heirloom. It's a 5–8-pound squash of high quality, with flesh that resembles a sweet potato—and a flavor that will remind you of the sweet tubers as well. It's very tough-skinned and has terrific storage ability. 90–100 days to harvest.

Australian Butter

This is an Australian heirloom variety that weighs 7–15 pounds and has a small seed cavity. The flesh is orange, thick, dry, and excellent for baking. 90–100 days to harvest.

Baby Butternut

These vines aren't as vigorous as some, but that can be a good thing if you're container gardening or have a small garden space. This 1958 heirloom produces sweet, ½–2-pound fruits. 90 days to harvest.

Big Max

Here's a pumpkin that's perfect for carving for Halloween. The fruits are bright orange and the flesh is a lighter orange. Big Max can weigh up to 100 pounds. Great for pies, too. 115 days to harvest.

Boston Marrow

This 10–20-pound squash originally came from Native Americans in New York State. Their skin is brilliant orange and the flesh is sweet and fine-grained. This is a great eating variety. 90–100 days to harvest.

Burgess Buttercup

This 1932 heritage squash may be different-looking, but it can certainly pass as a creative pumpkin. The rinds are deep green with a bit of ribbing and a button on the blossom end. This 3–5-pound squash's flesh is thick, flattened, and fine-grained. It has excellent flavor. 85–100 days to harvest.

Cheese

These really awesome-looking pumpkins were introduced in 1815, making them one of the very oldest varieties. They have a bluish color (or tan or slate-gray), are wide-ribbed, and resemble large cheese wheels. The flesh is bright orange, fibrous, and coarse, but also sweet and tender. It's an excellent keeper and perfect for stuffing and baking. 100–150 days to harvest.

Cheyenne Bush Pumpkin

This heirloom was developed in Cheyenne, Wyoming, in 1943 and is a very early maturing bush pumpkin. The plants are compact and produce fruits that are 5–8 pounds, which is perfect for a small garden. 80–90 days to harvest.

Chirimen

The Aggeler & Musser Seed Company first introduced this beautiful, dull bronze-colored fruit in 1922. The 5–8-pound fruit needs to have a long growing season to mature. Its flesh is sweet, dark orange, and moist. 95–110 days to harvest.

Connecticut Field (Big Tom, Yankee Cow Pumpkin)

This is a pre-1700 Native American heritage pumpkin. It holds the position of the most popular large Halloween pumpkin on the market. The fruits are 10–15 pounds, bright orange, and have slight ribbing. They're also great for baking, canning, and pies. 110 days to harvest.

Delicata Zeppelin

This is a super-sweet winter squash that has cream-colored skin with deep green stripes. The potato-shaped fruits grow to 2 pounds. It's a semi-vine that produces up to eight fruits per plant. 97 days to harvest.

Fordhook Acorn

W. Atlee Burpee introduced this hard-to-find acorn squash variety in 1890. The fruits don't usually grow past 2 pounds and can be eaten fresh or used for baking. 56 days to harvest for fresh eating; 85 days to harvest for baking.

Galeux d'Eysines

This French heirloom plant produces a beautiful, yellow winter squash that turns a rosy color as it matures. Growers first saw it at a pumpkin fair in France in 1996. The fruits develop a warty surface while they're being stored. They're a fast-ripening, 10–20-pound variety that's terrific in pies, soups, and sauces. 90–98 days to harvest.

Photo by Baker Creek Heirloom Seeds

Gele Reuzen

This is a large, German heritage variety whose name translates to "Yellow Giants." The vines are prolific and have monstrous leaves. These pumpkins can reach 65–120 pounds without needing to remove any blossoms for the advantage. 120 days to harvest.

Golden Hubbard

This hard-skinned hubbard was introduced by D. M. Ferry in 1898. The shell is a lovely dark orange and the flesh is golden yellow and sweet. A terrific baking and roasting pumpkin, it's one of the standards in American markets. Golden Hubbard also keeps wonderfully. 90–100 days to harvest.

Green-Striped Cushaw

This old variety's vines are large, squash vine borer–resistant, and very reliable. The 10–12-pound fruits have a bulb shape and have white-green skin and mottled green striping. The flesh is thick, fibrous, and has a slightly sweet flavor. It doesn't keep well, but it's good for baking and pies. 110 days to harvest.

Guatemalan Blue Banana

This interesting squash is long (16–20"), has thick flesh, and is great baked or roasted. It's a good storage variety. 90–95 days to harvest.

Jarradale

This is a wonderful pumpkin variety that is not only unusual-looking, but has excellent flavor. In the past, it has been rare in the United States, but it's now catching on. I have it on good authority that chefs adore getting their hands on it! This is a 12–20-pound, blue-gray fruit with deep ribs. It stores well and offers high yields. The flesh is deep orange, dense, and sweet. It's perfect for baking superb-tasting pies. 95–100 days to harvest.

Jaune Gros de Paris (Giant Yellow of Paris)

This is one of the most popular varieties in France. The beautiful fruits are pink-yellow in color, flattened, and have light ribbing. They can weigh up to 100 pounds and are great for soups, baking, and pies. 120 days to harvest.

Kikuza

The Oriental Seed Company of San Francisco introduced this excellent eating squash in 1927. The fruits are 4–7 pounds and have very thick flesh. It's a nice choice for baking or roasting. 90–95 days to harvest.

Lady Godiva

This variety makes a good Jack O' Lantern, but is also known for its seeds, which are green, hull-less, and nutritious. They're not only protein-rich, but they have good flavor whether eaten raw or roasted. The flesh really isn't of edible quality. 90–100 days to harvest.

Long Island Cheese

This East Coast heirloom's dark orange flesh is known to make wonderful pies. The squash's shape is flattened like a wheel of cheese, and it has buff-colored skin. 90–100 days to harvest.

Lumina

This 10–16-pound pumpkin has creamy white skin and bright orange or yellow flesh that's good for making roasted pumpkin soup, purées, and pies. It's a versatile variety that kids may want to paint or carve for Halloween. 80–115 days to harvest.

Marina di Chioggia

This is a large, gray-green, bumpy, turban-shaped squash that comes from Italy. It is 10–12 pounds and has a dry, sweet flesh that improves in storage. It's a good producer and keeps well. 95–100 days to harvest.

Musquee de Provence

This is a traditional Southern French variety that was introduced in 1899. Fat fruits averaging 20 pounds resemble big cheese wheels. They're green when young and turn to a deep, rich brown color as they mature. The flesh is dark orange and has good flavor that's nice in baking. 100–110 days to harvest.

North Georgia Candy Roaster

This early 1900s variety is rare. The fruits are banana-shaped, up to 18" long, and 6" in diameter. They're smooth, pink with blue tips, and have delicious orange flesh. 100 days to harvest.

Old-Fashioned Tennessee Vining Pumpkin

This variety was introduced in 1988 by Southern Exposure Seed Exchange. The vines are squash vine borer–resistant and produce pumpkins that weigh 12–15 pounds. The oval-shaped pumpkins turn tan when they're mature and have dark orange flesh. This variety has thin shells that are easy to carve. Days to harvest unavailable.

Pennsylvania Dutch Crookneck

This is a butternut squash that bears huge 10–20-pound fruits. This is one of the best squashes for making soups or pies. Deep orange flesh can be found throughout the neck of this strong squash. 100–110 days to harvest.

Pink Banana Jumbo

This was a popular winter squash in nineteenth-century American pioneer gardens. This banana-shaped squash is 2–3' long and weighs 10–40 pounds. It's pink-orange when it ripens and the flesh is yellow-orange. Perfect variety for pies, baking, and canning. 100–120 days to harvest.

Potimarron

This French winter squash produces 3–4-pound fruits that have a chestnut flavor. It stores well for the winter and is nice for roasting and baking. 85–95 days to harvest.

Queensland Blue

This is a lovely 1932 Australian variety. This blue, deeply ribbed fruit weighs 12–20 pounds and has a flat top and bottom with a thick and dense flesh. It's a very flavorful semi-sweet variety. Stores very well for the winter. 100–120 days to harvest.

Rouge Vif d'Etampes (Cinderella Pumpkin)

This is the pumpkin sitting in your garden that could change into a carriage at any moment. This French variety was first offered in the United States in 1883. It's a gorgeous, rich, almost dusky orange that's flattish with deep ribs. The fruits weigh in at 12–35 pounds. 95–120 days to harvest.

Seminole

This heirloom was cultivated by the Seminole Indians in the 1500s. The vines need lots of water and room to spread. It's vine borer– and heat-resistant, and bears buff-colord, bell-shaped, 7" fruits. The flesh is dark orange and tastes sweeter than Butternut. 95 days to harvest.

Sibley (Pike's Peak)

Sibley was introduced in New York in 1887. It's a hubbard-type squash that has a teardrop shape with slate-blue color and shallow ribs. They weigh 8–10 pounds and have super-hard skin, which is a plus if you're shipping them. The flesh has a great sweet flavor that becomes richer and dryer during storage. 110–120 days to harvest.

Small Sugar (New England Pie, Sugar Pumpkin)

Small Sugar is a pre-1860 heritage pumpkin that's one of the favorites of American gardeners. The round, orange fruits have a sweet and dry flesh. 100 days to harvest.

Spaghetti Squash (Vegetable Spaghetti)

This variety can actually be used like spaghetti with sauce poured over it. The flesh is tasty, pale yellow, and forms in spaghettilike strands. The fruits are 9" long with pale yellow skin. To remove the strings, you need to boil the squash for 20 or 30 minutes and then take the strands out with a fork. 90 days to harvest.

Styrian Hulless

Styrian Hulless is an heirloom variety from Styria, a region in Austria. These large, 10–20-pound, green and gold–colored pumpkins are grown for their large, hull-less seeds. It's also a good variety for soups, casseroles, and pies. 90–120 days to harvest.

Sucrine du Berry

This is an old, traditional French variety that has a musky scent and fabulous flavor. The 3–5-pound, oblong fruit is a tan-orange color and bell-shaped. It's used for jams and soups. Days to harvest unavailable.

Photo by Baker Creek Heirloom Seeds

Sweet Meat Squash

This is a prolific variety that grows vigorously. The slate-green squash has yellow flesh and weighs 12–15 pounds. The flesh has a butter flavor that sweetens as it matures. Sweet Meat has such a dry texture that it can be a good substitute for summer squash in recipes. It's also a great keeper. 110 days to harvest.

Table Queen Bush (Acorn)

This 1948 heirloom is perfect for small gardens or containers. You'll get about five fruits per plant. Great squash for baking. 80 days to harvest.

Table Queen Vine (Acorn)

This acorn squash was introduced in 1913. It has a deep green rind and fine-textured, golden yellow flesh that sweetens in storage. It's a good choice for baking and can be harvested while it's young to be used as a summer squash. 85 days to harvest.

Tan Cheese

Cheese pumpkins have a dense flesh that many people prefer to use when they need a baking variety. This one is productive, hardy, and weighs 6–12 pounds. 110 days to harvest.

Thelma Sanders' Sweet Potato

Of course, this isn't a sweet potato and I have no idea why it was given that name. It *is* a cool-looking fruit that was introduced in 1988. It starts out a cream color and ripens to a light gold. Its thick, gold flesh has wonderful flavor that sweetens as it's stored. 96 days to harvest.

Tonda Padana

This is a lovely Italian pumpkin variety that has vertical ribs in alternating gray, green, and orange colors. It's an unusual yet attractive variety that would make a beautiful centerpiece. It's a perfect pumpkin for soups, pies, breads, and gnocchi. 95–105 days to harvest.

Triamble (Triangle, Tristar, Shamrock)

This is a rare and unique squash that was first grown in the United States in 1932. It has very thick, excellent-quality flesh. This variety is great as a vegetable squash or for baking pies. It's a blue-gray-green color that looks a lot like a shrunken apple head. 110–120 days to harvest.

Turk's Turban

This variety was introduced in 1869 and produces fruits that are multi-colored with shades of green, gold, and orange. They are 8–12" in diameter and form a distinctive cap (or turban). The table quality is okay, but they're mostly grown as an ornamental. 80–100 days to harvest.

Waltham Butternut

This popular and reliable winter squash was introduced in 1977. It can be harvested while it's still small and used as a summer squash, yet as a mature specimen it stores very well. It has buff-colored skin and a sweet, orange flesh. The vines are vine borer–resistant. 95 days to harvest.

Winter Luxury Pie

This dark orange, 6½-pound pumpkin is an 1893 heirloom. It has a tender flesh that's known for being excellent for pies. 100 days to harvest.

Yugoslavian Finger Fruit

This variety was originally introduced to Americans in 1885 as Pineapple. These are creamy white squashes that have distinctive wing shapes. They can be eaten as summer squash, but usually end up as an ornamental. 90–100 days to harvest.

Radish

When you think of unusual vegetables, radishes probably won't pop into your mind. We all know that they're a red thing we find in salads or sliced thinly on sandwiches. That's where you'd be wrong.

The radishes found in the produce section of the grocery store are the ones that I've described. But radishes come in white, purple, green, and even black. They come in grape, carrot, and turnip shapes. Radishes can be eaten whole, grated, diced, or sliced. They can be eaten fresh or cooked, and they can be pickled.

Did you know that though radishes grow fast and need to be harvested quickly, they don't all have to be consumed right away? In fact, many radishes are planted in late summer for winter storage.

Black Spanish Round

This is a pre-1824 heirloom radish that has firm, white flesh and almost black skin. The roots grow 3–4" in diameter (sometimes larger) and have pungent flavor with a distinctive crisp texture. This is a radish for winter storage that is sensitive to day length, so plant them from late July to late August. 53 days to harvest.

Blauer Blue

This is a 4", German heirloom variety that's highly desirable on the market because it's hard to find. It has bright purple skin and crisp, white flesh that starts out with a sweet flavor and ends up a bit spicy. This is a winter storing radish that should be planted in late July to late August. 55 days to harvest.

Cherry Belle

This is a very sweet radish with firm, white flesh and bright red skin. It was a 1949 All-American Selection winner. 24 days to harvest.

China Rose (Rose Colored Chinese, Scarlet China Winter)

This heirloom was introduced around 1850 from Europe, but originated in China. This 5" variety has rose skin with white flesh. For storing, it needs to be harvested in late fall, before a hard frost hits. This for-winter-storage radish is daylength-sensitive, so plant them from late July to late August. 55 days to harvest.

Chinese Green Luobo (Qingluobo)

This is a tasty variety that's popular in China and has a bright green flesh. It's a rare old Chinese standard that only grows well in cool weather. 65 days to harvest.

Chinese Red Meat

This is a beautiful radish that resembles a watermelon when it's cut in half. It has 4", round roots with red flesh hidden by green and white skin. The flavor is clean, crisp, and sweet, which makes it perfect to add to salads and stir-frys. It's a cool weather lover and does best when planted in the fall. 30 days to harvest.

Chinese White Winter

This is a winter radish that should be planted in late July or late August for winter storing. The roots are 7–8" long with crisp and solid flesh. Eat them raw or cooked. 60 days to harvest.

Cincinnati Market

This dark red, pre-1870s heirloom grows 6" long and is tapered at the end. It has a tender and mild taste and is becoming a rare variety. 25–30 days to harvest.

Daikon, Miyashige White

This variety originated in Asia and is terrific for cooked vegetable dishes, salads, grated for sauces, and pickled. This is a juicy and flavorful radish that's usually harvested when it's 12" long and 2–3" in diameter. This is a daylength-sensitive radish for winter storage, so plant them from late July to late August. 65 days to harvest.

Early Scarlet Globe

This is an excellent choice for gardeners who want an extra-early harvest. The skin is bright red and the flesh is white. It's a 1" globe-shaped variety that's reliable and bunches well. 20–28 days to harvest.

French Breakfast

This is an interesting-looking radish variety that doesn't resemble a radish much at all; it looks more like a blunt-tipped carrot. It's an oblong, scarlet and white radish with crisp, white flesh. French Breakfast also has a top-quality, mild flavor. 30 days to harvest.

Formosa Giant Luo Buo

This variety used to be called Formosa and is an old favorite in Taiwan. The 2–3-pound, oval roots have a wonderful, sweet flavor and are terrific in soups. 90 days to harvest.

German Beer (Munchen Bier)

This is another winter radish that should be planted late July to late August for winter storing. It's a German heirloom that has a white, oval root that can get as large as a turnip. 52–67 days to harvest.

German Giant

This is a German variety that is very large and red in color. It's a popular heirloom with the Amish and it keeps its fine quality even after reaching its large, mature size. 29 days to harvest.

Giant of Sicily

This Sicilian heirloom is a large, bright red, summer radish with great flavor and good quality. 45 days to harvest.

Helios

This pale yellow, white-fleshed, sweet radish was named for the Greek god of the sun. It's a favorite oval-shaped spring radish. 30–35 days to harvest.

Japanese Minowase Daikon

This is a popular old variety in Japan. It has very big, white roots that grow 24" long and 3" wide. Its flavor is crisp and sweet. It's great eaten fresh, pickled, steamed, or stir-fryed. 45 days to harvest.

Jaune d'Or Ovale

The French have been enjoying this old variety for over 125 years. Its egg-shaped roots are medium hot and remain tender for quite a while. The root begins as a pale tan-white and turns yellow-tan while maturing. 28 days to harvest.

Long Black Spinach (Noir Gros Long d'Hiver)

Long Black Spinach is an old European variety that's hard to find. It has long, 9" black roots with pure white flesh that has a crisp and pungent flavor. Days to harvest unavailable.

Misato Rose

Misato Rose is very easy to please. Even if you crowd the plants or don't have the guts to thin the radish crop properly, it'll still provide you with proper bulbs. This variety has green and white skin and rose and white flesh. It looks lovely when sliced up for a salad. This is a daylength-sensitive radish for winter storage, so plant it from late July to late August. 60 days to harvest.

Philadelphia White Box

This mild-tasting heirloom dates back to the 1890s. It's a good variety for container gardens, as well as open cultivation. 30–35 days to harvest.

Plum Purple

This is a fun variety for the home garden and specialty market. Plum Purple has round, dark purple roots and white flesh with a sweet and mild flavor. It's a very adaptable variety that's never pithy. 25–30 days to harvest.

Rat-Tailed Radish

This radish oddity is native to South Africa. These radishes aren't grown for their roots. The part that's harvested is actually the fleshy, tapered seed pods that cover the top of the plant. The pods are 4–6" long and approximately the thickness of a pencil. They should be harvested before they're fully mature and can be eaten fresh, added to sandwiches, or chopped up for salads. 50 days to harvest.

Photo by Baker Creek Heirloom Seeds

Sparkler White Tip

The roots of Sparkler White Tip are bicolored with bright red on the upper part and a white tip on the lower third. Their flesh is sweet and white, and you'll want to harvest them at 1" diameter. 24 days to harvest.

White Icicle (Lady Finger)

This is a pre–1865, mild-flavored heirloom that has some unique characteristics. First of all, its roots are carrot-shaped and grow 4–5" long. While most people associate radishes with a red or pink blush, this one is white. The flavor is at its best when harvested young, but becomes milder when harvested at maturity. 29 days to harvest.

Rutabaga (Swedish Turnip)

The rutabaga resembles a turnip, but these two look-alikes are actually different vegetables. However, like the turnip, the roots are what we're after here. The flesh of a rutabaga can be yellow or white and has a mellow flavor. They're biennial plants and are usually directly seeded into the garden bed in early spring. Zones known for their blazing summers aren't a great home for rutabagas; they like to spend their summers on the cool side.

American Purple Top Yellow

This variety is an improvement on Purple Top Yellow (a pre-1850 variety) and was introduced in 1920. The yellow flesh is fine-grained and has a mild flavor. The roots should be harvested when they are 4–6" in diameter. 90 days to harvest.

Champion A Collet Rouge

This lovely little variety grows large roots that have a fine flavor that makes them popular fried or roasted. They're a purple-red color on the top of the root and yellow on the bottom. 25 days to harvest.

Collet Vert

This rutabaga has fine flavor with a bright green top and a yellow bottom. Many gardeners and gourmet chefs love this variety's rich flavor. 75 days to harvest.

Laurentian

Laurentian was developed as an improved Purple Top and has delicious yellow roots. The roots grow very uniform and they're wonderful and sweet whether fried or baked. 100 days to harvest.

Spinach

Spinach is ancient; the general consensus is that it originated in Asia, but spinach has been documented in Europe as far back as 1351. Spinach is a cool-loving annual that can take some pretty serious frosts, so it prefers to be planted in either early spring or late fall.

Spinach is a good crop for succession planting at about two-week intervals. Harvest your spinach's mature outer leaves until it bolts (flowers). At that point, you'll probably want to pull the whole plant and toss it to the chickens. Or let it go to seed if you're a seed saver.

I added a couple of other varieties of greens that are used interchangeably with spinach. New Zealand spinach is a substitute even though it isn't a true spinach. This variety is not only a perennial plant but will give you the spinach-type greens you want when you can't typically have them: all summer.

America

This is a compact Bloomsdale-type spinach. The plant grows to 8" tall, is slow to bolt, and is perfect for spring sowing in zones that have long days. It's heat- and drought-resistant. 43–55 days to harvest.

Bloomsdale

This fast-growing heirloom was introduced before 1908. Its leaves are a glossy, deep green and are thick, twisted, and savoyed. They're also extremely tender and have excellent flavor. Good for planting in the late spring or summer and a heavy producer. 39–60 days to harvest.

Giant Nobel

This huge, fast-growing, heritage spinach was introduced in 1926. Its tender leaves can spread to 25" long. It's a versatile variety that is great for fresh eating in salads, canning, or steaming. 40–56 days to harvest.

Gigante d'Inverno (Giant of Winter)

This is an Italian heirloom that grows large, broad, dark green leaves of terrific flavor. It continues to grow deep into the fall and winter. 50 days to harvest.

Long Standing Bloomsdale

This pre-1915 spinach has deep green, glossy, savoyed leaves. Long Standing Bloomsdale is super flavorful and does better in the heat than many varieties. 42 days to harvest.

Merlo Nero

An Italian spinach variety that has savoyed, dark green leaves and wonderful flavor. It matures on the early side and is very productive. 48 days to harvest.

Monstreux de Viroflay

This is a fast-growing, gourmet, French heirloom that has smooth, big leaves and is great for fall planting. 50 days to harvest.

New Zealand

This is not really a spinach, but we use it like one. The nice thing about this variety is that it produces leaves that can be used like spinach all summer. 60 days to harvest.

Red Malabar

This is a sun-loving variety that isn't a true spinach. It's an Asian vine with yummy stems and leaves. Like spinach, it's really wonderful in stir-frys or salads. 70 days to harvest.

Winter Bloomsdale

Winter Bloomsdale is a perfect variety if you'd like to plant spinach in the late summer or early fall. It has well-savoyed, deep green leaves. It's slow to bolt, and resistant to blight, mosaic, and blue mold. 47 days to harvest.

Summer Squash and Zucchini

Summer squash has a thin, tender skin and is eaten shortly after it's harvested. It's the opposite of its winter squash and pumpkin cousins that need to develop a tough shell for winter storing.

You want to harvest zucchini when it's no longer than 6–8" so you can enjoy its wonderful flavors. And lest you think that all summer squash is zucchini, I want to remind you that there are many more, such as crookneck squash, straightneck squash, Patty Pan, and scallop squash varieties.

Benning's Green Tint Scallop

Here's a beautiful, pale green squash variety that has uniform, saucer-shaped fruits with scalloped edges. The flesh is of fine texture and very good flavor. Harvest when the fruits are small for eating. 52 days to harvest.

Photo by Baker Creek Heirloom Seeds

Black Beauty Zucchini

Black Beauty is a 1957 heirloom. It's a standard summer squash with green-black-skinned fruits that are at their best when harvested and eaten at 6–8" long. The fruits are produced on spiny, compact bushes. It's a great variety for freezing. 44–65 days to harvest.

Cocozelle Italian

This is a pre-1934 heirloom squash variety that grows fruits that reach 10–12" long, but if you'd like to eat them you'd better harvest them while they are between 6–8" long. They are deep green with light green stripes and flesh that is firm and greenish-white. 59 days to harvest.

Costata Romanesca

This zucchini is a heavily ribbed Italian heirloom with light and dark green stripes. Its very large vines produce a delicious zucchini that is best if it's picked at 12". 62 days to harvest.

Dark Green Zucchini

This is a hugely productive bush variety that produces mottled deep green fruits with a pale green flesh. 50 days to harvest.

Early Golden Summer Crookneck (Early Yellow Summer Crookneck, Dwarf Summer Crookneck)

This is a very old heirloom that the Native Americans were growing before Europeans arrived in America. The fruit is a bright yellow-gold color with a curved neck. The flesh is creamy white and has wonderful flavor. It's at its best if picked at 5–6" long. 50 days to harvest.

Early Prolific Straightneck

This is a lovely little zucchini that's a straightneck variety with a bit of a club shape. It has lemon-yellow skin and wonderful flavor. It's best when picked at 3–7" long. It's a hardy and very productive plant. 48 days to harvest.

Early White Bush Scallop (White Patty Pan)

This is a pre-1722 heritage squash that has a white-green skin that matures to white with white flesh. This is a high-yielding variety that's 6–7" long and 3" in diameter. 54 days to harvest.

Golden Bush Scallop

Golden Bush Scallop produces a *Patty Pan*–type squash fruit with a golden yellow color. The fruits should be harvested when they reach 4–5" across. This one matures a full two weeks later than other types, but the fantastic flavor is worth waiting for. They're great for stir-frys, boiling, or frying. The bush is compact, so it's nice for the small garden. 68 days to harvest.

 DEFINITION

Patty Pan refers to a small, disc-shaped summer squash. It has a thick center, then tapers down as it reaches the edges. The edges are distinctly scalloped. Its flavor is similar to zucchini.

Golden Zucchini

This variety was introduced to gardeners in 1973 by W. Atlee Burpee. The cylindrical, glossy, gold-yellow fruits are formed on compact bushes. It's an excellent home garden variety. 50–55 days to harvest.

Grey Zucchini (Tender Grey)

This is a small-seed zucchini that has mottled gray-green skin. The flesh has excellent texture and flavor and the variety keeps well. 42 days to harvest.

Jaune et Verte (Pattison Panache)

This is a bowl-shaped fruit that produces high yields of yellow-cream fruits with bands of green on them. They can be eaten if they're harvested young, but when mature they're strictly ornamental because they're so hard-shelled. 55–70 days to harvest.

Round de Nice

Compact vines produce this 1" Italian heirloom. These little round zucchinis are green- and cream-streaked and have good flavor and delicate skin. This is a very nice squash for stuffing. 55 days to harvest.

Summer Crookneck

This is a heavy-bearing and semi-open bush variety that produces light yellow fruits with curved necks and smooth skin. Their flesh is creamy white and sweet. Harvest them for eating at 5–6" long. After the edible stage, bumps begin to form on the fruit. If you harvest continually, the fruit production continues. 55–60 days to harvest.

Tromboncino

This Italian heirloom produces vines that are best trellised. The fruit is mottled green in color and has a long curve with a bell shape at one end. Their flavor is sweet and excellent when the fruits are harvested at 8–10" long. 80 days to harvest.

Verte et Blanc

This French heirloom is an excellent summer squash with fruits that are round, flattish, and have scalloped edges. They should be harvested and eaten when they are a seafoam green color. The dark green stripes will appear as the fruit matures. 60–70 days to harvest.

Yellow Crookneck

Here's another squash that develops bumps as it comes into maturity. It has a bulb shape and yellow color. If you'd like to cook this variety, harvest it when it's no longer than 6". It's a very popular variety with gardeners. 55 days to harvest.

Sweet Potatoes

Sweet potatoes are related only very distantly to traditional potatoes. They're actually in the morning glory family. In fact, their blooms look exactly like morning glories, which is nice because they can pull double duty as an ornamental in the garden, too.

Sweet potatoes are not yams, either. Yes, like sweet potatoes, yams are a root crop. But the truth is that the two aren't related in any way. Yams are from South Africa and Asia, and our sweet potatoes are from South America—specifically Peru and Ecuador.

Sweet potatoes can have flesh colors such as yellow, orange, white, or purple. Their skin can be purple, orange-brown, or white. They're fat-free, high in fiber, and sweet.

Beauregard

This is a fast-maturing sweet potato that has reddish-orange skin and orange flesh. It's prolific and is crack-resistant. 90–100 days to harvest.

"Bunch" Porto Rico (Bush Puerto Rico, Vineless Puerto Rico)

This variety has copper-colored skin and light red flesh. It's a compact bush or "vine-less" plant. It has a wonderful old-fashioned flavor and makes a perfect baked potato. 110 days to harvest.

Centennial

This is a well-loved sweet potato that most people recognize. The skin has an orange-copper color and the flesh is orange. 90–100 days to harvest.

Georgia Jett

This sweet potato is a prolific producer of potatoes with deep red skin and dark orange flesh that's moist and tender. They're perfect for northern gardens. 90–100 days to harvest.

Nancy Hall

This sweet potato was the darling of the 1930s and 1940s with its light skin and yellow flesh. 110 days to harvest.

O'Henry

O'Henry is great tasting and a high yielder. It has white skin and cream-colored flesh that has a dryer texture after cooking. It's a good keeper. 90–100 days to harvest.

Vardaman

Vardaman is a bush variety that has golden skin and flesh that's a beautiful, bright red-orange. 100 days to harvest.

White Triumph (White Yam, Southern Queen, White Bunch, "Choker," and Poplar Root)

White Triumph is pure white from its skin to its sugary-sweet, dry flesh. It's one of the oldest sweet potatoes in America. 110 days to harvest.

Swiss Chard

 Swiss Chard is a beet that's grown for its leaves instead of its roots. The varieties are often so lovely that they're grown not only for food, but for ornamental value as well. Swiss chard has thick stems that'll remind you of celery, and the leaves are also large and thick. When new chard stalks come in, you can use the thinnings in your salad.

Later harvests will have you taking the outer leaves and leaving about 2" of stalk at the base of the plant. Of course, the chard will replace the leaves you harvest and you'll get more crops. Don't forget to feed the soil your chard is planted in by adding a layer of compost every few weeks.

Erbette

Underwood Gardens introduced this great chard in 2000. These are bushy plants full of large, flavorful leaves that are tender enough for salads when managed as a "cut and come again" variety. It's vigorous and drought- and heat-resistant. Winter-hardy to zone 5 in a cold frame. Tender sweet leaves continue to grow even as it goes to seed. 45 days to harvest.

Five Color Silverbeet (Rainbow Chard, Bright Lights)

Originally from Australia, this is one of the most stunning chards with its brilliant red, pink, orange, yellow, and white display of tasty stalks. Lovely in gardens and perfect for market growers. Some may even keep their color after cooking, but you'll have a better chance if it's prepared lightly steamed. It's often sold as Bright Lights. 60 days to harvest.

Flamingo Pink Chard

This gorgeous chard has ribs of neon pink and is beautiful when harvested young and tossed into salads. 60 days to harvest.

Fordhook Giant

W. Atlee Burpee introduced this prolific chard. The stalks are white and the leaves are dark green and very crumpled. 50–60 days to harvest.

Lucullus

Named after the Roman general Lucius Lucullus, who was known for his bountiful banquets, this heirloom was introduced around 1914. It has crumpled, pale green leaves and produces for most of the growing season as it tolerates the hot weather. 50 days to harvest.

Oriole Orange Chard

A delicious orange chard that's perfect for the home or market garden. 60 days to harvest.

Ruby Red (Rhubarb Chard)

This variety was introduced to the United States in 1857. The dark green, crumpled foliage is stark next to the bright red stalks that are tender and juicy. 50–60 days to harvest.

Vulcan Chard

Switzerland offers this improved rhubarb chard with its lovely red color and terrific flavor. Great as a market variety. 60 days to harvest.

Tomatillo

These warmth-loving little guys look like a small, green tomato variety—they aren't. They are in the same family, but tomatillos have a thin, paper-type husk that needs to be removed before cooking. Usually, the tomatillo's husk splits open and mostly off when they're ripe, but not always.

They're often used in Mexican salsas and enchiladas verdes. Like indeterminate tomatoes, tomatillo plants are sprawling vines that don't have tendrils but do need some support if you don't want the fruit on the ground. Many gardeners use tomato cages to keep them confined. They have a sweet yet tart flavor and are very easy to grow.

Cisneros Grande

This is a high-producing plant with large, 2½" fruits. There's quite a bit of variation with this variety in color, size, and flavor. Most Cisneros Grandes turn yellow when they're ripe, but some stay green. They can range anywhere from lime- to apple-size, but most will end up on the larger side. If you're after a tart flavor, you'll want to use the bright green ones while the husk is still green. If you'd like a sweeter, more fruity taste, wait until the husk is dry. 80 days to harvest.

Dr. Wyche's Yellow

This is a high-yielding variety that produces yellow tomatillos that have a slight purple blush to them. The flavor is sweet. 90–100 days to harvest.

Purple Coban

This is a 1" green tomatillo that has a varying amount of purple on the fruits. It's popular in Guatemala because it's super flavorful. Days to harvest unavailable.

Purple de Milpa

This variety is a little smaller and has a sharper flavor than other purples. They usually don't break open the husk when they're ripe. Used very often in Mexican cuisine. 70–90 days to harvest.

Tomatillo Purple

This fruit is large and much sweeter than the green tomatillos. When it's ripe, it turns purple, and many of them are a bright violet color. Its sweetness makes it perfect for grilling. 70–90 days to harvest.

Tomatillo Verde (Tomate Verde, Tomatillo Green)

This is the standard tomatillo variety. It's deep green in color with a rich taste. Although the vines are okay on the ground, this is a tall plant, so you may want to stake it. Used in Mexican dishes to add a sweet-sour flavor. Prolific producer. 95 days to harvest.

Tomato

America is truly smitten with tomatoes. This diverse vegetable is widely loved and considered the number one veggie planted in home gardens. With heirlooms, you're not only going to get the very best flavor, but an amazing array of tomato varieties.

Although most gardeners treat tomatoes as annuals, they're actually perennials in their native homes of western South America and Mexico. In the 1500s, Spanish explorers shared the tomato with Europe. The Italians immediately began cultivation.

Tomatoes dig compost, but be careful not to offer them too much nitrogen, or you'll have plenty of leaves and very little in the way of fruit. And don't store them in the refrigerator; refrigeration stops them from ripening fully and destroys the tomato's wonderful flavor.

Determinate tomato plants are those that reach a certain height at maturity and then set fruit all at once. Their habit is to grow into a bush-type plant that may not need staking. They usually reach anywhere from 2–4' high, bloom, and set fruit all at once. Determinate tomato plants can be a real plus for those looking to can tomatoes and needing a large harvest all at one time.

Indeterminate tomato plants are true vines in the sense that they sprawl, yet they don't have the clinging tendrils associated with many vine-type plants. Indeterminate vines continue to climb the entire growing season and usually to a hard frost. These tomato plants can reach up to 12' tall. They can take up a lot of space and definitely need to be caged or staked. Even then, many need continued support with ties or by trellising throughout production.

That said, the indeterminate varieties have a lot going for them. For one, these wild vines produce a higher fruit yield per square foot compared to their bushy cousins. Also, indeterminate tomatoes win the taste test every time. In general, their tomatoes are bigger and tastier. And the vines continue to produce right up until a hard frost kills them. It's perfect for those who want to harvest tomatoes all season for salads or slicing. Most (but certainly not all) heirloom tomato varieties are indeterminate plants.

Most tomatoes are started indoors before the last frost, so harvest dates refer to the date after transplanting them to the garden.

Black, Purple, and Brown Tomatoes

Bedouin

This meaty, deep brick–colored tomato has a pear shape and weighs 3–4 ounces. It has delicious flavor for fresh eating and is great for canning, too. 68–70 days to harvest.

Black Cherry

These 1", round tomatoes have a dusky purple-brown color with the rich flavor that black tomatoes are known for. Large vines produce a heavy yield. These make a gorgeous addition mixed with other cherry tomatoes in the garden and on the salad plate. 75 days to harvest.

Black from Tula

This rare Russian heirloom ties for best-tasting black with Black Krim. The deep, purple-brown variety is a large, 8–12-ounce tomato with a rich, sweet, and spicy flavor. Great for slicing or as a canning variety. 70–80 days to harvest.

Black Giant

This variety produces fruit that weighs in at 6–14 ounces. It's an early producer of large, purple-black fruit that have fantastic flavor. 55–68 days to harvest.

Black Krim

This is one of the best of the black tomatoes. It's a very juicy, dark red-purple fruit from Russia and was named for the Crimean peninsula in the Black Sea. Chefs are very happy with it, and it always places right at the top in taste tests. 69–90 days to harvest.

Black Oxheart

Brad Gates of Napa, California, at Wild Boar Farms introduced this dark, purple-brown variety that is said to be the first black Oxheart-type of tomato. The fruit is often irregular and more flattened than others. 75 days to harvest.

Black Plum

These Russian, 2" oval fruits start as a mahogany color and mature into a black-brown. Makes a rich-looking spaghetti sauce. 80 days to harvest.

Black Prince

This black–chocolate brown heirloom comes from Siberia. It has a deep and sweet flavor that's wonderful on salads. The crop is early and prolific. 70 days to harvest.

Black Sea Man

This variety has a number of odd qualities. It has a potato leaf but is a determinate plant. When it's peeled, it has skeletonlike veins underneath the skin. The fruits are dark brown, flavorful, and grow on small plants. 75 days to harvest.

Brown Berry

Brown Berry is a prolific plant bearing juicy, brown cherry tomatoes of excellent flavor. It's said to the first brown cherry tomato offered to gardeners. 75 days to harvest.

Carbon

This is one of the loveliest purple tomatoes. Its large and smooth fruit has a wonderful, complex flavor. Carbon has won taste tests across the country and in 2005 won the best-tasting heirloom award at the "Heirloom Garden Show." 90 days to harvest.

Cherokee Purple

Like the name says, this is a pre-1890 Cherokee Indian heirloom tomato that's an old favorite. It's a dark, purple-pink color and has a fabulously sweet flavor. 80 days to harvest.

Eva Purple Ball

This 1800s German heirloom comes from the Bratka family. This is a lovely, blemish-free tomato variety that's a terrific performer in hot growing zones. It is disease-resistant and has excellent flavor. The fruits are a rich, pink-purple color and weigh 4–5 ounces. 78 days to harvest.

Gypsy

This medium-size, colorful fruit is named for the Russian gypsies. It's a very deep purple-maroon color and has great flavor. 72 days to harvest.

Japanese Black Trifele

Despite its name, this pear-shaped tomato is supposed to have come from Russia. These unique-looking purplish tomatoes have skin that's perfect and smooth with no cracking. It's a prolific producer of rich and delicious fruits. 80–90 days to harvest.

Morado

This is a high-yielding plant that produces deep purple-pink, crack-resistant fruit with green shoulders. It's a rare variety that has great flavor. 85 days to harvest.

Nyagous

This is a very aromatic baseball-sized tomato that tastes as good as it smells. The flavor is rich and the flesh is meaty on this dark, 3–6-cluster tomato. Has almost no blemishes. 90 days to harvest.

Paul Robeson

This Russian variety was named in honor of the black opera singer and Russian equal rights advocate. It's an extremely popular variety with seed collectors and connoisseurs. Baker Creek describes it as having almost a cult following. It's black-brick in color and has a smoky, sweet, rich flavor that gardeners can't resist. 90 days to harvest.

Pierce's Pride

This is a nicely shaped, medium-size fruit that's a deep, black-red color. It has an excellent, rich flavor. 90 days to harvest.

Purple Calabash

This medium-size tomato is interesting because it's 3", flat, ribbed, and ruffled. Many people have never seen tomatoes like these; they're really wonderful to look at. It's a very popular purple tomato that has a sweet but tart flavor like a lime. 85 days to harvest.

Purple Russian

This is a Ukrainian heirloom that's right up there with the best. Purple Russian weighs in at 6 ounces and is shaped like a smooth egg with no blemishes. Because of its incredible flavor, it's a favorite for fresh eating, salsas, or preserves. 75 days to harvest.

Sara Black

Joe Bratka was given this sweet and spicy tomato by his great aunt in Germany. He introduced this purple-brown tomato in the 1990s. It is popular for its incredible flavor and matures a little earlier than most black tomatoes. 78 days to harvest.

Southern Night

This black tomato has its roots in the Soviet Union and is a dark maroon color. If you want the classic, sweet tomato flavor in a sexy package, you may want Southern Night in your garden. It's also an excellent canning variety. 85 days to harvest.

True Black Brandywine

Here's one for the collectors out there. Apparently, True Black Brandywine came from the Quaker family of the renowned William Woys Weaver. This black-purple tomato dates back to the 1920s. It's a heavy-yielding plant with delicious fruits that have a sweet, earthy flavor. 80–90 days to harvest.

Violet Jasper or Tzi Bi U

This high-yielding little fruit is an absolutely gorgeous violet-purple color striped with an iridescent green. It's a hugely productive, delicious tomato. 95 days to harvest.

Vorlon

This heirloom is from Bulgaria but named after a fictional alien race. Baker Creek Seeds is introducing it this year and is touting this lovely purple-black tomato as having a rich, smoky flavor. 69–80 days to harvest.

Green Tomatoes

Aunt Ruby's German Cherry

These bite-size, green, cherry tomatoes are from Aunt Ruby's German Green beefsteak tomato and look like a perfect miniature. They also have the big flavor of the original. 78 days to harvest.

Aunt Ruby's German Green

This German heirloom is one of the largest beefsteak tomatoes. It's bright, neon green in color and can weigh in at over 1 pound. Surprisingly, it's juicier and sweeter than many of the red tomatoes and was the 2005 taste-test winner at the "Heirloom Garden Show." You'll know they're mature when the blossom end blushes pink and they feel soft to the touch. 85 days to harvest.

Chile Verde

Tom Wagner bred this awesome variety that looks very similar to a green chili. It has a pointed pepper shape and a soft green skin. This green paste tomato has great flavor and is perfect for canning or making ketchup. 85 days to harvest.

Emerald Evergreen (Tasty Evergreen, Evergreen)

Introduced by Gleckers Seed Co in 1956, this plant is prolific. It produces beautiful lime-green fruits that are rich with excellent flavor. It's one of the best of the green tomatoes and is a popular special market variety. 80 days to harvest.

Green Grape

Here's a winner by private breeder Tom Wagner that has chefs, home gardeners, and specialty markets all atwitter. This determinate, grape-sized tomato has an even better flavor than its big sister, Green Zebra. You'll be spoiled by it; traditional cherry tomatoes pale in comparison. 70–80 days to harvest.

Green Moldovan

This heirloom from Moldova is rare. These 10-ounce, beefsteak-type tomatoes are lime-green and have a round, flattened shape. Their flesh is neon and has a tropical flavor. 80 days to harvest.

Green Sausage (Green Sleeves)

This is an outstanding, banana-shaped, paste tomato on a determinate plant. It's striped lime-green and yellow with a rich and tangy flavor. Beautiful fruit in the garden and on the table. 86 days to harvest.

Lime Green Salad

This variety was introduced by private breeder Tom Wagner in the 1990s. Lime Green Salad is another determinate plant that bears yellow-green fruit with lime-green flesh that has a tangy flavor. Great plant for containers. It makes a beautiful addition to a salad and is perfect for spicy salsas. 58–85 days to harvest.

Malakhitovaya Shkatulka

This is a Russian heirloom whose translated name means "Malachite Box," named for the green jewelry boxes made from the mineral malachite. It's an early variety that has a light to olive green color and a lot of flavor. 70 days to harvest.

Spear's Tennessee Green

This is an heirloom that has been grown by the Spear family of Tennessee since the 1950s. They weigh 8–10 ounces and have an old-fashioned tomato taste. 80 days to harvest.

Orange Tomatoes

Amana Orange

This Iowa heirloom is named for the Amana Colonies. The 1-pound beefsteak tomatoes are super-flavorful and lovely to look at. 75–80 days to harvest.

Amish Paste

This big, brilliant orange-red paste tomato can weigh as much as 12 ounces. It has a reputation for super flavor and prolific production. 80–90 days to harvest.

Barnes Mountain Yellow

These heirlooms came from Kentucky and have a delightful, old-fashioned flavor. The plants tend to be disease-resistant. They're a meaty, 1–2-pound beefsteak. 85–90 days to harvest.

Big White Pink Stripe

The name is confusing, but these beauties are a creamy peach color with sweet, tropical flavor. They are low producers, but your neighbors will drool. 95 days to harvest.

Currant (Gold Rush)

This tiny cherry tomato is a golden-orange color and has excellent flavor—perfect little snacking tomatoes. The fruits are a slight ¼" and hang in trusses of 10–12 fruits. It's a prolific plant. 75–80 days to harvest.

Dad's Sunset

These tomatoes grow very uniform and have a golden orange color like the setting sun. They're not only lovely, they have a wonderful zesty-sweet flavor as well. 75 days to harvest.

Djena Lee's Golden Girl

Southern Seed Exposure introduced this delicious variety in 1987. It's been a family heirloom for Djena Lee since the 1920s. Absolutely lovely golden orange, 8-ounce fruits that have a nice blend of sweet and tang. 80 days to harvest.

Dr. Wyche's Yellow

The late Dr. John Wyche introduced this variety to the Seed Savers Exchange. He owned circus elephants at the time, which provided plenty of manure to fertilize his gardens. This smooth, tangerine-orange fruit has a sweet, tropical flavor. 80 days to harvest.

Earle of Edgecombe

This plant is a New Zealand heirloom that grows very handsome, orange, globe-shaped fruits in clusters of two or more. It resists cracking, blossom-end rot, and most diseases. The little tomatoes are smooth and have a sweet but tangy flavor. 73 days to harvest.

Golden Jubilee

This is an old standard orange variety that produces a good yield of mild and sweet fruit. 70–80 days to harvest.

Golden Sunray

Golden Sunray has the rich, sweet, and tangy flavor of the old-fashioned varieties. The productive vines produce this uniform tomato with a golden orange color. Perfect for fresh eating as well as sauces. 80 days to harvest.

Illini Gold

These meaty, golden orange tomatoes were developed by the well-respected seed researcher/developer Merlyn Neidens. The heavy-producing plant bears beautiful, Roma-type fruit that's great for processing or as a market variety. 75 days to harvest.

Jaune Flamme (Flamme)

A French heirloom that has terrific flavor with a bite, this is a prolific plant with deep orange, 2–3-ounce fruits growing in clusters of two or more. It has an apricot shape and is excellent for drying because it keeps its lovely orange color. 70–80 days to harvest.

Kellogg's Breakfast

This large beefsteak tomato courtesy of Darrell Kellogg of Michigan grows to 1–2 pounds. They're very orange in color and are juicy and meaty. 80–90 days to harvest.

Kentucky Beefsteak

This eastern Kentucky heirloom can weigh in at 2 pounds at maturity. It's a nice market variety that has a superb, sweet flavor. 80–90 days to harvest.

Mini Orange

Mini Orange's color is so extremely orange that it almost glows. It's a productive plant that keeps producing salad-size, 2-ounce tomatoes all summer long. They have a mildly tangy flavor and are perfect for gardeners living in the hottest areas of the south. 66 days to harvest.

Moonglow

This is a wonderful producer of perfectly globe-shaped, medium-size fruit that's a golden orange. It has an excellent, fruity flavor. 80–90 days to harvest.

Nebraska Wedding

This variety has a wonderful reputation. It's reliable, adaptable, prolific, and has well-balanced flavor. Excellent variety for midwest gardens. The 3–4", round, orange fruits are formed in clusters on this determinate plant. 85–90 days to harvest.

Orange Banana

There aren't a lot of orange paste tomatoes out there, but Orange Banana is one of them. They're banana-shaped with a delicious fruity flavor. Although perfect for paste, they're great for drying and canning as well. 80–85 days to harvest.

Orange-Fleshed Purple Smudge

This is a gorgeous tomato that you really have to see to believe. It's a ribbed variety that's also flattened out. But the amazing part is its color: a brilliant tangerine color with incredible true purple splashes all over the upper half of the fruit. They tend to get more purple as they mature. This tomato has a nice, mild flavor. 80–90 days to harvest.

Persimmon

Persimmon was first introduced around 1982 and is a rose-orange, 12–16-ounce fruit that grows on vigorous vines. It has a beautiful persimmon-looking tomato and delicious flavor. 88 days to harvest.

Pike County Yellow

This heirloom came from Pike County, Kentucky, and produces well over a long season. The orange tomatoes weigh in at 12–16 ounces and have great flavor. 90 days to harvest.

Rosalie's Early Orange

This variety was introduced by Underwood Gardens in 1996. It produces very early, heart-shaped, orange fruits that have green shoulders. They're juicy and sweet with a good acid balance. It's prolific, heavily branched, and disease-resistant. 70 days to harvest.

Roughwood Golden Plum

This is a golden orange paste tomato that you don't want to overwater. The sweet flavor weakens with too much watering. This is a handball-sized tomato with golden orange mottled skin and bright red flesh. The flavor is delicate yet richly sweet. Perfect for foccacia bread or pizza. 76–85 days to harvest.

Sungold Select II

This one came from Reinhard Kraft of Germany and is derived from the original cherry, Sungold. It's a very tasty little tomato that's perfect for garden snacking. It's not 100 percent stable yet, so sometimes you'll get a red one here and there. 51 days to harvest.

Verna Orange

These monstrous, oxheart-shaped tomatoes were introduced in 1990 by Southern Exposure Seed Exchange. This is a meaty variety and has few seeds. It's a high-yielding plant that offers mild-tasting fruit. It can be susceptible to foliage diseases late in the season. 84 days to harvest.

Woodle Orange

This large, smooth, fancy heirloom came from Iowa. It's a prolific variety of bright, tangerine-colored fruit. Its flavor is very sweet and complex. 75 days to harvest.

Pink Tomatoes

Amerikanskiy Sladkiy

Amerikanskiy Sladkiy translates to "American Sugared," which should indicate what this Russian pink variety tastes like. This rare variety is super-sweet and borne in clusters on the vine. 70–90 days to harvest.

Anna Russian

Russian tomatoes are known for their fantastic flavor and this pink, heart-shaped fruit is no different. It's an heirloom that produces a high yield of thin-skinned, flavorful fruit. 69–80 days to harvest.

Arkansas Traveler

This Arkansas variety is heat-, disease-, and crack-resistant. It's smooth skinned and a lovely rose color. This medium-size fruit produces well under high heat and drought conditions and has good flavor. 80 days to harvest.

Babywine

This is a little, pink, plum tomato that's basically a miniature of the legendary Brandywine. It has firm flesh and wonderful flavor. Plants produce fruit for a long time. 75 days to harvest.

Bali

This is a prolific, raspberry-pink heirloom from Indonesia. The fruits are 2–3", have a flat shape, and are ribbed. They taste both sweet and spicy and have wonderful fragrance. Days to harvest unavailable.

Barnes Mountain Pink

Although this prolific Kentucky variety bears rather late in the season, it produces gorgeous, pink, beefsteak fruits with good flavor until frost. 90–95 days to harvest.

Belize Pink Heart

This is a heart-shaped, tender, and juicy variety from Belize. It's a nice burgundy-pink in color and has perfect flavor. 78 days to harvest.

Blosser Pink Beefsteak

This is an old heirloom from the Virginia Mennonites. It's a hardy plant that produces a pretty, pink, beefsteak fruit. The flavor is sweet and tasty. 90 days to harvest.

Brandywine (Pink Brandywine, Suddath's Strain)

This is one of the most well-known (and well-loved) heirloom tomatoes ever. It's a Tennessee family heirloom that was passed down from mother to daughter. Brandywine is a variety from 1885 that bears large fruit with sweet, fantastic flavor. The lovely pink tomatoes weigh 1–1½ pounds each. 90 days to harvest.

Brave General

This Russian variety boasts a sweet taste and a pretty raspberry-pink color. The fruits are 1 pound and flattened, making them excellent as slicing tomatoes. Days to harvest unavailable.

Bread and Salt

This big, lovely, pink heirloom was named for an old tradition in Russia. When special guests visited a home, they were given a loaf of bread (hospitality) and salt (long friendship). Days to harvest unavailable.

Brimmer (Pink Brimmer)

This Virginia heirloom's fruits are pink-purple in color and can easily weigh 2½ pounds when mature. They're meaty with a low acid/high sugar content. Nice as a slicing tomato, Brimmer is also a useful canning variety. It's not a good choice for northern climates. 82 days to harvest.

Caspian Pink

One of my personal favorites; I've been smitten with this Russian heirloom since the moment I tasted it. It originates from the Caspian and Black Sea region. The fruit is generally 1 pound but can be larger. Like all the Russian tomatoes, this variety does best in cooler growing zones. Caspian Pink always comes out near or on top of the taste tests, often winning over Brandywine. 80 days to harvest.

Crnkovic Yugoslavian

Yugoslavia brings us this 1-pound, low-acid beefsteak tomato. It's a high-yielding variety that's disease-resistant, meaty, and juicy. It has a complex tomato flavor. 85 days to harvest.

Depp's Pink Firefly

This is an heirloom that's been grown by the Depp family in Kentucky since 1890. It's a dusky-pink beefsteak tomato that has iridescent freckling (the "fireflies"). The flavor is creamy with a sweet-tart combination. 85 days to harvest.

Dr. Walter

Here's an heirloom from New Zealand that's perfect for market gardeners. This variety produces 8-ounce tomatoes with low acid content. 75 days to harvest.

The Dutchman

One of the first rare seed dealers, Merlin W. Glecker, introduced this large, pink-red fruit that grows to 3 pounds or more. The Dutchman has very sweet flavor. 85–90 days to harvest.

Ferris Wheel

John A. Salzer Seed Co. introduced this big, pink, and sweet tomato variety in 1907. At one point it was all but extinct until it was grown by Seed Savers Exchange. 90 days to harvest.

German Johnson

German Johnson resembles Mortgage Lifter, as well it should: it's one of the four parent lines used to create the famous Mortgage Lifter. But the color is a deeper pinkish-red than Mortgage Lifter. German Johnson's fruit weighs in at 1–2 pounds and are crack-resistant and prolific. 80–100 days to harvest.

German Lunchbox

This is an heirloom that was given to Baker Creek Heirloom Seed Company by a gentleman whose family had been growing it before they came to the United States. This vibrant pink, egg-size variety has perfect fruit for salads or slicing and is super-sweet. 70–80 days to harvest.

German Pink

This heritage plant has a potato leaf and produces meaty, 1–2-pound fruits. There's not much cracking with this variety and it's terrific for slicing, canning, and freezing. 85 days to harvest.

Grace Lahman's Pink (Lahman Pink)

This variety bears heavy, 4–6-ounce, round, pink fruits that are perfect for slicing or canning whole. These fruits are rich, sweet, and juicy. The plant produces well over a long season. 75–80 days to harvest.

Grandfather Ashlock

This is a family heirloom from Carl Ashlock. During the Revolutionary War, three Ashlock brothers served George Washington; Carl is a direct descendant of one of the brothers. This beefsteak tomato variety produces 10–16-ounce, pink fruit with very good flavor. They're not great keepers, but because of their awesome flavor, that probably won't be a problem; they won't last long enough to worry about. 85 days to harvest.

Henderson's "Pink Ponderosa"

This pink beefsteak variety is huge, meaty, and delicious. Peter Henderson & Co. introduced it in 1891. 87 days to harvest.

Henderson's "Windsall" (Wins All)

Peter Henderson & Co originally introduced this variety in 1924 as Number 400 but it was renamed in 1925 courtesy of a tomato-naming contest. This is a variety that's continuously requested among tomato growers despite the fact that it's a low producer. It's a large fruit that's pink and slightly flattened with delicious flavor. 80–85 days to harvest.

Hungarian Heart

This productive variety bears big, pink, oxheart-shaped fruits. It was brought to the United States in 1901 from Budapest. It's an excellent choice for slicing, freezing, and canning. 85 days to harvest.

Japanese Plum

These lovely, pink fruits are bottle-shaped and slightly ribbed. They're a paste-type tomato and are bigger than Amish Paste. Elvin Martin of Minnesota introduced it and said it was being swapped around in his area. It's supposed to have originated in Japan. 75 days to harvest.

June Pink (Pink Earliana)

First offered in 1900, this heritage tomato was developed during the turn of the century while tomato breeders and gardeners were racing to see who could create a variety that brought tomatoes to market the earliest. June Pink is almost exactly like the Earliana variety with the exception that it's rosy pink in color and produces fruit longer. 68 days to harvest.

Lady Lucy

This high-yielding variety comes from Georgia and produces 6–8-ounce reddish-pink fruit. It has a complex flavor of sweetness with a little acid zip to it. It's good for either slicing or canning. 85 days to harvest.

Millionaire

Millionaire was born in the Ozark Mountains in the 1950s. It was famous there for over 50 years for its sweet flavor and as a terrific canning and fresh eating variety. It's a beautiful coral-pink variety with a delectable flavor. 80 days to harvest.

Missouri Pink Love Apple

The Barnes family of Missouri has been growing this variety since the Civil War. Of course, at that time they grew it as an ornamental because tomatoes were considered poisonous. Missouri Pink Love Apple has potato-type leaves and bears large, pink fruits that have rich flavor. 80 days to harvest.

Monomakh's Hat (Shapka Monomakha)

Here's a fantastic-tasting heirloom from Siberia. It's raspberry in color, has a wedge or heart shape, and its flavor has been described by Baker Creek as honeylike. Its name comes from the diamond-decorated coronation crown worn by the Russian czars. 69–80 days to harvest.

Mortgage Lifter (Radiator Charlie's)

M. C. Byles of West Virginia ("Radiator Charlie") bred this heritage variety to bring in more money during bad times in the 1940s. He bred the plant for six years and achieved stability in the variety. He then sold his plants for $1 each and paid off his $6,000 mortgage. These are 1-pound, pink tomatoes with a top-notch sweet flavor. 85–95 days to harvest.

Mrs. Benson

This indeterminate potato-leaved variety was introduced by Underwood Gardens in 1997 and made famous by top chef Rick Bayless. The seeds came from Mrs. Benson in Oswego, Illinois, who brought it with her from Italy as a bride in the early 1900s. Large yields of these beautifully shaped, voluptuously pink, and crack- and blemish-free fruits averaging 1 pound appear from mid-July to frost. Few seeds, old-time flavor, and good acid balance. 70 days to harvest.

Omar's Lebanese

This is a huge, pink beefsteak that weighs 3–4 pounds. This monstrous tomato has been described as having a multi-dimensional flavor that puts its best foot forward when grown in northern areas. It's a little less predictable in the hot southern climates. Omar's Lebanese has good resistance to foliage diseases. 80 days to harvest.

Oxheart

The oxheart tomato shape originally came about as a genetic mutation in the fruit. This heirloom appeared around 1925. The vines are big producers of pink, very large, meaty tomatoes. The fruits weigh 1–2 pounds and have a mild flavor. 88 days to harvest.

Ozark Pink VF

You can thank the University of Arkansas for this pretty, pink, and smooth-skinned variety. This tomato grows well in hot and humid zones. Ozark Pink is a medium to large variety, is a high yielder, and has great flavor, making it popular in home gardens and for market, too. 65 days to harvest.

Pearly Pink

These little, bright pink, cherry tomatoes grow on prolific vines—very pretty. 75 days to harvest.

Pink Accordion

This deeply ribbed variety is odd-looking yet beautiful. D. Landreth Seed Company describes it as looking ruffled like an accordion. Inside, it's quite hollow and perfect for stuffing. It has a sweet-fruity flavor. 105 days to harvest.

Pink Bertoua

From the Republic of Cameroon in West Africa comes this lovely 3–6-ounce fruit. Their shape is flattened and slightly ruffled. The plant is prolific and has disease-resistant qualities. Days to harvest unavailable.

Pink German Tree Tomato

The German Amish farmers in Ohio created this pink, 2-pound variety that has a mild, sweet taste. The plants resemble trees in that they have thick, sturdy stalks. They're a prolific potato-leaf variety with excellent flavor. 90 days to harvest.

Pink Honey

A variety from Western Siberia, Pink Honey is described as having a honeylike sweetness. The fruits are 1–3 pounds and of irregular shape. They're delicious eaten fresh as well as cooked. Days to harvest unavailable.

Pink Oxheart

This is an old-time favorite tomato that's used as an all-purpose variety. It is oval-shaped and pointed with old-fashioned sweet flavor. Very pretty fruit. 85 days to harvest.

Pruden's Purple

This variety matures quite early considering its large, 1-pound size. The fruit is deep pink, sweet, and very similar to Brandywine in flavor as well as size. It's a potato-leaf variety. 70 days to harvest.

Redfield Beauty

These are very productive plants that produce 3–4", pink, flattish fruits. This heirloom was selected from the variety Livingston's Beauty. 80 days to harvest.

Rosalie's Large Pink (Big Rosy)

This wonderful variety was grown in Maryland for about 200 years and introduced by Underwood Gardens. It challenges Brandywine in taste tests, where it does tremendously well. The fruits are smooth, pink, and huge (some weigh in at over 3 pounds). 80 days to harvest.

Rose

Dr. Grace Kaiser preserved Rose when she got it from an Amish woman named Hannah Lapp of Pennsylvania. It rivals the flavor and production of Brandywine. It's a large tomato with meaty, dark, dusty-rose flesh. It's an early producer and is disease-resistant. 75–80 days to harvest.

Rose de Berne

This is Switzerland's contribution to sweet, rose-pink tomato varieties. These are beautiful, 4–6-ounce fruits born on good-producing vines. 70–80 days to harvest.

Rose Quartz

This is one of the earliest-maturing tomato varieties. Rose Quartz is a Japanese heirloom that comes in several shapes: cherry, marble, oblong, and pear. They form in clusters on vigorous vines that are disease-resistant. The balance of the sugar and acid in this little tomato is perfect. 65–75 days to harvest.

Royal Hillbilly

In 1997, Darrell Merrell introduced this large, purple-pink variety. He selected and developed this variety from Hillbilly in the 1990s. It has an exquisite sweetness that has just enough tang to give it the perfect tomato flavor. 80–90 days to harvest.

Sheboygan

These pink paste tomatoes have been grown by Lithuanian immigrants in Sheboygan, Wisconsin, since the early 1900s. These 4–6-ounce fruits have great flavor and are perfect for canning. 80 days to harvest.

Tappy's Finest

This is a West Virginia family heirloom that came from Italy before 1948. It was introduced in 1983 by Southern Exposure Seed Exchange. The 5' plants produce pink-red, flattened globes that weigh between 14 ounces and 2 pounds. Tappy's Finest performs best in zones where the summers are mild to cool. It's a meaty tomato, so it makes an excellent processing variety as well as a slicing tomato. It's not a heavy producer, but the sweet tomatoes are worth it. 77 days to harvest.

Thai Pink Egg

This grape tomato comes from Thailand and is perfect for snacking, markets, and restaurants. The delicious, pink fruits weigh 2 ounces. The plant is a good producer. 75 days to harvest.

Tlacolula Pink

This rare tomato is from Mexico and has a mild, pink, sweet flesh. 75–85 days to harvest.

Uncle Mark Bagby

Mark Bagby brought this heirloom to Kentucky in 1919 and it's grown by his grand-niece to this day. The plants are vigorous and have a potato leaf. The pink fruits are 8–12 ounces and have terrific flavor. They've been compared to Brandywine, but Uncle Mark Bagby produces better than Brandywine in the warmer climates. 75 days to harvest.

Vinson Watts

This old Virginia heirloom is a large, flattened variety that's won many taste tests and has smooth texture. The pink fruit has a nice balance between acid and sweet flavors. 85–90 days to harvest.

Red Tomatoes

Abraham Lincoln (Early Abraham Lincoln)

If your area tends to have tomato foliage diseases, this may be the variety you're looking for. Introduced around 1975, these are red, medium-size fruits with a slightly acidic but distinctive flavor. The original Abraham Lincoln was introduced around 1923, and was a late-maturing variety. 70 days to harvest.

Alaskan Fancy

This early, semi-determinate variety is a good choice for those gardening in a zone that's cooler and has a short growing season. The fruits are 2 ounces, red, and juicy. 55 days to harvest.

Amish Paste

This is a red, 6–8-ounce Amish heirloom that was discovered in Wisconsin. It's oxheart-shaped and has fantastic flavor. Great variety for fresh eating and sauces. 85 days to harvest.

Aurora

This determinate variety is from Siberia and grows very well on the West Coast and the cooler climates. The fruit is medium-size and delicious. 60 days to harvest.

Austin's Red Pear

This little pear-type tomato bears 2" red tomatoes that have terrific flavor. The plants are high yielding, and once in a while a yellow fruit will pop up. 80 days to harvest.

Beefsteak

This is an old standby as far as big, red tomatoes go. Beefsteak has a rich, old-time tomato flavor. 85 days to harvest.

Belii Naliv

The fruits from this early maturing variety can vary in size and flavor a little, but it's a sweet and tangy tomato that's also crack-resistant. 60 days to harvest.

Big Month

This is a Roma-type tomato that's sweet and tasty. The fruits are 4 ounces and oblong. Big Month's texture is firm and it's great eaten fresh or as a canning variety. It's a heavy producer that has a tendency to ripen all at once—a "big month" of ripe tomatoes. Days to harvest unavailable.

Brandywine (Red Brandywine)

Johnson and Stokes introduced the original Brandywine in 1889. It's known as a productive plant with seriously sweet-tasting, 8–12-ounce fruit. 80 days to harvest.

Break O'Day

This heirloom was introduced in 1931. It's a big, bright red tomato that's lovely to look at and a big producer. It has a rich, full, and tangy flavor that's nice for fresh eating and terrific for canning. 70 days to harvest.

Buckbee's New Fifty Day

This medium-size, red tomato with an old-fashioned taste is a pre-1930 heirloom. It's also an early producer. 70–75 days to harvest.

Burbank Red

This is a semi-determinate variety that produces 4–5" fruits of excellent taste. It's a super high-yielding tomato. 58 days to harvest.

Burpee Long Keeper

Introduced in 1979, this is a terrific tomato for harvesting just a bit before it's ripe and keeping somewhere dark and cool. It'll remain unripe for a couple months and then ripen to a red-orange color. 78 days to harvest.

Cardinal

W. Atlee Burpee introduced the lovely Cardinal in 1884. The red fruits are small- to medium-size, flattened, and have good flavor with a bit of tartness. 86 days to harvest.

Chadwick Cherry (Camp Joy)

This is a 1-ounce cherry tomato that has a sweet flavor. It's popular with home gardeners because its vines produce huge yields of the small, delicious fruit. 80 days to harvest.

Chalk's Early Jewel

In 1910, James Chalk of Norristown, Pennsylvania, introduced this 4–6-ounce tomato variety with heavy yields and delightful flavor balance. 70–80 days to harvest.

Cherry Roma

This smaller cherry tomato looks very much like the ones you'll find in the produce section of your grocery store, but these guys have awesome flavor. Their sweet-spicy taste and 1" fruits make them a terrific snacking tomato. 75–80 days to harvest.

Costoluto Genovese

This is a very old Italian variety that produces soft fruits that are juicy and a little bit tart. It's a determinate plant that also grows wide-angle stems that help support it. The tomatoes are flattened and bright red, with edges that are heavily scalloped. 80 days to harvest.

Cosmonaut Volkov

This heritage tomato comes from the Ukraine and was named for a Russian cosmonaut. It's a medium to large variety that has smooth skin and a full, rich flavor. It's a high-yielding plant even in extremely hot weather and is also disease-resistant. Great for fresh eating or canning. 75 days to harvest.

Cour di Bue

This Italian heritage tomato is said to have a sweet, perfect flavor. It is oxheart-shaped and is formed on large, vigorous vines. The 12-ounce fruits are terrific for slicing or cooking. 70 days to harvest.

Cuostralee

This monster of a tomato plant grows a ton of foliage then bears 2–3-pound, ribbed fruits. They have an intense tomato flavor. 85 days to harvest.

Currant (Sweet Pea)

There are hundreds of little currant-type fruits on each plant. The little fruits form in clusters of 10–12 and don't drop off. Lovely, clean tomato flavor and perfect as a garnish. 75–80 days to harvest.

Czech's Bush

Originally from Czechoslovakia, these stocky little plants produce tons of 4–6-ounce, nicely flavored fruits. Perfect for container planting, but it might need a stake to help. 70 days to harvest.

Delicious

Burpee developed this variety that produces big, 1–3-pound fruit with fabulous flavor. It actually set a world record for weight in 1986 when one Delicious came in at 7 pounds, 12 ounces! 90 days to harvest.

Dr. Walter

These 6–8-ounce red tomatoes are smooth and pretty fruits. The plant is a prolific producer and is somewhat disease-resistant. It's a very popular commercial variety in New Zealand. 75 days to harvest.

Druzba

This Bulgarian heirloom was introduced in 1995 by Southern Exposure Seed Company with seed from Dr. Carolyn Male. The 5-ounce fruits have excellent, sweet flavor. They're also disease- and crack-resistant. The productive clusters have two to four fruits each that ripen uniformly. A favorite at farmer's markets. 75 days to harvest.

Earliana

This heirloom was introduced in 1900 and developed by George Sparks of Salem, New Jersey. The 4–5-ounce, flavorful fruits grow on short, 30–36" plants. 85 days to harvest.

Egg Tomato

This variety is so-named because although it's red, it's about the size and shape of a medium-size egg. It has very rich, thick flesh, which makes it perfect for canning. It's a flavorful tomato that also happens to keep well. 75–80 days to harvest.

Eva Purple Ball

This smooth and round, 4–5-ounce tomato variety is a 1800s German heirloom. The plants are hardy and grow well in humid growing zones. 75 days to harvest.

Federele

This paste variety is 6–7" long and simply amazing-looking. When you first see them, you'll think someone switched out your tomato plants for peppers. They're great for salsa as well as preserving. 85 days to harvest.

Fireworks

This variety matures on the early side, which is nice for a tomato. It's medium-size and has classic tomato flavor. It's a very beautiful red fruit that home gardeners will appreciate. 60–70 days to harvest.

Floradade

This is a prolific tomato variety even though it grows on a determinate plant. The fruits are 5–7 ounces and resistant to the many diseases that affect tomatoes in the south. 78 days to harvest.

Fox Cherry

This heirloom cherry tomato is one of the big ones—about 1 ounce. It has been touted as one of the best-tasting large cherry tomatoes available. It's a reliable and hardy plant. This is the perfect salad tomato. 80 days to harvest.

German Red Strawberry

Dr. Carolyn Male gave these German heirloom seeds to Southern Exposure Seed Exchange, who introduced them in 1995. This seriously flavorful tomato looks like a strawberry—but it's a lot larger. These juicy fruits are 10 ounces and can be smooth-shouldered or slightly ribbed. 80 days to harvest.

Giant Italian Red Whopper

This variety was introduced by Underwood Gardens in 2000. Indeterminate vines produce 1–2-pound, intensely red fruits with a "ruffled" stem end and a rich, old-fashioned flavor. Strong and very productive plants. 100 days to harvest.

Giant Syrian

These are big, deep pink-red tomatoes that can weigh in at over 1 pound. They're meaty fruits with very little seed and have excellent flavor. 80 days to harvest.

Goldman's Italian-American

Amy Goldman found this variety at a roadside stand in Italy and named it after her father's grocery store. These gorgeous tomatoes have a unique look—pear-shaped and rather squatty. They're also a ribbed and pleated variety and have a super blood-red color. They have very nice flavor and are terrific for fresh eating or canning. Days to harvest unavailable.

Good Neighbor

These 6–8-ounce, flavorful tomatoes are formed on 7' plants. They're disease- and crack-resistant. 80 days to harvest.

Granny Cantrell German Red/Pink

This Kentucky heirloom is a large beefsteak variety grown by Lettie Cantrell, who reportedly received the seeds from a German soldier returning from World War II. Since the 1940s, she grew them in her Kentucky garden, saving the seeds from the largest fruits each year. Lettie died in November of 2005 at 96 years old, and didn't get to see her wonderful tomato win "Best of Taste" in an heirloom show in the fall of 2006. This pink/light red beefsteak can reach 2½ pounds, is very flavorful, and can be used for both fresh eating and canning. 69–80 days to harvest.

Hazelfield Farm

The creator of this variety had it pop up as an unexpected volunteer in the garden, and it outperformed the other tomatoes. The rest, as they say, is history. It's an early maturing variety that produces tons of 8-ounce, flat red fruit. Hot, dry summers don't bother it a bit. 75 days to harvest.

Heinz 1350 VF

This variety has a big commercial name, but it's a bonafide heirloom tomato. H. J. Heinz company introduced this 6–8-ounce, crack-resistant, high-yielding variety in 1963. It's widely adaptable, great in a salad, and, of course, excellent for canning. These qualities make it a pretty terrific home garden variety. I'll bet you never look at your ketchup the same way again. 75 days to harvest.

Homestead

Homestead is a firm variety with very tasty flesh. It's productive as well as wilt-resistant and was developed in the 1950s for Florida growers (and all the southern states). 80–83 days to harvest.

Hungarian Italian Paste

This determinate plant produces 2–3-ounce, pear-shaped fruits formed in clusters of four. This is a disease-resistant paste tomato that bears until frost. 79 days to harvest.

Illini Star

Illini Star is an early maturing variety that is known for its reliable and steady fruit production. It was selected by growers Merlyn and Mary Ann Niedens from a cross of a Hungarian heirloom tomato and an old potato-leaved variety. It bears 6-ounce, round, red tomatoes that have excellent flavor. It's perfect for both home gardeners and market growers, and is disease- and crack-resistant. 65–75 days to harvest.

Illinois Beauty

This was originally an accidental variety cross that turned out to be lucky for tomato lovers. Illinois Beauty is a high yielder of lovely 4–6-ounce fruits that are typically perfect in form and are blemish-free. It sets fruit in the hottest, driest summers and is disease-resistant. It's a terrific, flavorful variety for the home garden as well as the market. 80 days to harvest.

Ingegnoli Gigante Liscio

This is an Italian heritage variety from around 1900. It started out as a cross between Ponderosa and Saint Louis. The fruit is mega-large at 2 pounds or more, with flavor to match. It is rich-tasting and very sweet—perfect for home gardeners. 75 days to harvest.

Italian Heirloom

This Italian heirloom has both tremendous tomato flavor and beauty going for it. The plants are heavy with fruit that's perfect for fresh eating or canning. 70–80 days to harvest.

Jersey Giant

Here's a tomato that's on the edge of extinction; so plant them, save some seed, and pass them on! This New Jersey tomato is 6" long and pepper-shaped. The large fruits make them easy to can, but their wonderful flavor will make it hard for you to stop eating them long enough. In fact, their flesh is so thick, rich, and old-fashioned that the modern paste varieties can't hold a candle to it. Days to harvest unavailable.

Joe Thienemann's Australian Heart

This is a 12-ounce, bright red fruit that's an oxheart type with a pointed strawberry shape. It's a high-quality variety that has few seeds and a lot of taste. 75–80 days to harvest.

John Baer

John Baer is a prolific producer of bright red, meaty fruits with really nice flavor. Perfect for canning or fresh eating. 70 days to harvest.

Jujube Cherry

Reinhart Kraft of Germany offers this red grape tomato variety. They're awesome little snacking tomatoes that are crisp and refreshing. Days to harvest unavailable.

Koralik

This Russian cherry tomato is an early variety formed in trusses of six to eight fruits on a determinate plant. The bright red, flavorful tomatoes are sweet and super productive. Excellent for small gardens. 65 days to harvest.

Large Red

This was the most commonly grown tomato variety before the Civil War. It's one of the best-documented tomatoes in our country. These 2"×4" fruits are flattened and heavily ribbed—very different than modern tomato varieties. They're sweet tomatoes with a little tangy zing to them. 85 days to harvest.

Large Red Cherry

These super-productive plants bear large, 1½" cherry tomatoes that have great flavor. Try canning these little guys whole, tossing into a salad, or for snacking. 75 days to harvest.

Long Tom

Long Tom is a sweet, 2"×5" tomato that has firm texture. It's a prolific plant and the fruit is perfect for paste, but nice for salads, too. 85–90 days to harvest.

Marglobe (Marglobe Improved)

This variety was bred from the original Marglobe that was introduced in 1925. It's a determinate plant that bears medium-size, 5–8-ounce fruits that are firm and have good flavor. Terrific disease resistance and vigorous plants. 70 days to harvest.

Marmande

This is an old French heirloom that bears scarlet-colored, slightly ribbed fruit on semi-determinate vines. This medium-size variety has full, rich flavor and makes an excellent market tomato. 70 days to harvest.

Martian Giant Slicer

This is a big, juicy, beefsteak tomato. Its texture is firm and the flavor has just the right balance between sweet and acidic. 95 days to harvest.

Martino's Roma

This Italian heirloom variety is super reliable and produces 2–3-ounce fruits that are perfect for salsa, paste, and sauce. The foliage has puckered leaves. The fruits tend to fall off the vine when they're ripe. 75 days to harvest.

Mexico Midget

This is a terrific, prolific tomato that produces all through the growing season. You'll see hundreds of little, round, ½" fruits that have rich tomato flavor. 60–70 days to harvest.

Moneymaker

Here's an old English heirloom that grows beautifully in hot, humid zones and greenhouses. The tomatoes are 6 ounces and super red. Moneymaker is a high-quality, flavorful tomato that's becoming a rarity. 75–80 days to harvest.

Mong

Sturdy, indeterminate plants full of true-red 2–3-pound tomatoes that are very meaty; have small seed cavities; and have a mellow, sweet, fruity flavor. Underwood Gardens introduced this in 2003, and it was voted "Best Tomato" in *Organic Gardening* magazine's 2003 test gardens. 90 days to harvest.

Mountain Princess

This is a determinate heirloom variety from the mountains of West Virginia. It's a very early maturing and productive variety that bears 4–6-ounce fruit. It has a nice, mild flavor. 50–68 days to harvest.

Mule Team

Introduced in 1997, this 8–12-ounce fruit is a workhorse in the tomato kingdom. It's not only a big producer; you can rely on it to produce for a long season. The tomatoes are slightly egg-shaped and have sweetness with a little tanginess. 86 days to harvest.

Neptune

Neptune is an early to mid-season variety that was bred especially for heat tolerance as well as resistance to bacterial wilt, which is a problem in the southeast and Florida. 67 days to harvest.

Old Italian

Here's an old Italian heirloom that was collected by a soldier stationed in Italy during World War II. It's a big, delicious beefsteak that makes a perfect slicing tomato. Days to harvest unavailable.

Old Virginia

This 6–12-ounce, dark red tomato was commonly grown in Virginia during the early 1800s. It has that old-time sweet-yet-tart tomato flavor. It offers good flavor and high yield. 80 days to harvest.

Opalka

This 1900s heirloom was given to Carolyn Male by a Polish co-worker. This variety produces a fantastic set of 3"×5" paste tomatoes that have terrific fresh flavor. The vines are vigorous but wispy. It's a good processing tomato. 85 days to harvest.

OTV Brandywine

Dr. Carolyn Male and Craig LeHoullier named and introduced this variety that they bred from crossing Yellow Brandywine" with a red beefsteak. "OTV" stands for "Off the Vine," which is the newsletter the two breeders edit. They say it's the very best strain of Brandywine because the fruit is so creamy with buttery texture and sweet flavor. The tomatoes are a rich red color with some orange undertones. They average about ¾–1 pound. This is the most productive and heat-tolerant Brandywine strain. 72 days to harvest.

Pantano Romanesco

This is a Roman heirloom variety that's rare and delicious. The fruit is dark red with a purple tint. It has rich, juicy flavor and makes an excellent home or market tomato. 70–80 days to harvest.

Pearson

During the 1950s, Pearson was one of the most popular varieties grown in California. This determinate plant produces large fruits that can tolerate hot, semi-arid zones. A perfect canning tomato. 80–90 days to harvest.

Placero

This little tomato was cultivated in Cuba and has a super-high beta-carotene content. The fruits are flavorful and the plant is productive. Days to harvest unavailable.

Ponderosa Red

American gardeners got their introduction to this variety in 1891. It's a thick-fleshed tomato of terrific quality that tastes mild and sweet. It may have been the one to put the beefsteak types on the map. 80–90 days to harvest.

President Garfield

This medium-size, ruffled tomato is said to be from the 1880s. The fruits are very flavorful and a brilliant red color. It was named for our twentieth American president, who was only in office for four months when he was fatally shot on July 2, 1881. Days to harvest unavailable.

Principe Borghese

This Italian heirloom tomato is a semi-determinate plant, which means it only climbs half as high. Still, you're going to have to stake it. The fruits are 2" and have a small point on the end. They're predominantly used for sun-dried tomatoes because they hang on to their wonderful flavor after they're dried better than other varieties. 78 days to harvest.

Red Fig (Pear-Shaped)

This eighteenth-century heirloom was used as a fig substitute years ago because it has a nicely sweet flavor. It was dried, preserved, and packed away for winter use. It produces big yields of 1½", pear-shaped tomatoes. 85 days to harvest.

Red Zebra

Here's the red version of Green Zebra. These 2½" tomatoes are nothing short of gorgeous with their fiery-red skin and golden yellow stripes. It's a very productive variety with wonderfully sweet flavor. 75–80 days to harvest.

Rei Dos Temporoes

This is a Portuguese market tomato whose name means "King of the Earlies"—which should give you an indication of its character. For a ½-pound tomato, it certainly is an early maturing variety and it has nice flavor, too. The flattened, blemish-free fruits are resistant to cracking and make a terrific slicing or sandwich tomato. For a semi-determinate vine, it's nicely compact. 70 days to harvest.

Reisetomate

If you see one of these amazing-looking tomatoes, you'll think something is very, very wrong. But it's supposed to look like cherry tomatoes all melted together. Reisetomate is one of the most unique-looking tomatoes available. It has also been called Traveler Tomato because it's possible to tear off one piece of the tomato at a time—without using a utensil. 68–80 days to harvest.

Photo by Baker Creek Heirloom Seeds

Reverend Morrow's Long Keeper

This northern Illinois, determinate vine produces 6–10-ounce, globe-shaped fruit that has pink flesh and orange-red skin when mature. It lives up to its name and is touted as having the longest storage time of all tomatoes. Rumor has it that it's been kept until January! 78 days to harvest.

Riesentraube

This tasty European heirloom was grown by the Dutch as early as 1856. William Woys Weaver sent the seeds to Underwood Gardens, who introduced it in the mid-1990s. Its curious name translates to "bunch of grapes," which is exactly what the fruits look like—only red. They're formed in clusters of 20–40 fruits that are 1", round, and have a distinct nipple at the bottom. The plant is extremely productive. 80 days to harvest.

Roma Rio Grande

These plants are high-yielding during hot, dry summers and produce 4" long, pear-shaped fruits that make excellent slicing or sauce tomatoes. 70–80 days to harvest.

Roma VF

This determinate, pear-shaped variety is one of the most popular paste tomatoes. It ripens uniformly, produces high yields, and has good disease resistance. 75 days to harvest.

Rosalie's Large Paste

These indeterminate vines bear tons of large, 6–8-ounce single-red and occasionally double-red paste tomatoes. Underwood Gardens introduced this in 1996. The fruits have a marvelous flavor and very few seeds. Outstanding for sauces. 80 days to harvest.

Rouge d'Irak

This variety is a prolific producer of medium-size fruit that has good flavor. It is becoming a rarity as farmers are encouraged to grow more modern types of tomatoes. 75 days to harvest.

Royal Chico

This variety is becoming rare, although it's a perfect home garden and market variety. It's a bright red, Roma type with a pear shape formed on a determinate plant. It's disease-resistant and terrific for paste and canning. 80 days to harvest.

Rutgers

This determinate, New Jersey heirloom produces large, 8-ounce fruits with good flavor. The plants are high yielders and the tomatoes are great for slicing or canning. 60–100 days to harvest.

Seattle's Best of All

This mild-tasting tomato was developed by a Seattle market grower and listed in the Gill Brothers Catalog in the 1960s. The prolific vines grow tall and have good foliage. The tomato is medium-size and has good flavor. It's a good all-around tomato variety. 80 days to harvest.

Siberian

This variety is a sprawling dwarf plant that sets fruit very early. The tomatoes are egg-shaped, 2–3", and have very nice flavor. Don't confuse Siberian with Siberia, because this is the superior variety. 57–60 days to harvest.

Silver Fir Tree

Here's an unusual Russian heirloom that's a determinate, 24" variety with terrific foliage. Its leaves are feathery—almost like carrots—and their color is a silvery gray. It yields a ton of 3–3½" fruits that are red and slightly flattened. Really lovely, show-stopping tomato variety. It also grows very well in hanging baskets and other containers. 58 days to harvest.

Sioux

Introduced in 1944, Sioux was one of the most popular varieties grown in the midwest during the late 1940s. The beautiful, tasty fruit matures early and heavily. 70–80 days to harvest.

Soldacki

This is a 1900 Polish heirloom that has potato leaves and produces large, pink-red fruits. The tomatoes can weigh up to 1 pound and are outstandingly sweet in flavor. 80 days to harvest.

St. Pierre

This deep red French heirloom's fruits are large and have a full, rich flavor. It's a terrific producer and is perfect for fresh eating or canning. 78 days to harvest.

Stone

Stone is an heirloom from 1889. It's a flattened, globe-shaped, 5–7-ounce tomato that's great for everything. It's a nice canning variety because the fruits are on the acidic side. They may not be as sweet as some others, but they're very dependable, drought-hardy, and fairly disease-resistant. 78 days to harvest.

Stupice

This is a Czechoslovakian heirloom that grows 4' tall vines and produces 2½"×2" tomatoes. It's a heavy-yielding, potato-leaf variety that produces very early, clustered, and delicious tomatoes. The mature fruit is red with orange undertones. Perfect as a salad tomato. 55–65 days to harvest.

Sub-Arctic Plenty (World's Earliest)

This determinate variety was developed by Dr. Harris in Alberta, Canada. Many 2-ounce fruits are formed on this compact plant that is one of the earliest-maturing varieties. It's also one of the best choices for a gardener living in a cooler growing zone because it sets fruit in lower temperatures than most varieties. 49–59 days to harvest.

Super Choice

This Kentucky heirloom has been grown for over 100 years. It grows vines 7' tall and produces 1–1½-pound beefsteak tomatoes that have terrific flavor and texture. 85 days to harvest.

Tappy's Heritage

This 6-ounce, meaty tomato was bred from a cross between Tappy's Finest and another red tomato. It was developed and recommended by growers Mary Ann and Merlyn Niedens. It's said to be an improved strain with the best traits from Tappy's Finest but with more red color and fruit uniformity. It's a very sweet-tasting tomato that has good pest and disease resistance. 85 days to harvest.

Tommy Toe

This tomato won a taste test in Australia against 100 other varieties. The plant continuously produces red fruits that are 1" (apricot-size). 70 days to harvest.

Trophy

The sweet and mild-flavored Trophy weighs 5–7 ounces and is a good slicing tomato. Colonel George E. Waring introduced this variety in 1870 for $5 a packet. Translated to today's prices, that would make them $70 a packet. 80 days to harvest.

Tropic VFN

This sweet tomato is perfect if you're a gardener in the mid-Atlantic area. Tropic is extremely disease-resistant and has little problem growing well in hot and humid areas. The fruit is 8–9 ounces, thick-walled, and has green shoulders when fully ripe. 80 days to harvest.

Trucker's Favorite

Introduced in the early 1800s, Trucker's Favorite is a good producer of delicious, 3" fruits. 75 days to harvest.

Velvet Red

Velvet Red has a silvery gray, Dusty Miller–type foliage. These sweet, 1" cherry tomatoes have excellent flavor and are prolific. Once in a while you'll have a plant pop out without the silver color. 75–80 days to harvest.

Weeping Charley

This variety is nearly a paste tomato, but the flavor is much sweeter and juicier than most paste varieties. The fruit is big, fat, Roma-shaped, and has very strong tomato flavor. 80–85 days to harvest.

Wisconsin 55

This is a terrific all-around tomato that's great for canning. The 5–8-ounce fruits have good flavor. Rich soils have this variety performing at its best. 80 days to harvest.

Striped and Bicolored Tomatoes

Beauty King

These are some of the most beautiful tomatoes you'll find anywhere. This clearly defined red- and yellow-striped fruit has a fruity, sweet flavor and is excellent for specialty markets or chefs. 70–90 days to harvest.

Beauty Queen

This fruit is a small- to medium-size tomato that also has clearly defined red and yellow stripes. They have terrific flavor and the plant is a prolific producer. 80 days to harvest.

Big Rainbow

Here's a huge heirloom variety that produces 2-pound tomatoes. It has green shoulders, a yellow midsection, and neon red streaks running through it and makes a lovely slicing variety. 80–102 days to harvest.

Copia

This newer open-pollinated variety was developed by Jeff Dawson and is an extremely unique-looking tomato. The skin has fine striping of brilliant gold and neon red. The flesh is swirled red and yellow. It's a flavorful variety and very juicy. 80–90 days to harvest.

Csikos Botermo

This is a cluster tomato that has lovely yellow stripes on red skin. It's not only rare and colorful, it also has sweet flavor. 65–75 days to harvest.

Gajo de Melon

These little pink and yellow marbled cherry tomatoes taste like tomato, melon, and sugar stirred all together. The plants produce these little melon-toned, gourmet beauties in spades. 69–80 days to harvest.

Georgia Streak

This Georgia heirloom is a big beefsteak-type that reaches 2 pounds and has yellow and red flesh with yellow skin and a red blush. It has nice flavor. 91 days to harvest.

Gold Medal

This gorgeous variety is predominantly yellow but has a rose blush radiating up from the blossom end of the fruit. It has a super-smooth, firm flesh that tastes mild and sweet. Because it has very little acid, it makes a great slicing tomato. 75–90 days to harvest.

Green Zebra

Here's a favorite chef's variety that's extremely striking in color with yellow-gold skin and stripes of lime green. It was introduced in 1985 by Tater Mater seeds. Lovely in the garden or in the kitchen, its flavor won't disappoint you. Green Zebra has a rich, sweet flavor that gives just a little bite—excellent taste. 75–86 days to harvest.

HillBilly (Flame)

This is a 4–6", yellow, flattened fruit with rose "flames" on its skin and throughout the flesh. It's a smooth variety that's been described as meaty, creamy, rich, and sweet. It's also crack-resistant and makes a gorgeous slicing tomato. Prolific plant variety. 80–90 days to harvest.

Isis Candy Cherry

This is a cherry tomato that's popular with the kids. Not only are the little fruits sweet and fruity, but they come in different shades with blush patterns on them. Usually they have a "cat's eye" at the blossom end. 67 days to harvest.

Marizol Gold

This German heirloom comes from the Bratka family and was brought to the United States in the 1800s. These are flattened, deeply ribbed, red and gold bicolored tomatoes. It's a prolific producer with delicious flavor. 85 days to harvest.

Mary Robinson's German Bicolor

This variety has vigorous vines that produce a large, yellow fruit that has lots of red shading and stripes. It's a pretty fruit that's sweet and mild in flavor. 80–90 days to harvest.

Nature's Riddle

This Russian tomato is golden yellow with salmon-pink streaks and blushes. It's a pretty smooth fruit that's sweet-flavored with a meaty texture. Days to harvest unavailable.

Old German

Southern Exposure Seed Exchange introduced this Mennonite family heirloom in 1985. It has outstanding flavor and its color is yellow with a red center through the whole tomato. The fruits often weigh more than 1 pound. 75 days to harvest.

Pineapple

This tomato is beautiful to serve, with yellow skin and red marbling. The fruit is very large—up to 2 pounds. It has a sweet and fruity taste. 75–95 days to harvest.

Plum Tigris

This plant produces 4-ounce fruits of unusual bright red and yellow stripes. It has a plum shape and good flavor. 80 days to harvest.

Red Zebra

This is Green Zebra in a fire-engine-red dress with bright yellow stripes. It's a very productive plant and a sweet tomato full of flavor. 85–95 days to harvest.

Striped Cavern (Schimmeig Seoo)

These good-size fruits are shaped like a bell pepper and have red skin with vibrant yellow stripes. Great stuffing tomato (try it with cheese). 80–100 days to harvest.

Striped Roman (Speckled Roman)

Striped Roman is an amazing-looking variety that you'll never recognize as a tomato. It was a fortuitous cross of Banana Legs and Antique Roman tomatoes that occurred in the Illinois garden of noted plantsman John Swenson. The fruit's unique shape is cylindrical, 3–5" long, and pointy. Their base color is red, but they have wavy yellow stripes. This meaty, excellent-flavored tomato is popular with chefs and specialty foodies. 80–90 days to harvest.

Tigerella

These 2" round tomatoes are a popular variety from England. It's an early producer and very prolific even in cool summer areas. Tigerella is dressed in bright red with orange stripes and is disease-resistant. 55–75 days to harvest.

Turkish Striped Monastery

This heirloom comes from Turkey and was collected at a monastery just outside of Istanbul. This 2" variety is striped red and gold, has great flavor, and is a heavy producer. 80–85 days to harvest.

Williams Striped

Williams Striped is a beautiful tomato with skin and flesh colors of red and white. The large fruits are 1 pound or more and have luscious flavor. 85–90 days to harvest.

White Tomatoes

Cream Sausage (Banana Cream)

This determinate plant produces white to light yellow, sausage-shaped fruit that has a nice, sweet flavor. It's perfect for salsas and makes a lovely cream-colored sauce. 70–80 days to harvest.

Duggin White

Lloyd Duggin sent this rare, white heirloom tomato to Dorothy Beiswenger. It's a medium-size beefsteak tomato with a strong, fruity taste. 80 days to harvest.

Great White

This large, 1-pound, creamy white, beefsteak tomato is smoother than most of the beefsteak types. Baker Creek describes the flesh as tasting so fruity that it reminds them of a fresh pineapple, melon, and guava mixture. Quite an endorsement, indeed. 80–85 days to harvest.

Ivory Egg

A seed-saver in Sweden sent this rare cream-colored tomato to America. Ivory Egg has the shape and size of a chicken egg and the flesh is sweet and rich in flavor. Very prolific plants. 70–75 days to harvest.

Shah/Mikado White

The history of this variety is supposed to date back to 1886. It was introduced by Underwood Gardens in the mid-1990s after William Woys Weaver sent them seeds. The creamy white fruits are flattened globes with a hint of blush at the blossom end when it's ripe and weigh 8–10 ounces. Seriously sweet flavor with a hint of pear. The flavor becomes more intense if it's dried. 80 days to harvest.

Snowberry

Snowberry is a popular little cherry tomato in Europe but isn't easy to find in the United States (Baker Creek has them). It's a creamy light yellow, 1" fruit with a mellow, fruity flavor. 75 days to harvest.

Transparent

This is an uncommon, pale lemon-colored, 3-ounce tomato variety. It has a smooth texture and sweet flavor. Very prolific plant. 70–75 days to harvest.

White Queen

This almost white, 3", round and flat tomato has ribbed shoulders and possibly some pink streaks on the blossom end. Yields admirably throughout the summer and is perfect for white pasta sauces. 85 days to harvest.

White Tomesol

The gourmets of the world are going to love this heirloom. The fruit is cream-colored and beautiful with a wonderful fragrance and an exceptionally sweet flavor. It's a high-yielding plant with an exotic appearance. 80 days to harvest.

White Wax

William Woys Weaver passed this heirloom down from his Mennonite grandfather. The fruit has a flattened shape and is waxy and sweet. 75 days to harvest.

White Wonder

This white tomato variety was chosen for the famous Chez Panisse restaurant owned by Alice Waters. These are medium-size, creamy white fruits that have a sugary-sweet flavor and are easy to grow. Wonderful when blended with a variety of colored tomatoes. 84 days to harvest.

Yellow Tomatoes

Azoychka

This Russian heirloom has a sweet citrus flavor and weighs in at 6–8 ounces. It's brilliant lemon-yellow, round, and flat. 70–80 days to harvest.

Big Yellow Zebra

This neon yellow fruit with darker yellow markings is courtesy of Wild Boar Farms in California. It's large and has good flavor. 65 days to harvest.

Blondkopfchen (Little Blonde Girl)

These 1", golden yellow fruits are produced in big clusters and have monstrous yields. They have very sweet flavor and never crack. This variety bears fruit until frost. 75–80 days to harvest.

Dr. Carolyn

This heavy-producing yellow cherry tomato was named for Dr. Carolyn Male, who wrote the book *100 Heirloom Tomatoes*. The fruit has a velvety feel. 65 days to harvest.

Egg Yolk

This tomato is aptly named; it's the color and size of an egg yolk. This variety has a rich, fruity flavor and grows on long vines. The heavy producer was developed by Larry Pierce. 80 days to harvest.

Furry Yellow Hog

You almost have to grow this because of its name. Like the peach-type tomatoes, this one has a slightly fuzzy feel to the skin. The flavor is citrusy and more acidic than most yellow tomato varieties. It produces over a long season. 80 days to harvest.

Garden Peach

These vigorous vines produce 2–3-ounce fruits that resemble a peach, right down to the peach-fuzz on the yellow skin. On occasion the skin will also have a pink blush to it. It's a split-resistant variety with outstanding sweet flavor. 73 days to harvest.

Gold Nugget

This is a golden cherry tomato that is quite prolific and matures early. It has fabulous flavor and is perfect for containers. 56 days to harvest.

Golden Ponderosa

This West Virginia heirloom is a productive plant of showy, yellow-gold fruits with mild flavor. It's rather large-cored and doesn't resist leaf diseases very well. The first Ponderosa was introduced in 1891 by Peter Henderson & Co. 78 days to harvest.

Golden King of Siberia

This big, yellow variety from Russia is a favorite of many gardeners. It's a 1-pound, heart-shaped, smooth fruit with a sweet taste that's very balanced. It's a productive plant with some disease resistance. Days to harvest unavailable.

Golden Monarch

This variety with bright yellow, 10–14-ounce fruits was listed in the 1940s by the Buist Seed Company. They have terrific flavor that's both sweet and tart. 80 days to harvest.

Golden Roma

If you're looking for a yellow paste tomato, this might be just the ticket. Golden Roma is an excellent variety that has a smooth and sweet flavor. They can be anywhere from bright yellow to a bit orange in color. 75 days to harvest.

Golden Sunray

These up to 1-pound, golden yellow fruits have nearly zero blemishes and grow uniform in size and shape. The flavor is excellent. 80–90 days to harvest.

Hartman's Yellow Gooseberry

This heirloom was originally introduced by the J. M. Hartman & Daughters Seed Company. This variety produces hundreds of yellow, sweet-tasting, cherry tomatoes. 75 days to harvest.

Huge Lemon Oxheart

This is a very uniform, noncracking heirloom with good, sweet flavor. The fruit is huge and pale yellow. 90 days to harvest.

Hughs

This 1940 heirloom from Madison County, Indiana, was first introduced by the Southern Exposure Seed Exchange in 1990. Hughs is meaty and extremely sweet. This light yellow beefsteak tomato rivals some of the best red tomatoes out there. It's a prolific producer, has some disease resistance, and matures late in the season. 89 days to harvest.

Lollipop

These are lovely little light yellow cherry tomatoes that have a sweet and fruity flavor. It's a high-yielding variety and quite popular. 70 days to harvest.

Manyel

Manyel's Native American name translates to "many moons." Its creamy yellow skin resembles the moon when nestled among green foliage. It's smooth-shouldered and thin-walled (resulting in some minimal cracking). The 6-ounce fruits are formed in clusters of two to four and have a sweet, lemonlike flavor. 78 days to harvest.

Morning Sun

This compact variety produces prolific amounts of sweet, grape-shaped tomatoes in clusters of up to eight little fruits. 60 days to harvest.

Pale Yellow Egg

These fruits have an egg shape and size. They're a light yellow color (nearly translucent) and have a mild and sweet flavor. 80 days to harvest.

Pink Grapefruit

This medium-size tomato resembles its namesake in that it has a lovely yellow skin but flushed pink flesh. The taste is described as sweet-tart with citrus overtones. 75 days to harvest.

Plum Lemon

Chefs will gladly take this medium-size (3"), bright yellow lemon look-alike off your hands. It has a delicious, refreshing flavor. 80 days to harvest.

Poma Amoris Minora Lutea

This is one of the oldest known tomato varieties and was written about in historic botanical books. Heralding from Italy in 1553, this variety offers good yields and has a very nice flavor. 75–80 days to harvest.

Powers Heirloom

Bruce McAllister from Indiana first offered this variety in the 1990 Seed Savers Exchange Yearbook, but the seed originated in southwest Virginia over 100 years ago. It produces heavy yields of 3–5-ounce yellow paste tomatoes with excellent flavor. 85–90 days to harvest.

Reinhard's Goldkirsche

These German vines produce tons of little gold-yellow, 1" snacking tomatoes. 75 days to harvest.

Roman Candle

This new, yellow, banana-shaped fruit was created from Speckled Roman. It has an intense sweetness and is extremely colorful. Roman Candle is meaty and perfect for tomato paste or salsa base. 85 days to harvest.

Tasmanian Blushing Yellow

This is a Kentucky beefsteak heirloom that has silky flesh and grows to at least 5–6 ounces. The yellow fruit has traces of pink inside and has been described as having a sweet, pronounced, yet mild flavor like most yellow varieties. 85 days to harvest.

TC Jones

This yellow beefsteak comes from five generations of the Jones family in Kentucky. It has a blush stripe on the blossom end. The vines grow tall and produce 8–12-ounce, super-tasty fruits. 80 days to harvest.

Topaz (Huan U)

This prolific plant named for the topaz stone is light yellow with gold specks. This mild-tasting, great slicing variety comes from China. 95 days to harvest.

Wapsipinocon Peach

This Iowa heirloom is one of the varieties that has that lightly fuzzy-feeling skin like that of a peach. It is creamy yellow to nearly white with flesh that has excellent taste and texture. Its flavor is complex and has sweet, spicy, and fruity notes all at once. 80 days to harvest.

Yellow Bell

This yellow paste tomato was introduced in 1986 by the Southern Exposure Seed Exchange. This is a prolific variety that bears heavily until the frost and produces fruit in clusters of five or six tomatoes. The Roma-shape fruits have excellent, sweet flavor and ripen from green to creamy yellow and then to yellow. 60 days to harvest.

Yellow Brandywine

This Illinois heirloom is a large, beefsteak-type tomato with flavor that's tangy and sweet. This is an excellent tomato in both beauty and flavor as is the nature of Brandywines—and every bit as delicious as the red variety. Its strong plants produce golden, flavorful fruit in high yields. 90 days to harvest.

Yellow Mortgage Lifter

Mortgage Lifter of any color is always a hit both in size and flavor. Developed by Underwood Gardens and introduced in 1997, it is identical to the Pink Mortgage Lifter in all but color. It has wonderfully sweet, creamy flesh and an iridescent, glowing yellow color. Fruits hold well on the plants and after picking. 80 days to harvest.

Yellow Pear

These plants are very prolific (practically endless) and produce 1½" yellow, pear-shaped tomatoes that are very sweet. While they're heat-resistant, they'll need to be watered on a regular basis. If you let tomatoes dry all the way out and then water them, they'll tend to split because they won't retain enough moisture. Eat them fresh or make tomato preserves with this small variety. 78 days to harvest.

Yellow Riesentraube

Here's a superb grape tomato that you won't want to miss out on. It's extremely prolific and produces clusters of deliciously sweet little fruits that even out-sweet the red version of the same name. 75–85 days to harvest.

Yellow Stuffer (Bell Pepper)

These bell pepper–looking tomatoes that were popular in the 1970s and 1980s have large cavities that are perfect for stuffing. The flavor isn't flashy—in fact it's kind of bland—but it tastes better after it's been cooked. 110 days to harvest. 80 days to harvest.

Turnip

 Blessed are the veggies that are versatile like turnips, which can be grown for their roots or their greens. Turnips are part of the *brassica* family along with cabbage, Brussels sprouts, broccoli, cauliflower, and mustard. So it stands to reason that they prefer to be grown in fall weather, but there are varieties that grow just as beautifully in the spring.

One nice thing about turnips is that they aren't overly picky about soil type. They'll grow in a wide array of soils but prefer the loamy, friable type if possible.

Amber Globe (Yellow Globe)

This is a pre-1840 heirloom with 6", smooth, globe-shaped roots. The soft yellow flesh is fine-grained and sweet. Amber Globe is at its best when planted in the fall. Harvest it when the roots are 3–4" in diameter. 63 days to harvest.

Boule d'Or

This beautiful turnip is still grown and cherished in France. The yellow flesh is said to be sweeter, milder, and of much finer quality than most white-fleshed varieties. Days to harvest unavailable.

Golden Globe

This is a lovely turnip with sweet, golden flesh that's nice for the spring or fall. Very tasty flavor. 55 days to harvest.

Ice-Bred White Egg

This is a popular variety in the south because it's fast-growing and tender. It should be planted in the fall and is winter-hardy. 45 days to harvest.

"Ideal" Purple Top Milan

This nineteenth-century Italian heirloom is a great market variety. Its roots are white and flat with purple tops and sweet, mild flavor. Days to harvest unavailable.

Navet Des Vertus Marteau

In the late 1800s, this variety was extremely popular with French market growers. It has 5–6" long and 2" wide, cylindrical roots with mild and sweet flavor. Days to harvest unavailable.

Petrowski

This is a terrific variety for both home and market. This yellow turnip with flat roots matures early and tastes sweet. 40–60 days to harvest.

Purple Top White Globe

This is a pre-1880 heritage turnip that produces round, white roots and has bright purple around the top where the sun hits it. This one is at its best when harvested at 3" in diameter. Stores very well. 45–65 days to harvest.

Red Round

This hard-to-find turnip produces small, round roots with stunning bright red color (the stems are red, too). The roots are crisp and perfect for eating raw or cooked. 55 days to harvest.

Shogoin

This Japanese turnip is excellent for steaming or frying. It's an early variety that produces smooth, white, delicious roots. 30 days to harvest.

White Egg

This pre-1880s heirloom is another popular variety for the south. It matures quickly and has egg-shaped roots that grow partially above ground. Its crown has a green tint and the flesh is white. 48 days to harvest.

Watermelon

We know that people have been growing watermelon for consumption for at least 4,000 years. Their roots are in the Kalahari desert in South Africa, but they were actually cultivated in Egypt. We also know that once people bit into the juicy flesh they became smitten and never looked back. Mark Twain once said, "When one has tasted watermelon he knows what the angels eat." You'll get no argument here. In fact, most people won't turn down the offer of a slice of the juicy fruit.

Heirloom watermelons provide us with colors in various shades of red, white, yellow, and pink. The rinds can be solid-colored, have zig-zag stripes, or have an entire galaxy recorded on them (Moon & Stars). Their flavors range from mild to sublime.

When a watermelon is half grown (or the size of a basketball if you're growing a giant variety), gently lift the melon up slightly and slip a board underneath it to ward off any rotting while the watermelon is growing.

If you want the utmost sweetness for your harvest (and who doesn't?), about a week before it's ripe, back off on the waterworks. Just give it enough to survive that last week so the sugar concentrates into the melon. If the vines are waterlogged, your melons won't be as sweet.

How do you know when it's ready for the table? There are a few signs to look for. Thump it with your middle finger and thumb; if it sounds hollow, then it's ripe. Do you see a little tendril on the same vine by the stem of the watermelon? If it's shriveled and brown, that's another good sign. Now, look at the outside of the melon (the rind): is it dull or shiny? Dull is what you're looking for in a ripe watermelon.

Ali Baba

This is an Iraqi heirloom that produces oblong, 15–20-pound melons. It has sweet, red flesh that offers good texture and fantastic flavor. In fact, it's touted to be the best-tasting watermelon. 90 days to harvest.

American Champion (Kolb's Gem)

American Champion has been producing huge, round watermelons since at least the 1880s. Melons from this vine have been recorded at 130 pounds! They have sweet, red flesh. 100 days to harvest.

Astrakhanski

This round, 10–11" melon has a dark green rind with light mottling and streaks. Its flesh is pink, juicy, and delicious. A good choice for gardens that have short growing seasons. 75–85 days to harvest.

Black Diamond—Yellow Belly Strain

This one is a favorite of many home gardeners. It has a dark green rind and sweet, red flesh. It's capable of growing extremely large, so give it room. 90 days to harvest.

Black Diamond—Yellow Flesh

This yellow-fleshed variation of Black Diamond is rare and very sweet. It can grow to really huge sizes. 90 days to harvest.

Black-Seeded Ice Cream

This is a prolific little watermelon that matures early and keeps well. The rind is pale green and cream with very sweet, pink flesh. 90 days to harvest.

Black-Tail Mountain

This fast-maturing little 9" watermelon is a highly productive variety that does well in both the cooler northern regions and the hotter southern regions. It's perfectly round and has a dark green rind with narrow, even darker green stripes. The orange-red flesh is very sweet and rich. The small seeds look like they have a black tail. 73 days to harvest.

Charleston Gray

Charleston Gray dates back to 1954. It is long, gray–green, and has fiberless, red flesh. It offers high yields and has great flavor. 87 days to harvest.

Chelsea

This 15–20-pound variety was popular in the early 1900s and has delicious, pink flesh and white seeds. It's a sweet one and will keep for several weeks after harvesting. 90–100 days to harvest.

Chris Cross

This is an heirloom from Iowa that was once thought to be lost, but Seed Savers Exchange preserved it. Chris Cross came about when Chris Christensen bred Hawksbury and Dixie together. It has light green rings with jagged stripes and weighs 15–20 pounds. 85–90 days to harvest.

Congo

Congo is very high in sugar as well as big watermelon taste. Talk about your natural sugar rush! It's about 30–40 pounds and has a tough, striped rind. Its flesh is dark red and firm. 90 days to harvest.

Cream of Saskatchewan

This 4–10-pound heirloom was brought to Saskatchewan by Russian immigrants. It has a pale green rind with dark stripes that is so thin (¼") it has to be handled gently. That means this variety is only suitable for home gardens and local markets—it doesn't travel well. The flesh is white and very sweet with black seeds. Grows well in northern gardens. 80–85 days to harvest.

Crimson Sweet

This is a very reliable variety for southeast gardens. Crimson Sweet is a medium–size, striped melon that weighs in at 23–27 pounds. It has some terrific attributes that keep gardeners coming back for more. The first is that it is disease- and anthracnose-resistant. It also has the unique capability to promote beneficial bacterial fungi in the soil, which inhibits fusarium wilt. 85 days to harvest.

Crimson Sweet (Virginia Select)

Just when you thought Crimson Sweet couldn't be improved, Ms. Pam Dawling has selected seeds from the largest, earliest melons since 2001 and come up with this super-sweet variety. 85 days to harvest.

Daisy (Yellow Shipper)

The rinds on the 13–20-pound Daisy are striped and very tough, which works well for shipping. The flesh is bright yellow and very sweet. 85 days to harvest.

Desert King

Desert King has a light, pea-green rind and yellow flesh that has a sweet flavor. It's extremely drought-resistant. This variety is very popular in Arkansas and weighs about 20 pounds. 85 days to harvest.

Dixie Queen

This is a pre-1935 variety that's round with stripes of dark green and a creamy green rind. The flesh is bright red and has fine flavor. It grows to 50 pounds. 80 days to harvest.

Early Moonbeam

This variety has short vines, making it a great choice for small gardens. It produces 5–8-pound melons that have a green rind and crisp, sweet, yellow flesh. 76 days to harvest.

Fairfax

This oblong melon was developed in 1952 and is a nice market variety. It weighs in at 30–40 pounds and has bright red flesh with excellent flavor. 86 days to harvest.

Georgia Rattlesnake

There isn't a true date to this sweet melon, but it's thought to have been developed in the 1830s. Its light, crimson flesh is a favorite in the south. The stripes on the rind resemble a rattlesnake. 90 days to harvest.

Golden Midget

This 1959 heirloom has sweet, salmon-pink flesh and black seeds. This is a really cool melon because when it's ripe it sends out big signals: the fruits and the entire plant turn golden yellow. It's a really early variety, which only adds to the fun of this little, 3-pound melon. 70 days to harvest.

Japanese Cream-Fleshed Suika

At the trial at Washington State University, this variety won "Best Tasting Cream-Fleshed." This is an early and prolific vine producing 6–12-pound melons that have a mild and refreshing flavor. 85 days to harvest.

Jubilee

This is a large, oval watermelon that has red flesh and super-crisp texture. It's an old, sweet favorite. 90 days to harvest.

Katanya

This Russian heirloom, introduced by Underwood Gardens in 2004, produces 10–30-pound, round, green melons that have a red-pink flesh with small seeds. It's a sweet variety that needs plenty of room but isn't aggressive. 85–90 days to harvest.

Kleckley's Sweet (Monte Cristo)

Introduced by W. Atlee Burpee in 1897, this dark green, oblong melon doesn't ship well but is perfect for the home garden. The flesh is bright red and loaded with sugar. 70–75 days to harvest.

Klondike Blue Ribbon Striped

This variety is really tasty—and really rare. It's medium-size and has red flesh that's sweet and delicious. 85 days to harvest.

Malali

Here's the perfect little melon for home gardens. Malali weighs about 10 pounds and is green-striped. The flesh is light red and sugary-sweet. 90 days to harvest.

Melitopolski

This is a 10" Russian variety that's early maturing and has a striped rind and sweet, bright red flesh. 90 days to harvest.

Missouri Heirloom Yellow Flesh

This Missouri heirloom produces 20-pound fruits that are round with a pale green rind. The golden-yellow flesh is both sweet and refreshing. This is a nice yellow watermelon that's hard to find. Days to harvest unavailable.

Moon & Stars (Moon & Stars Van Doren Strain, Amish Moon & Stars)

This legendary variety was offered back in 1926, but eventually it fell off the map. Gardeners and plant breeders thought the variety had been lost, but it was rediscovered and then reintroduced in 1987. The oval fruits reach 20–30 pounds and have a dark green rind with yellow stars and at least one big moon on them. The flesh is red and the seeds are a brown that's slightly beige-mottled. The foliage of the vine is also covered in stars. Moon & Stars has a fantastic sweet flavor. 80–90 days to harvest.

Moon & Stars (Yellow-Fleshed)

This variety replicates the original Moon & Stars on the outside, but has yellow flesh with white seeds. The melons weigh 10–16 pounds and are super-sweet. 95 days to harvest.

Moon & Stars Cherokee

A variation of Moon & Stars, the Cherokee strain has the same golden moon and stars on the dark green rind and leaves, but the flesh is bright pink with black seeds. It's very sweet just like all of the Moon & Stars variations. 95 days to harvest.

Mountain Hoosier

This is a pre-1937 heirloom watermelon that can grow to 80 pounds. It has a deep green rind with dark red flesh that has excellent flavor. 85 days to harvest.

Mountain Sweet Yellow

This prolific variety is from the same strain of Mountain Sweet that was popular in the 1840s. It's a long, 20–35-pound melon with dark yellow flesh and black seeds. It has a seriously high sugar content. 95–100 days to harvest.

Northstar (Planet and Stars)

This terrific strain of Moon & Stars was bred for the northern Illinois climate by Merlyn and Mary Ann Niedens. This is a large melon (up to 30 pounds) with a dark green rind covered with small dots and pink flesh with white seeds. 90–100 days to harvest.

Orange Flesh Tendersweet

This variety lives up to its name and produces an excellent watermelon with dark orange flesh and extremely sweet flavor. Super delicious! 85–90 days to harvest.

Orangeglo

This is an excellent producer of 20–30-pound melons that have light green rinds with jagged light green stripes. The flesh is dark orange, crisp, and flavorful. Also a high-yielding variety. 85–90 days to harvest.

Osh Kirgizia

This Russian heirloom is a productive variety of 10–15-pound melons that have a light green rind with jagged dark green stripes. The flesh is pink and very sweet. 90–100 days to harvest.

Peacock Striped

This watermelon has bright red flesh, fine texture, and a sweet and tasty flavor. It ships well, too. 87 days to harvest.

Petite Yellow

Petite Yellow melons are 6–10 pounds with bright yellow flesh and small seeds. They're compact fruits that fit well inside the refrigerator ("icebox melons") and easily adapt to northern climates. Great market variety. 65–80 days to harvest.

Picnic

Picnic produces nice-size, 8–14 pound melons that have sweet, red flesh and small seeds. Its rind is extremely tough, which makes it good for shipping. It is also fusarium wilt–resistant. 90–100 days to harvest.

Quetzali

This 7–13-pound melon has a thick, dark green rind that's covered with alternating dark and light green stripes. The flesh is pink-red with white seeds. 83 days to harvest.

Red-Seeded Citron (Colorado Preserving)

This isn't a typical picnic watermelon—you don't eat it raw. This variety is used to make candied fruits, preserves, sweetmeats, cookies, fruitcake, and puddings. It's a prolific plant and the fruits store well. 90–100 days to harvest.

Small Shining Light

The Russian variety Small Shining Light is very tolerant of northern climates as well as high altitudes. It's a nice little dark green melon with sweet, red flesh that fits neatly into the fridge. 80–90 days to harvest.

Stone Mountain

This is a 1923 heirloom watermelon that weighs just over 30 pounds. It has a dark green rind and red flesh that's sweet and juicy. 60–80 days to harvest.

Strawberry

These are 15–25-pound watermelons that have a dark green rind with darker green stripes. Its strawberry-red flesh has a delicate texture and fabulous sweet flavor. 85 days to harvest.

Sugar Baby

This is a 1959 heirloom variety that produces 6–10-pound fruits with a rind that turns green-black when ripe. It has red flesh and white seeds. Sugar Baby is a reliable variety that doesn't mind a little drought and is good for small gardens. 77 days to harvest.

Sugarlee

This green-striped melon grows 15–18 pounds and has pink-red flesh that's very sweet. It is disease-resistant and ships well. 90 days to harvest.

Sweet Siberian

This is an early Russian watermelon that's oblong and has a deep green rind. The flesh is an apricot color and has wonderfully sweet flavor. 80–90 days to harvest.

Tendergold

This is a 22-pound variety that matures on the early side. It has orange flesh with great taste and texture. The rind is tough, so it's also a nice market variety. 80 days to harvest.

Thai Baby Watermelon

This is an easy-to-grow baby watermelon that's harvested at about 3" long for stir-frys, soups, curries, etc. Popular variety in Thailand. 86 days to harvest.

Tom Watson

The 20–40-pound Tom Watson is becoming a hard-to-find variety. It's a pre-1900 heirloom that has deep red flesh. Its flavor is sweet and crisp. It is popular with the old-timers and ships well. 87 days to harvest.

Verona

Mississippi State University developed this variety in 1965. This is a large watermelon with nice, dark green skin. It has a wonderful, sweet taste and good disease resistance. Good keeper and shipper—all-around great melon. 70–86 days to harvest.

White Sugar Lump

Henry Field's Seed Company carried this variety as far back as the 1950s. The fruits weigh 5–10 pounds and have a thin-striped rind and white flesh. The flavor is sweet and refreshing. Days to harvest unavailable.

White Wonder

This white-fleshed melon was more common in the 1800s than today. This 3–10-pound variety has a green rind with darker green stripes. The creamy flesh has a fresh, sweet, and crisp taste. Take the opportunity to keep this centuries-old variety alive—plant it and save the seeds. 80 days to harvest.

Wilson Sweet

This melon was nearly extinct when Sandhill Preservation Center and Merlyn Niedens began growing and saving the old variety. There's now enough seed to share this red-fleshed, sweet variety with gardeners once again! Its rind is unusually green with mottling. Some people claim that they've never tasted a better watermelon. 85 days to harvest.

Glossary

adaptability   The capability to adjust readily to a climate, environment, or habitat. This is usually a process that happens over many generations.

annual   A plant that germinates, flowers, produces seed, and dies in one year.

bagging   A technique wherein a gardener places a bag of any kind over a pollinated flower in a way designed to keep out other pollens. This prevents cross-pollination with other plants.

beneficial insects   Insects that either prey on garden pests, spread pollen to flowers in the garden, or in any other way help plants thrive and complete the pollination process. This is an organic method of pest control as well.

biennial   A plant that completes its life cycle in two years. Leaves are grown the first year, and fruit and seeds are produced in the second.

biodiversity   This is the variety of life. In the plant kingdom, it is the genetic diversity within a plant species in a particular environment. Biodiversity often is used as a way to measure health within a biological system.

caging   The technique of placing a cage over a plant to prevent it from cross-pollinating with another plant.

commercial heirloom   Generally, a commercial heirloom is an open-pollinated variety introduced prior to 1940. Gardeners will also refer to commercial heirlooms as those that are readily available to the public through seed catalogs as opposed to those that are only available through trading with other seed collectors.

community garden   A piece of land cultivated by members of a community, particularly in an urban or suburban setting. Community gardens encourage citizens to grow their own food and/or donate to local food banks.

companion planting   This is the practice of planting one type of plant species next to or near another—the theory being that they will benefit each other. One example is using French marigolds in the vegetable garden to help ward off nematodes under the soil.

compost   Organic waste that's been biologically reduced to humus. The term is used for both the process as well as the end product.

cross-pollination   The transference of pollen from the anther of one plant to the stigma of another. This term is also used to refer to situations in which two different varieties have crossed.

drip line   The ground directly under a plant's outermost leaves.

dry processing   The technique used to collect seeds from plants that produce their seeds inside a pod or husk. Good examples are peas and beans.

F1 (filial 1) hybrid   This is the offspring of two varieties (parents) that are genetically different, although they're usually within the same species.

fermentation   The breakdown of carbohydrates by microorganisms.

friable soil   Soil with an open structure that crumbles when handled. Also referred to as tilth.

genetic diversity   The total range of genetic differences that are displayed within the same species. This applies to all species, including humans.

genetically modified organism (GMO)   A plant or organism that's been genetically altered, typically through the transfer of DNA to another organism. This includes combining genes from different organisms, resulting in the expression of new characteristics not naturally belonging to the original organism.

germination   The very beginning of plant growth, when a seed begins to sprout into a plant.

growing zone   The USDA hardiness zone map that most gardeners consult so they know which plants will grow well in their area. This map assigns zone numbers to each area for clarification.

hand-pollination   A technique that gardeners and plant breeders use to help pollination of their plants. This technique can include using a paintbrush to transfer pollen or shaking the branch of a self-pollinating plant.

heirloom (heritage) vegetables   Most gardeners agree that a variety becomes an heirloom when it's 50 years old. Most varieties are considered heirlooms when they've been handed down through the generations of a family. Heirlooms are consistently of high quality and have been saved because of their superior characteristics and ease of growing.

humus   The material that's formed after the breakdown of organic matter. It makes complex nutrients in the soil easily accessible to plants.

landrace   A variety that has adapted to its environment through careful natural selection within a seed pool. Many varieties adapt to a non-native location and thrive, becoming a landrace of that new area.

landscape cloth   A synthetic material that's used to prevent weeds, control erosion, and retain moisture in the soil. Also called landscape fabric.

loamy soil   A soil that generally contains more humus and therefore more nutrients than sandy soils, is easier to work than clay-type soils, and has better infiltration and drainage than silty soils. The sand, silt, and clay are fairly balanced in this type of soil (40–40–20 respectively). It's considered the ideal gardening soil.

microclimate   A climate of a smaller, specific place within an area as contrasted with the climate of the entire area. An example would be the microclimate of your neighborhood as opposed to your city, or the north side of your house as opposed to the neighborhood.

microorganisms   Those organisms (plants or animals) that are too small to be seen with the naked eye.

monoculture   The agricultural practice of producing or growing one single crop over a wide area.

mulch   A protective covering of organic material laid over the soil around plants to prevent weeds and erosion, retain moisture, and enrich soil.

open-pollination   Those plants that are produced by crossing, in nature, two parents that are the same variety. Open-pollination ends up producing nonhybrid offspring that look almost identical to their parents.

organic matter   Any material that originates from living organisms, including all animal and plant life, whether still living or in any stage of decomposition.

perennial   A plant that continues its life cycle for three or more years. It can produce flowers and seeds from the same roots year after year.

pistil   The reproductive part of a female flower, including the style, stigma, and ovary.

savoyed   The puckered and crinkled leaves of some vegetables, such as certain cabbage varieties.

self-pollination   The transference of pollen from an anther to a stigma of the same flower. It can also be the transference of pollen from the anther to the stigma of another flower on the same plant.

Silica gel   A drying agent made of a gelatinous silica in a form that readily absorbs water from the air.

stamen   The male reproductive part of the flower; it carries the pollen grain and has filaments and anthers.

stigma   The part of the pistil (on a female flower) that receives the male pollen grains during fertilization.

threshing   The act of breaking the seeds free from dried plant material or seed pods.

topography   Local details, including natural and man-made features of the land.

wet processing   A technique used to remove and dry the seeds from a pulpy fruit such as tomatoes.

winnowing   A technique used to separate the grain or seed from the chaff.

Resources

Here you'll find some top-notch seed companies for purchasing heirlooms, as well as books, websites, and organizations that can take you further down the road to heirloom vegetable gardening. Enjoy the journey and share the bounty!

Heirloom Seeds

Here are the companies that can help you get started on the road to growing your own heirloom vegetables. Some of these companies carry heirloom seeds exclusively, and some have hybrids as well.

Abundant Life Seeds
www.abundantlifeseeds.com
Open-pollinated, certified organic seeds available here.

Baker Creek Heirloom Seeds
www.rareseeds.com
Baker Creek offers 1,400 heirloom varieties. All of the seeds they carry are open-pollinated, and all of them are non-GMO. The photography in this catalog is ridiculously stunning. You'll want to get it for that reason alone.

BBB Seed
www.bbbseed.com
This company has open-pollinated, non-GMO seeds available for veggies, wildflowers, and herbs.

Beekman 1802
www.beekman1802.com
These guys have heirlooms, but they'll also keep you hanging around their site with the other organic goodies and information they offer.

Botanical Interests
www.botanicalinterests.com
Botanical Interests carries both heritage and hybrid veggie, flower, and herb seeds. Lovely artwork in this catalog.

Bountiful Gardens
www.bountifulgardens.org
This site is all about heirlooms, open-pollination, and sustainable agriculture.

Burpee
www.burpee.com
Burpee has a lot of hybrids, but they have some good heirlooms, too.

The Cook's Garden
www.cooksgarden.com
This company has both heirlooms and hybrids of some of the tastiest varieties.

D. Landreth Company Heirloom Seeds
www.landrethseeds.com
Started in 1784, Landreth is the oldest seed house in America.

Fedco Seeds
www.fedcoseeds.com
These guys cater to the northeastern climate and have heirlooms and cultivar varieties available.

Freedom Seed
www.freedomseeds.org
This company sells open-pollinated seed varieties.

Good Seed Company
www.goodseedco.net
Heirloom seeds especially adapted for northern gardens.

Heirloom Seeds
www.heirloomseeds.com
This site has a ton of heirloom seeds to offer.

Johnny's Selected Seeds
www.johnnysseeds.com
Johnny's has been around a very long time and carries both heirloom and hybrid seeds.

Kitchen Garden Seeds

www.kitchengardenseeds.com
Here's a great site with lots of seeds and growing tips.

Marianna's Heirloom Seeds

www.mariseeds.com
This one is for tomato and pepper lovers with some eggplant thrown in for good measure.

The Natural Gardening Company

www.naturalgardening.com
In Sonoma, California, sits the oldest certified organic nursery in the United States. Come get your seeds.

New Hope Seed Company

www.newhopeseed.com
This family-owned company specializes in rare and noncommercially available seed.

Peaceful Valley

www.groworganic.com
They've got seeds; they've got supplies; they've got a good attitude. What's not to love?

Pepper Joe's

www.pepperjoe.com
A little burn doesn't bother you? Here's where you'll find the hottest peppers.

Reimer Seeds

www.reimerseeds.com
These guys have more than 4,500 quality non-GMO vegetable seeds, herb seeds, and flower seeds for the home garden and market growers.

Renee's Garden

www.reneesgarden.com
This is a fun site to peruse and is owned by the plant-world-renowned Renee Shepherd. When you order your seeds, they come in lovely little packages that Renee's Garden Seeds are known for—with little watercolor portraits of the plant.

Revolution Seeds

www.walkinginplace.org/seeds
This is a family-owned company that sells heirloom and open-pollinated seeds, free of genetically modified organisms.

Sandhill Preservation Center

www.sandhillpreservation.com

These guys are doing their part to preserve our heritage—which means heirloom seeds. They have chickens, too.

Seed Savers Exchange

www.seedsavers.org

These guys offer oodles of open-pollinated seeds. If you become a member, you'll have access to thousands of heritage vegetable varieties.

Seeds of Change

www.seedsofchange.com

Seeds of Change has both heirloom and hybrid seeds—all are 100 percent organic.

Seeds of Diversity

www.seeds.ca/en.php

Focused on heirloom seeds and located in Canada.

Seeds Trust

www.seedstrust.com/joomla/

This is a 25-year-old family-owned seed company. They have heirloom and open-pollinated veggie and flower seeds.

Southern Exposure Seed Exchange

www.southernexposure.com

This seed company offers only varieties that are open-pollinated.

Sustainable Seed Company

www.sustainableseedco.com

A fantastic open-pollinated seed resource from California, 90 percent of their seeds are grown on the west coast; 65 percent of them are grown on organic farms in the state itself. Plus, these guys are really awesome to deal with.

Terrior Seeds (Underwood Gardens)

www.underwoodgardens.com

This is a family-owned company that offers heirloom vegetables and flowers exclusively. It's been around since the very beginning of the heirloom seed movement.

Territorial Seed Company

www.territorialseed.com

This seed company has both open-pollinated seeds and hybrid seeds.

Tomato Growers Supply Company

www.tomatogrowers.com

Heirloom and hybrid tomatoes, eggplant, peppers, and tomatillos are the focus here.

Totally Tomatoes

www.totallytomato.com

This website is completely devoted to tomato seeds and plants—almost. They also carry some pepper varieties and a few other gardening gadgets.

Victory Seeds

www.victoryseeds.com

This is a small, family-owned and -operated company that offers heirloom and rare open-pollinated seeds to home gardeners.

Websites, Blogs, and Organizations

I've added some informative websites and blogs on this list for you to peruse as well as organizations that can put rare and commercially unavailable seeds into your hands.

American Community Gardening Association

www.communitygarden.org

If you want to join a local community garden, start here.

The Complete Idiot's Guide to Heirloom Vegetables

www.cigheirloomvegetables.com

This is the photo guide companion site to this book, so it's the first place you're going to want to visit. We'll be adding images as we receive them as well as when new heirlooms or open-pollinated varieties become available. We'll also add images of those varieties that aren't commercially available so you'll know what you're hunting down.

Foodie Mama

www.foodiemama.com

This website has vegetable growing hints, but mostly it's about great ways to cook the food you grow for your family.

Garden State Heirloom Society

www.historyyoucaneat.org

This heirloom organization is a great source for heritage historical facts.

I Dig My Garden

www.idigmygarden.com/forums/

All kinds of veggie and gardening chat is going on around this forum.

Local Harvest

www.localharvest.org

This is a terrific hub site. It has forums for discussing crops and events and a locator to find your nearest fresh produce farm or farmer's market.

Seed Savers Exchange

www.seedsavers.org

This is a terrific place to order seeds, but actually becoming a member unlocks all kinds of other opportunities. You'll connect with other heirloom growers as well as have an exclusive quarterly yearbook mailed to you with more than twice the amount of seeds available in the regular catalog.

Seeds of Diversity

www.seeds.ca/en.php

Here's another organization that offers open-pollinated seeds to the general public, but if you join you'll have access to the seed exchange yearbook and be more in the loop.

Slow Food USA

www.slowfoodusa.org

This grassroots movement began in Italy and is meant to be the polar opposite of fast food. It's all about fresh food, people, and the environment.

Southern Seed Legacy

www.uga.edu/ebl/ssl/about

This organization is all about reversing the erosion of plant genetic diversity in the American South. They encourage and support local seed-saving exchanges and the conservation of plant genetic resources.

Thomas Jefferson Center for Historic Plants

www.monticello.org

It turns out President Thomas Jefferson was a major vegetable gardener, to say the least. Come see for yourself.

Vegetable Gardener

www.vegetablegardener.com

This is a wonderful website with tips on growing all vegetables. It also has terrific recipes for cooking with your homegrown veggies.

Books

I enjoy having print books on hand as a physical gardening resource. If you're like me, here's a list of some of the best heirloom and gardening books.

- Acevedo, Karen Keb. *Cooking with Heirlooms: Seasonal Recipes with Heritage-Variety Vegetables and Fruits*. Lexington, KY: Hobby Farms Press, 2007.

This book has 150 delicious recipes created with our precious heirloom veggies.

- Ashworth, Suzanne. *Seed to Seed*. Decorah, IA: Seed Savers Exchange, Inc., 2002.

Hands-down the single most comprehensive seed guide.

- Bowman, Daria Price, and Price, Carl A. *The Complete Idiot's Guide to Vegetable Gardening*. Indianapolis: Alpha Books, 2009.

A very hands-on vegetable guide that's full of all-around great vegetable gardening information.

- Bubel, Nancy. *The New Seed Starters Handbook*. Emmaus, PA: Rodale Press, 1988.

This is another extremely in-depth book about saving and starting seeds. One of my favorites.

- Coulter, Lynn. *Gardening with Heirloom Seeds*. Chapel Hill, NC: The University of North Carolina Press, 2006.

This is a thick book full of great information on heirloom vegetables and heirloom flowers. Ms. Coulter's book is one of my favorites.

- Creasy, Rosalind. *The Edible Heirloom Garden*. Berkeley, CA: Periplus Editions (HK) Ltd, 1999.

This is a terrific all-around heirloom book that offers the basics on heirlooms, as well as some growing tips and recipes.

- Goldman, Amy. *The Heirloom Tomato: From Garden to Table*. New York: Bloomsbury USA, 2008.

This is a lovely book that you'll want to set out on the coffee table. Fun heritage stories and recipes, too!

- Male, Carolyn. *100 Heirloom Tomatoes for the American Garden*. New York: Workman Publishing Company, 1999.

There is in-depth tomato planting information in this one. Great to have on your shelf.

- McLaughlin, Chris. *The Complete Idiot's Guide to Composting*. Indianapolis: Alpha Books, 2010.

Find out just how easy it is to create your own garden gold for your heirloom vegetable beds.

- Smith, Edward. *The Vegetable Gardener's Bible*. North Adams, MA: Storey Publishing, LLC, 2009.

Mr. Smith's book has a ton of information to guide gardeners to create the garden of their dreams.

- Stickland, Sue. *Heirloom Vegetables*. London: Gaia Books, Limited, 1998.

This book gives terrific information on the genetic diversity of heirloom vegetables.

- Watson, Benjamin. *Taylor's Guide to Heirloom Vegetables*. Orlando: Houghton Mifflin Harcourt, 1996.

With 500 varieties of heirloom vegetables and 200 photos, this is a nice guide.

- Weaver, William Woys. *Heirloom Vegetable Gardening*. Brighton Victoria, Australia: Owl Publishing Company, 1999.

More heirloom wisdom from one of the very best heirloom authorities.

- Weaver, William Woys. *100 Vegetables and Where They Came From*. New York: Algonquin Books of Chapel Hill, 2000.

This handy book was written by heirloom vegetable royalty himself. It's a fun and very interesting read.

- Yepson, Roger B. *A Celebration of Heirloom Vegetables*. New York: Artisan, 1998.

This book includes gardening and cooking tips as well as recipes.

Index

Q-R

U–V

You can have your own backyard farmer's market with these *Complete Idiot's Guides*®

"Everything you need to know to get started and keep composting successfully."
—Joe Lamp'l (aka "joe gardener™"), author of *The Green Gardener's Guide*

COMPLETE IDIOT'S GUIDE TO

Composting

Turn your organic waste material into black gold

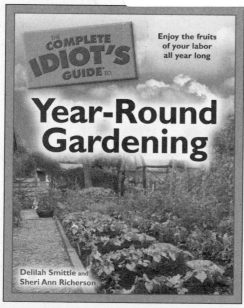

THE COMPLETE IDIOT'S GUIDE TO

Enjoy the fruits of your labor all year long

Year-Round Gardening

Delilah Smittle and Sheri Ann Richerson

978-1-59257-970-9

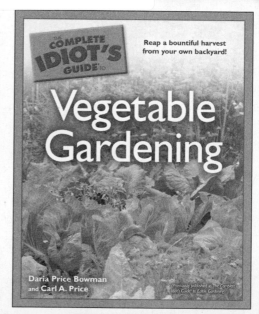

THE COMPLETE IDIOT'S GUIDE TO

Reap a bountiful harvest from your own backyard!

Vegetable Gardening

Daria Price Bowman and Carl A. Price

(Previously published as The Complete Idiot's Guide to Edible Gardening)

978-1-59257-907-5

ALPHA

idiotsguides.com